*Yale Western Americana Series, 17*

# JOE LANE OF OREGON

*Machine Politics*

*and the Sectional Crisis, 1849–1861*

James E. Hendrickson

YALE UNIVERSITY PRESS, NEW HAVEN AND LONDON

1967

*Designed by Beverly Kruger,*
*set in Garamond type,*
*and printed in the United States of America by*
*The Carl Purington Rollins Printing-Office*
*of the Yale University Press, New Haven, Connecticut.*
*Distributed in Canada by McGill University Press.*

*Library of Congress Catalog card number: 67–13436*
*Published with assistance from the Catherine Barker Hickox Fund*

*To Sonja*

J. D.

# PREFACE

Western territories attracted a particular breed of politicians—Western carpetbaggers, they have been called, who went out to take advantage of the unusual opportunities awaiting those who were able to exploit them. Whether conditions on the frontier bred or attracted persons with peculiar qualities has been a matter of considerable debate among historians since the time of Frederick Jackson Turner. Undoubtedly, Truth finds defenders in both camps.

The Democratic leaders who dominated politics in Oregon during the territorial period seem generally to have been ambitious for power before they went west. In fact, some of the most prominent among them had formerly been Whigs and changed their politics along with their residence. And once in Oregon they pursued power with consummate passion and devotion, prompting a correspondent to a California newspaper in 1857 to declare, "The Oregonians have two occupations, agriculture and politics."

That aspiring politicians should opportunistically modify their political allegiance is of less consequence than the more obvious but little appreciated fact that the frontiersman brought his politics with him from "the States." Oregonians were "hards" and "softs" and "independents" and "disaffected" and "tender-footed," but only because they were first Democrats and Whigs and Native Americans and Republicans. The organization of territorial politics along national party lines was one of the most potent forces for integrating the life of the territory with that of the nation.

The cluster of politicians that made up the territorial Democratic machine, the Salem Clique, was in general a remarkably able and articulate lot. The doughty machine boss, Asahel Bush, assumed and exercised power through the columns of the *Oregon Statesman,* which he established in 1851 and edited until after the territory achieved statehood. Bush's rule was sometimes arbitrary and often autocratic, as victims of his wrath were quick to discover, but his enlightened despotism was in large measure responsible for making the Democratic party the viable political force that it was. And the despotism was enlightened. For despite the high-handed tactics Bush pursued, the Clique gave Oregon efficient and responsible government, remarkably free of the graft and corruption so commonly associated with political machines.

The Clique was successful, in part, because of the role of Joseph Lane, who represented the machine in Washington, even while individual members of the Clique became increasingly antagonistic to him. Lane was important because he was the best vote-getter in the territory and because—through his acquaintance with Presidents Pierce and Buchanan—he controlled patronage, the *élan vital* of territorial life. And as the sectional conflict broke, Lane was able to capitalize on his Western residence, his sincere devotion to Southern rights, and the national forum provided him by Congress.

This study is neither a biography of Lane nor a history of the Clique. Rather, by focusing on Lane's political career, it seeks to explore his relationship with the machine, to probe the motivations of his political behavior, and to examine the impact of the sectional controversy upon the people of Oregon. The hitherto unused Lane Collection of the Lilly Library, Indiana University, Bloomington, covers Lane's career after 1855 and throws much valuable light upon events in Oregon prior to the outbreak of civil war.

In attempting to recover this segment of the past, I have sought to recapture in all their vitality the personalities and events and ideas of the turbulent fifties. To this end I have relied extensively upon the personal correspondence and newspaper files of the period, permitting the leading characters as much as possible to speak for themselves in their own language. This, in turn, has involved the risk of excessive quotation, but I trust that the risk is more than justified by the cumulative effect of the detail in illustrating the methods, illuminating the relationships, and re-creating the personalities of Lane and his contemporaries in Oregon. Except where correction seemed necessary to make meaning clear, I have attempted throughout to retain the original spelling, punctuation, and syntax. Any words I have added are enclosed in brackets.

This manuscript, like others, is the product of many hands, and I would like to express my sincere appreciation to the several individuals, named and unnamed, who have rendered assistance and offered encouragement. I am particularly grateful to my wife, Sonja, who assisted in ways that even she cannot fully realize; to Martin Schmitt, who suggested the topic and did much more; to Earl Pomeroy who with his usual tolerance directed this study as a doctoral dissertation. I would like also to acknowledge the helpful co-operation of the staffs of the Oregon Historical Society, Portland, the Lilly Library, Indiana University, Bloomington, and the University of Oregon Library, Eugene, without whose aid this study would have been impossible. Materials in the Bancroft Library, University of California, Berkeley, are cited by permission. The University of Victoria generously provided summer research grants in 1965 and 1966.

J.E.H.

*Victoria, B.C.*
*July 1966*

# CONTENTS

# LIST OF ILLUSTRATIONS

## *Chapter 1*

# NEW HORIZONS

Just after breakfast on an August morning in 1848, a stranger with massive frame and waggish ways pounded imperatively on the door of an Indiana farmhouse. Some weeks earlier, bedecked in the blankets and buckskins of a mountain man, he had created a minor sensation in Washington City by announcing himself as the "Envoy Extraordinary and Minister Plenipotentiary from the Republic of Oregon to the Court of the United States." He now introduced himself to the owner of the farmhouse as Joseph L. Meek, United States Marshal, and presented him with a commission from President James K. Polk, naming him governor of the new Territory of Oregon. Would he accept?[1]

1. Frances Fuller Victor, *The River of the West. Life and Adventure in the Rocky Mountains and Oregon; Embracing Events in the Life-Time*

General Joseph Lane, the "Marion of the Mexican War" and "Cincinnatus of Indiana," interrupted his writing and looked up from his desk. He was not a very large man, not more than five feet eight or nine, but his heart was big and his body lean and wiry, his constitution rugged. His dark hair fell loosely across a high forehead, crowning a long leathery face that seemed to respond contagiously and spontaneously to the twinkle in his eyes. A frontiersman accustomed to the vicissitudes of outdoor life, he was really quite handsome. Yes, the postmaster at Louisville had forwarded the President's telegram, and he had already sent a reply. He would accept.

Joe Lane was not accustomed to hesitation or indecision. Born in 1801 in North Carolina of old pioneer stock, he was but three years old when the Wilderness Road beckoned his parents westward to a Kentucky farm on the banks of the Ohio; when he was fourteen he left home to clerk in a dry goods store on the Indiana side of the river. By the time he was twenty-one, he was engaged in the flatboating business and had acquired a farm, a wife, and a seat in the state legislature—even before he was entitled to vote. Bold and even impetuous action in the war with Mexico brought him promotion from the rank of brigadier general, a political appointment, to that of brevet major general. More important, his experience in the war brought him to national attention and provided him with an invaluable political asset, a favorable military record.

---

*of a Mountain-Man and Pioneer* (Columbus, Long's College Book Co., 1959), p. 449; Harvey Elmer Tobie, *No Man Like Joe: The Life and Times of Joseph L. Meek* (Portland, Binfords & Mort, 1949), p. 165. Cf. James Buchanan to Lane, Aug. 18, 1848, Lane Papers (Lilly Library, Indiana University, Bloomington; microfilm in University of Oregon Library, Eugene), cited hereafter as Lane Papers, InU. In his "Autobiography" (Bancroft Library, University of California, Berkeley), pp. 2, 134, Lane claimed that he accepted the appointment because of Polk's solicitations rather than his own desires.

Oregon had recently received considerable publicity in the expansion-prone Union, thanks to missionaries like Jason Lee and Marcus and Narcissa Whitman and to "prophets" like Hall Jackson Kelley and Thomas Hart Benton. "Oregon fever," a disease particularly infectious in the upper Mississippi Valley, led to sizable overland migrations in 1843, 1844, and 1845. In 1844 the Democrats capitalized on the feeling of "manifest destiny" by proposing Oregon as a northern counterbalance to annexations to the south, a proposal made possible by a treaty with England two years later. In 1843 Oregonians established a provisional government, and five years later, after the Whitman massacre and subsequent "Cayuse War," it was this quasi-legal body that sent Joe Meek with a petition to Washington requesting the speedy organization of a territorial government.

Territories were traditionally the spawning ground for ambitious politicians, and Lane was nothing if not ambitious. Oregon was twenty-five hundred miles away, but that was where the patronage was and where the opportunities lay. Federal appointees would man courts, land offices, customhouses, and Indian agencies; enterprising businessmen would win military and postal contracts; the people would elect a delegate to Congress. In fact, so attractive were the prospects that Lane had been interested in Oregon even before he left Mexico.[2]

"How soon can you be ready to start?" asked Meek.

"In fifteen minutes!" replied Lane.

Actually, Lane spent the next two days making preparations for the trip. Then early in the morning of August 29, he bade farewell to his wife, Mary Hart Lane (Polly), and eight children and, with his eldest son, Nathaniel (Nat), and Joe Meek, boarded a steamboat for St. Louis.[3]

2. Archibald B. Campbell to Lane, Aug. 28, 1848, Manuscript Collection (Oregon Historical Society, Portland), cited hereafter as MS OrHi.

3. Victor, *River of the West,* p. 471; Tobie, *No Man Like Joe,* pp. 179–80.

General Stephen Watts Kearny, commanding officer of Jefferson Barracks, St. Louis, Missouri, was a man of authority, but he could not discourage Lane and Meek from attempting an overland crossing in the winter. What Lane lacked in caution, he made up for in courage. And persistence. "Well, General," he said, as he breakfasted with Kearny and his wife, "I did not come to consult you about the trip but about an escort; will you give me an escort?"[4]

The old soldier yielded. From a regiment slated to leave for Oregon the next spring, he detached twenty-five riflemen and a surgeon under the command of Lieutenant George W. Hawkins. Because of the lateness of the season, they selected a route similar to that Kearny had taken to California two years earlier. With wagon masters, teamsters, and servants, the party that left Fort Leavenworth on the morning of September 10 numbered about fifty persons; they required ten wagons to transport their supplies and several additional mounts. An officer there noted that Lane was something of a driver, a "pushing" fellow, but on the whole a "fair sample of a Western man." He has "a pleasant smile on rather hard features," he continued. "Has been a successful working man. Has slight education but talks sensibly about common things. Is good-hearted and ambitious."[5]

At Santa Fe the party learned it would have to abandon its wagons because of insufficient grass ahead. Repacking their provisions on mules and ponies, the men set off on the old road for El Paso and Chihuahua. Before reaching El Paso the little band left the main trail and turned west. Before long the rigors of the trip began to tell. At Tucson two riflemen deserted; when Hawkins sent another with a guide to retake them, the deserters killed both.

4. Lane, "Autobiography," p. 3.

5. W. A. Croffut, ed., *Fifty Years in Camp and Field: Diary of Major General Ethan Allen Hitchcock, U.S.A.* (New York, G. P. Putnam's Sons, Knickerbocker Press, 1909), p. 347.

Conditions steadily deteriorated until the travelers reached the Gila River, which they followed to its junction with the Colorado. Here they constructed crude rafts of bulrushes and, except for the loss of some mules, crossed safely to a Yuma village on the California side. Shortages of food and water soon became critical, and the company increasingly demoralized. The desert took a dreadful toll. Animals died nearly every day, and more men sought release by deserting. At Cook's Wells the carcass of a mule polluted the water hole. Sizing up the situation, Lane boiled some of the water and made coffee for all to drink, declaring that "maggots were more easily swallowed cooked than raw."[6] On another occasion their thirst was so great that they punctured the stomach of a mule to find liquid. In the vicinity of the Vallecito Desert, they stopped for a day with a company of American soldiers, one of whom noted in his diary that their numbers had been reduced to fifteen, adding dourly that they "are now as far from *Oregon City* as when they left Santa Fe, or even Leavenworth. . . . Stopped with us but one day, and pushed on. Had been living on nothing but beans for six days."[7] By this time the men were all on foot; the remaining animals were needed to carry the supplies. It was a weary and footsore band that finally made its way to Williams' Ranch on the Santa Ana River some three or four weeks later, its numbers further reduced by the electrifying news of nearby gold strikes.

The rest was easy. Securing fresh mounts, the adventurers followed the Santa Ana River to San Pedro Bay, where they found a government vessel ready to sail for San Francisco with a company of dragoons. There they were amazed to find themselves at the scene of a frantic gold rush. Particularly astonishing was the number of Oregonians who had forsaken their farms and businesses to

6. Victor, *River of the West,* pp. 475–77; Tobie (*No Man Like Joe,* p. 182) says Meek took the initiative and had to urge Lane to drink the coffee.

7. "Diary of Cave Johnson Couts," MS (Bancroft Library, University of California, Berkeley), Dec. 23, 1848.

try their luck in the diggings. Both Lane and Meek must have been sorely tempted to set off for the mines, but time was against them. Seeing the United States sloop of war, the *St. Mary's,* lying at anchor in the San Francisco harbor, Meek tried to persuade Lane that they ought to require her services to take them to Oregon in a manner befitting their dignity. But Lane, whether for financial or political reasons, insisted that they take passage for one hundred dollars each on the brig *Janet,* along with a host of other returning Oregonians. As the *Janet* slipped out of San Francisco harbor, the *St. Mary's* guns boomed in salute to the first governor of Oregon Territory.

For eighteen days the brig made its way up the coast to the mouth of the Columbia—eighteen days in which Lane had a chance to rest and relax and learn something about the territory he was soon to see. From Oregonians on board he learned particulars of the Whitman massacre and its perpetrators, who yet roamed at large. He was doubtlessly also informed of the activities of the Hudson's Bay Company and of the local political factions, which tended to polarize around the company and the "mission party" of the Willamette Valley. Perhaps the most satisfying aspect of the voyage was making the acquaintance of James W. Nesmith, a man of charm, intelligence, and an inimitable, if earthy, sense of humor. The two men became fast friends.[8]

The *Janet* deposited her passengers at Astoria, leaving them to find their own transportation up the Columbia. Lane made the

8. Nesmith to Lane, April 24, 1854, MS OrHi; Lane to James Guthrie, Aug. 31, 1854, MS OrHi.

James Willis Nesmith (1820–85) was born in New Brunswick, Canada, and came to Oregon with the overland migration of 1843. Before going to the gold fields in California, he served as justice of the provisional supreme court, member of the provisional government, and captain in the Cayuse War. In 1853 he became U.S. marshal, in 1857 superintendent of Indian affairs, and in 1861 U.S. senator from Oregon. He was elected to the House of Representatives in a special election in 1873 and served until 1875.

last hundred and twenty miles by canoe, "working his passage," as he phrased it, by taking his turn at the paddle.[9] Only eight members of the original escort under Lieutenant Hawkins completed this last leg of the journey. On March 2 the men nosed their craft into the waters of the Willamette River and debarked at the little village of Portland where the residents, hardly more than twenty souls, received them with warm hospitality and a simple but substantial meal. It was nearly evening when they reached their final destination of Oregon City, a town of more than one hundred homes, two churches, and a handful of stores and mills. A committee received the governor and his party with a great display of ceremony and escorted them to the spacious home of William L. Holmes. There, on a long porch in front of the house, they sat down with almost the entire population of the town to a veritable banquet, replete with toasts and responses to mark the establishment of Oregon Territory. With the formalities suitably concluded, the celebrants cleared the floor for an "Inaugural Ball," and the jubilant Oregonians danced until daybreak.[10]

The new governor lost little time setting in motion the machinery of government. On March 3, 1849, one day before the close of Polk's administration, Lane took the oath of office before a justice of the peace and, assisted by George L. Curry, drafted a proclamation inaugurating the territorial government, which Curry published in broadside. The young Oregonian quickly became Lane's

9. Lane to ed., Sept. 15, 1852, *Oregon Weekly Times,* Dec. 4, 1852.
10. *Oregon Weekly Times,* May 21, 1853; [Samuel C. Damon], "Tour Through the Willamette Valley," *The Friend; a Monthly Journal Devoted to Temperance, Seamen, Marine and General Intelligence,* 7 (1849), 57–60; Keeler H. Gabbert, "The Fine Old Home at Oregon City in Which the First Inaugural Ball Was Held," Scrapbook 43, p. 126, OrHi; *Sunday Oregonian* (Magazine), Nov. 24, 1940, p. 7.
For accounts of the journey to Oregon, see also *Oregon Statesman,* April 18, 1851, July 17, Aug. 7, 1852.

confidant, serving unofficially as secretary and public printer until the appointed secretary arrived from the East.

Lane's first official action was to order a census by counties to fix the apportionment of representation to the territorial legislature. To Secretary of State James Buchanan, he expressed fears that it would be "difficult to get a Legislature, so unwilling will those be who are qualified, to stay and serve, so great is the desire to go to the mines." Entrusting the job to Marshal Meek, he busied himself with the multiplicity of other considerations that faced a new executive. The mass exodus to California prevented enumeration on any accurate basis, but Meek and his deputies nonetheless recorded the names of 8,903 residents, of whom 2,509 were eligible to vote.[11] Lane issued his second proclamation, April 2, calling the first territorial election for the first Monday in June.

A week later the new governor swore in the chief justice for the territory, an old friend from Indiana, William P. Bryant. By proclamation on May 23, Lane laid the foundations for the legal system, dividing the territory into three judicial districts and assigning the first or central one to Bryant and the second or southern to Orville C. Pratt. The third or northern one remained vacant.[12]

A fourth proclamation summoned the legislative assembly to convene on July 16, and Lane delivered his first official address before the body the following day. The Reverend George W. Atkinson helped write the message, and the result was a happy combination of high-flown rhetoric and practical politics. Pledging his support to the interests of the territory, Lane reviewed its needs: the punishment of the Whitmans' murderers and payment of the Cayuse War claims; the donation of land by the federal government; improved navigational facilities and a system of territorial roads; the exploitation of agricultural and mineral resources; a "judicious system" of raising revenue; the organization of the

11. Lane to Secretary of State, March 10, April 9, 1849, U.S. Senate *Executive Document,* No. 52 (31 Cong., 1 Sess.), pp. 4–6.

12. Lane to Secretary of State, May 23, 1849, ibid. pp. 6–7.

militia; and a thorough revision of the "loose and defective condition of the statute laws declared by the organic act to be operative in the territory." If priorities can be assigned, perhaps education and Indian affairs were given special emphasis. Deprived of the advantages of an education himself, Lane was keenly interested in the benefits it bestowed and advocated a system of common schools for all the children of the territory. Two weeks later he joined Atkinson in a successful effort to bring six teachers to Oregon from New England. Finding the Indians eager to sell their lands and the whites "exceedingly sensitive on the subject," he recommended the speedy removal of all Indians from the settled areas before "civilization, by destroying the resources of the Indians, doom them to poverty want and crime." But he also asked for the repeal of a law banning the sale of firearms to all Indians and the substitution of one that would discriminate only against unfriendly tribes. The message was highly popular. "If the judicious suggestions of his excellency were fully carried out," said Wilson Blain of the *Oregon Spectator,* "it would be a happy thing for Oregon."[13]

If Oregonians found their chief executive much to their liking, Lane also received a favorable impression of Oregon. He wrote Buchanan shortly after his arrival that he found the people "most orderly, intelligent, industrious, and good citizens." Moreover, the climate was salubrious and the country appealing to his eye. Within a few weeks his duties as superintendent of Indian affairs took him as far up the Columbia as The Dalles and as far north as Puget

13. *Oregon Spectator,* Oct. 4, 1849. The *Spectator* reprinted the entire message in this issue, resuming publication for the first time since Feb. 22, when its printer left for the mines. To Nesmith, Lane wrote with heavy-handed sarcasm on Sept. 25: "Blane has got a printer at last, so the press will go to grinding, and then we will catch Hell Generally as I suppose, so you may look out. Now my Dear Friend I am not sure but the Legislative Assembly will immortalize themselves, and every body will grow rich, by virtue of their valuable enactments." MS OrHi. Cf. Lane to William Slade, July 31, 1849, Lane Papers, InU; Slade to Lane, Oct. 26, 1849, MS OrHi.

Sound. Since the executive office held a veto over the legislative assembly, he was free after it began to function to explore the coast south from Astoria and to inspect the conditions of the Indian tribes there. With a native pilot in an Indian canoe, he and Nesmith were probably the first white men to cross the bar at Yaquina Bay.[14]

Such excursions gave Lane a welcome relief from his paper work, which he never did relish. A man of restless energy, he craved physical activity, particularly when excitement or adventure was involved—activity, that is, of the rifle or the trail rather than of the axe or the plow. Rare indeed was the man of half his years who could surpass his vigor or spend longer hours in the saddle.

Next to action he liked people. Affable and gregarious, he always appreciated situations that permitted him to demonstrate his natural capacity for leadership. Perhaps this is why he was attracted to politics, for he loved an audience and enjoyed the limelight. Endowed with an ego sufficient for two men, he kept it in check by a sincere devotion to the interests of people around him.[15] Consciously posing as a champion of the common man, he found a significant—and politically advantageous—prototype in Andrew Jackson, whom he idolized. With as much of the South as the frontier in his veins, Lane did not have to affect a Jacksonian rhetoric about states' rights, the Constitution, and the Union, or a Jackson-like attitude toward women, duels, and the institution of slavery. Above all, his politics were devotedly Democratic, reli-

14. Lane to Secretary of State, April 9, 1849, U.S. Senate *Executive Document,* No. 52 (31 Cong., 1 Sess.), pp. 4–6; Fred Lockley, "In Early Days," *Oregon Daily Journal,* Feb. 21, 1915, p. 4.

15. Hubert Howe Bancroft relates an incident illustrating this point. While governor, Lane "permitted himself to be chosen arbitrator in a land-jumping case, and rode a long distance in the rain, having to cross swollen streams on horseback, to help a woman whose husband was absent in the mines to resist the attempt of an unprincipled tenant to hold the claim of her husband. His influence was sufficient with the jury to get the obnoxious tenant removed." *History of Oregon,* 2 (San Francisco, History Company, 1888), 93.

giously so, and in this respect most Oregonians proved entirely compatible.

By the end of the summer, Lane had decided to settle permanently in the territory. In November he purchased a half interest in a grist and sawmill located on an island in the Willamette River just below the falls at Oregon City. His son Nat secured a quarter interest in the same business and left for San Francisco to sell a shipload of lumber, intending to return to Indiana and bring the rest of the Lane family to Oregon. About the same time Lane heard rumors that he had been removed by the Whig administration of Zachary Taylor and that a new governor was on his way to replace him. He was not unduly disturbed, as the prospect for economic success for a moment outweighed political aspiration. "If they dont take the mills," he confided to Nesmith, "I dont care a dam."[16]

Lane had no sooner arrived in Oregon than he was besieged by numerous Indians who had heard that a "White Father" had arrived from Washington—"chiefs, head men, warriors, and, in many instances, entire bands, expecting presents, making known to me that the whites had promised, from time to time, that when the laws of the United States were extended over Oregon, the Governor would bring them blankets, shirts, and such other articles as would be useful to them." As acting superintendent of Indian affairs, Lane was somewhat embarrassed because neither funds nor instructions had arrived from Washington, but fortunately the Indians were patient and well disposed.[17]

16. Lane to Nesmith, Nov. 15, 1849, MS OrHi. Cf. Nat H. Lane to Lane, Dec. 15, 1849, Lane Papers, InU.

17. Lane to Secretary of War, Oct. 13, 1849, U.S. Senate *Executive Document,* No. 52 (31 Cong., 1 Sess.), pp. 167–77. For a discussion of the problems involved in combining the office of governor and superintendent of Indian affairs, see William M. Neil, "The Territorial Governor as Indian Superintendent in the Trans-Mississippi West," *Mississippi Valley Historical Review, 43* (1956), 213–37.

Until military reinforcements arrived, the governor could do little to apprehend the Cayuse responsible for the Whitman massacre. When a government draft of $10,000 arrived early in April, of which some $3,000 was earmarked for Indian purposes, he was able to begin a program of visitations. To ensure friendly relations with the tribes along the immigrant route, he held a council with the Indians at The Dalles, distributing some $200 worth of cheap presents to the Deschutes and Yakima tribes who, in turn, promised to permit the whites to pass through their lands unmolested. At the request of the Yakima chief, Lane was instrumental in working out terms of peace between that tribe and its upcountry brothers, the Walla Wallas. Finally he made a strong appeal to the Cayuse to surrender the murderers of Whitman.[18]

While visiting the Cowlitz Indians early in May, Lane received alarming news of an uprising by the Snoqualmie Indians near Fort Nisqually on Puget Sound in which an American citizen, Leander C. Wallace, was killed. Taking Lieutenant Hawkins, five of the eight riflemen—the only troops in the territory—and what muskets and ammunition he could procure, Lane promptly set off for the Sound. A few miles from his destination he was met by an old employee of the Puget Sound Agricultural Company, who was able to offer suggestions for the preservation of peace. "D - - - them," sputtered Lane before the astonished clerk, "it would do my soul good to be after them." A remark like this, wrote the Englishman later, "would never have escaped the lips of either [John] McLoughlin or [James] Douglas."[19]

The next day Indian messengers from the Hudson's Bay Company arrived with a dispatch from Major James S. Hathaway, announcing his arrival in Fort Vancouver with two companies of artillery. Deciding to return and have Hathaway establish a post

18. Lane to Secretary of War, Oct. 13, 1849, U.S. Senate *Executive Document,* No. 52 (31 Cong., 1 Sess.), pp. 167–77.

19. "The Round Hand of George B. Roberts: Letters to Mrs. F. F. Victor, 1878–83," *Oregon Historical Quarterly,* 63 (1962), 194.

near Nisqually (Fort Steilacoom) and demand the surrender of the murderers, Lane sent a letter to William F. Tolmie, the Hudson's Bay Company's factor at Nisqually, asking him not to furnish the Indians with ammunition but to warn them that troops had arrived and that further outrages would be visited "by sudden and severe punishment." Upon his return to Oregon City, however, Lane finally received instructions from Washington, including the appointments of three Indian subagents. Since one of them failed to claim his commission, Lane divided the territory into two districts, assigning J. Quinn Thornton the area north of the Columbia. When Thornton visited the Sound he took the initiative in offering the Indians a substantial reward of eighty blankets if they would deliver the guilty to the proper authorities, a decision concurred in by Tolmie, Hathaway, and several of the American settlers. This Lane considered little better than a bribe—"bad policy, under any consideration, to hire them to make reparation"—since it would only encourage them to murder again and deliver some slave for a reward. Moreover, he explained to the commissioner of Indian affairs, it would "underrate our ability and inclination to chastise by force, or make war upon them for such conduct, which in my opinion, is the only proper method of treating them for such offences." Prompted by Thornton's generosity, the Indians surrendered six of their number to the commander of the new post at Fort Steilacoom. Refusing to honor Tolmie's bill for the blankets until he knew if the prisoners were guilty, Lane requested special legislation by the territorial legislature to attach the Sound area to the first judicial district so that Chief Justice Bryant could hold a special court at Fort Steilacoom early in October and impress the natives with the efficacy of the white man's justice. So sparse was the population around the Sound that citizens from Vancouver County had to be brought to fill the grand and petit juries, which acquitted three of the six accused. The guilty were hanged. Not counting lawyers' fees or the price of the blankets ($480), the total cost of the trial was $1,899.54, but Lane thought the salutary effect upon the Indians in that rather remote portion of the territory fully justified the expenditure.[20]

Although Lane's deprecatory attitude toward the Indians was that of the frontier, he occasionally showed more insight into and appreciation of their problems than did many of his contemporaries. In August 1848 an incendiary had sought to drive the Falls Indians from their village near Lynn City, across the river from Oregon City, by setting fire to their homes and destroying their winter provisions. When they appealed to Lane for justice, he conducted a public hearing, decided that the Indians had been wronged, and permitted them to resettle on their land. Although this decision was certainly unpopular in some quarters, it instilled a new confidence in the minds of the Indians and laid an effective foundation for future treaty negotiations.[21]

The regiment of mounted riflemen, which had left Fort Leavenworth in the spring, did not reach Oregon until October, after detaching two companies each at Forts Laramie and Hall to guard the immigrant trail. Lane was reluctant to commit himself to a full-scale military campaign against the Cayuse so late in the year, but he did what he could short of war. Quietly conferring with James Douglas and Peter Skene Ogden of the Hudson's Bay Company at Fort Vancouver, he found them ready and willing to assist in bringing the Whitmans' murderers to justice. With the approval of Archbishop Francis N. Blanchet and Dr. John McLoughlin and disregarding rumors of his impending removal, he ad-

20. Lane to Tolmie, May 17, 1849, Tolmie Papers (University of Washington Library, Seattle); Lane to Secretary of War, Oct. 13, 1849, U.S. Senate *Executive Document,* No. 52 (31 Cong., 1 Sess.), pp. 167–77. Thornton's resignation on Sept. 21 was prompted not only by Lane's disapproval of rewarding the Indians, as Bancroft suggests (*History of Oregon, 2,* 71), but also by Lane's insistence that the subagent reside within his district—in Thornton's case, north of the Columbia. Lane to Thornton, Sept. 14, 20, 1849, Lane Letterbook 5, OrHi; Thornton to Lane, Sept. 19, 24, 1849, ibid.

21. *Oregon Spectator,* Aug. 10, 1848; [Damon], *The Friend,* 7, 57–60.

dressed a communiqué to the Cayuse in which he insisted that they surrender the guilty persons. The reply was evasive; the Indians wanted time. Learning from the Nez Perce early in November that the young chief of the Cayuse was well disposed to the whites—the regiment of mounted riflemen had just passed through their land—Lane renewed his demand in another dispatch, which threatened to destroy the Cayuse nation if it would not yield. In February 1850 he received word from the Hudson's Bay factor at Fort Walla Walla that the Cayuse would comply. The two sides agreed to meet at The Dalles.[22]

Before the appointed rendezvous occurred, more than one third of the regiment of riflemen deserted for the California gold mines; many of them had doubtless enlisted for that very purpose. In the temporary absence of Colonel W. W. Loring, Lane promptly issued a proclamation offering a reward of thirty dollars for each deserter and took about twenty men to overtake the fugitives. Although he believed that the men would not succeed in their eight-hundred-mile escape, he felt their return essential for the welfare of the territory. "For God's sake," he wrote to Nesmith, "get as many men as you can, armed with Rifles, and mounted on the best horses you can get." At Grave Creek in the Rogue River Valley, Lane overtook some 75 of the 120 deserters; the majority, without clothing and provisions, willingly submitted to their captors. Returning with the prisoners through Umpqua Valley, he met Colonel Loring, who continued south in pursuit of those still at large.[23]

Back in Oregon City, Lane learned that a Cayuse chief had been there to see him but had left after waiting two weeks. Proceeding to Fort Vancouver, where he got a boat and escort of ten men,

22. Lane to ed., Nov. 29, 1879, *Morning Oregonian,* Dec. 3, 1879; Lane to "Young chief of the Cayuse," Nov. 9, 1849, Lane Letterbook 5, OrHi; *Oregon Spectator,* May 10, 1849. Cf. Lane, "Autobiography," pp. 136–37.

23. Lane to Nesmith, March 5, 1850, MS OrHi. See also *Oregon Spectator,* July 22, 1851, May 10, April 18, 1850, and Cyrenius Mulkey, "Eighty-One Years of Frontier Life," typescript, pp. 40–41, OrHi.

Lane purchased $240 worth of supplies and presents—shades of Thornton—from the Hudson's Bay Company, including eleven blankets, twelve handkerchiefs, seven shirts, twenty pounds of twist tobacco, and one gallon of brandy. With this collection of threats and bribes, he set out for The Dalles, where most of the Cayuse nation was encamped. In a lengthy talk there, he explained that a trial would be held in which the prisoners would be defended by a lawyer in the same manner as were white men, that if found guilty they would be hanged, and that their chiefs should be present to witness the operation of the white man's courts. After camping with the Indians a second night, he took possession of the five accused, invited their friends to bid them a last farewell, and returned to Oregon City.[24]

There being no jail in the territory, the governor took his prisoners to Oregon City rather than Fort Vancouver and incarcerated them in one of his mill buildings on Abernethy Island, which was accessible only by a long bridge to the upper part of the town. The departure of Chief Justice Bryant from Oregon required Lane to ask the legislature for an act to allow Pratt to hold a special court session at Oregon City. After deliberating seventy-five minutes, the jury found all five guilty, and their friends and relatives hurried away without waiting to hear the sentence. Pratt sentenced the condemned to be hanged on June 3. Lane left for Rogue River and California on the 27th of May, so he was not present to receive the petition for a reprieve, which was drawn up by some of the citizens and presented to Acting Governor Kintzing Pritchett. Nor was he a part of the crowd that gathered the following week around the crude scaffold that had been constructed just south of

24. *Oregon Spectator,* May 10, 1850; receipt from Peter Skene Ogden, April 9, 1850, Lane Papers, OrHi; Lane, "Autobiography," p. 138. Lane could hardly have appreciated how self-incriminating was his actual statement in the "Autobiography": "Then I told the interpeter to tell their friends to come and bid them good by, that I did not think that they would ever see them again." Disclosures like this effectively prejudiced Bancroft against Lane.

McLoughlin's house. At nine o'clock that morning the prisoners were baptized and confirmed into the Roman Catholic faith; at two in the afternoon they stood before the scaffold, as Archbishop Blanchet pronounced a last blessing. The trap was sprung, and five bodies dangled in mid-air. "Some of them died almost without a struggle," a reporter observed; "others seemed to suffer more, and one showed signs of life after hanging fourteen minutes."[25]

Dr. John McLoughlin, for years the chief factor of the Hudson's Bay Company and a man who perhaps contributed more to the settlement of Oregon than any other individual, was the first to realize the potential value of the land adjacent to Willamette Falls. He laid claim to it in 1829, but in the early 1840s persons connected with the Methodist Mission trespassed upon his claim, organized the Oregon Milling Company, and erected two mills on the island just below the falls. The company disregarded McLoughlin's protests and sold out in 1846 to Provisional Governor George Abernethy and others, who in turn sold to Chief Justice Bryant in May 1849. Since the Island Mills, as they were called, were located within Bryant's judicial district, McLoughlin could hardly resort to court action to obtain his rights.[26]

The gold rush to California caused lumber and flour prices to skyrocket, and when Lane and Nat bought into the mills they were valued at $100,000. The mills were sawing about $10,000 worth of lumber a day, expenses were minimal, and there were ten or twelve ships lying in the river awaiting lumber. Lane paid Bryant $20,000 in cash and gave him a note for the remaining $30,000,

25. Observer [Francis N. Blanchet], "Reminiscences of Early Days," Scrapbook 112, pp. 94, 96, 98, OrHi; Lane to Secretary of War, May 27, 1850, Lane Letterbook 5, OrHi; *Oregon Spectator,* June 27, 1850.

26. McLoughlin to Alex H. H. Steward (copy), July 15, 1851, MS OrHi; Sidney Teiser, "The First Chief Justice of Oregon Territory: William P. Bryant," *Oregon Historical Quarterly, 48,* (1947), 45–54.

satisfied, as he wrote to Nesmith, that he now had "entire control of . . . a fortune."[27]

Had conditions remained static Lane would indeed have been well on the way to fortune. But disaster struck. At Christmas time a great freshet swept down the Willamette Valley, severely damaging the Island Mills and carrying away logs and a great deal of sawed lumber. As soon as the waters subsided, Lane set about to effect the necessary repairs and recoup his losses. Before he could accomplish this, lumber prices began a rapid decline, and the mill became a millstone around the necks of its unlucky owners. Making the best of a bad situation, they put Nat in charge of the mill operations, but as time passed Lane despaired of meeting his obligations to Bryant. He speculated briefly in real estate without apparent success. For example, in January 1850 he paid Elijah White $5,000 for a ten per cent interest in the Willamette town of Lancaster. Eventually he sold his farm on the banks of the Ohio River to Bryant as final payment for the Island Mills.[28]

Newspapers in "the States" published rumors of Lane's removal as governor as early as September, but not until January 1850, after Joseph G. Marshall of Indiana and one Abraham Lincoln of Illinois

27. Lane to Nesmith, Nov. 15, 1849, MS OrHi. See also Lane, "Autobiography," p. 149, and *Oregon Spectator,* Nov. 1, 1849. A notation appended to his "Autobiography" (p. 149) reports the operating expenses of the mill, including logs, were $40 per day. Where Lane got the $20,000 down payment is not known.

28. *Oregon Spectator,* Dec. 27, 1849, Jan. 10, 1850; Lane, "Autobiography," p. 149; agreement with Elijah White, Jan. 16, 1850, Lane Papers, InU; *Weekly Oregonian,* Dec. 20, 1851. Robert R. Thompson, who had a one-eighth interest in the mills, estimated the damage to them at $20,000 in a letter to his mother, Elizabeth Thompson, Sept. 12, 1851, MS OrHi.

Lane's opening remarks to the legislative assembly, May 7, 1850, were noticeably personal: "Although the past winter has been an unusually rainy one, occasioning higher water than has hitherto been known—seriously injuring many of our citizens, engaged in milling operations, it has pleased Almighty God to grant us general good health and prosperity." *Oregon Spectator,* May 10, 1850.

had declined the appointment, did the *Spectator* announce that another Indianan, John P. Gaines, had accepted the position. This news created quite a furor among Oregonians, especially those of the Democratic persuasion, who were quick to denounce Whig appropriation of the spoils system. A resolution passed by a mass meeting in Oregon City expressed the prevailing sentiment: "We *believe* that Gov. Lane has faithfully, vigilently, and honorably discharged all the duties incumbent upon him as Governor and Superintendent of Indian Affairs in and for this Territory; we *know* that he has endeared himself to this people by his uniform kind, generous, and manly bearing as a neighbor, friend, and citizen, and we deeply regret his removal."[29]

About the same time Lane became the subject of another controversy when an Oregonian, subscribing himself as "Lansdale" (probably J. Quinn Thornton), wrote a scurrilous letter to Horace Greeley's *New York Tribune.* The letter charged Lane, "who, although he may be brave enough to fight, is not wise enough to govern," with ineffective leadership in the Legislative Assembly. The author further censured him for "throwing himself into the hands of men of bad character and intemperate habits." Again Oregonians rose to their governor's defense and passed resolutions condemning the author and supporting Lane.[30]

The same issue of the *Spectator* that announced the appointment of Gaines noted the holding of a public meeting on January 20 to subscribe capital for a new Willamette and Columbia Steamboat Company. Enthusiasm ran high, and that night in Lane's office a meeting was held to complete the organization (Lane was elected a director) and to choose an agent to secure vessels and to represent the company in Pittsburgh. Because of his "long experience . . . in

29. *Oregon Spectator,* May 21, 1850. Similar resolutions were passed by meetings in Yamhill and Polk counties and by the territorial legislature.

30. The letter is reprinted in the *Oregon Spectator,* May 16, 1850. See also Bancroft, *History of Oregon,* 2, 153, and R. D. Campbell to Lane, Nov. 27, 1849, Lane Papers, InU.

matters connected with the running of steamboats," reported the *Spectator,* the directors decided to send Lane, who consented to represent them after "much persuasion." For reasons unknown, Lane abruptly changed his mind and resolved not to abandon his governor's post until Gaines arrived. Perhaps upon more mature consideration he decided that a successful prosecution of the Whitmans' murderers would be the greater service. In any event, the *Spectator* found it necessary to append a footnote as it went to press to the effect that the governor found it "wholly inexpedient" to leave the territory at present, and that the company had regretfully accepted his resignation.[31]

Passage of gold seekers between California and Oregon had sorely tried the patience of Indians in the Rogue River Valley. The increasing activity of the miners, coupled with isolated acts of violence by the Indians, foreshadowed a clash. In the spring of 1850, the Indians surprised and plundered a party returning from California with a considerable amount of gold dust. The miners appealed to Lane, who promised to do what he could about the matter as soon as his duties would permit.

Although he had not received official notice of his removal as governor, Lane resigned effective June 18 and left immediately after the trial of the Cayuse for the Rogue River and a mining expedition into northern California. Taking with him a dozen or more whites and an equal number of Klickitat Indians under Chief Quatley, a life-long enemy of the Rogue River band, Lane paused briefly to prospect the canyon region between the Umpqua and Rogue rivers. Crossing to the south side of the Rogue, the party met Indians just above the present town of Gold Hill, where the chief agreed to assemble his people, unarmed, in two days to negotiate a treaty of peace. At the appointed hour some seventy-five

31. *Oregon Spectator,* Jan. 26, 1850; Lane to Samuel R. Thurston, Jan. 27, 1850, MS OrHi.

warriors sat down with the whites in a large circle around Lane and their two principal chiefs. Just as the parley was about to begin another seventy-five warriors advanced on the camp, some armed with guns, the rest with bows and arrows. With great aplomb Lane invited the new arrivals to put away their arms and to sit down in peace. He then asked Quatley to come inside the circle near the main chief. "I took a good look at the new comers," he related years afterwards, "and then looked quick at Quatley; he caught my eye and motioned his head; I saw that he understood me; and then I gave a look at my men, saw that they were all right, and commenced my talk."[32] Recounting in detail the several "outrages" committed against the whites, Lane insisted that whites be allowed to pass through the country unmolested and that all property stolen since the extension of United States law over the territory be surrendered, if the government were to afford the Indians protection and if the two races were to live in peace. The speech was coolly received. After the leading chief made a few remarks, his warriors leaped to their feet with a sudden war whoop. As the chief broke for his men, Quatley caught him from behind and, under orders from Lane, held a knife to his throat. Shouting to his men to hold their fire, Lane sprang to the line of Indians, six-shooter in hand, commanding them to sit down. When one large fellow hesitated too long, he struck down his gun. Reluctantly the chief called on his men to put down their arms. After a brief consultation, Lane ordered the Indians to withdraw for two days while he held their leader hostage.

Lane's audacity paid handsome dividends. Treating his prisoner with studied kindness, he soon gained the chief's confidence as much by his winning manner as by his demonstrated courage. When the chief's favorite wife cautiously asked to be allowed to join her husband in captivity, he met the request with courtesy and presents. The chief was impressed. Requesting an audience, the

32. Lane, "Autobiography," p. 92.

hostage asked if he might have Lane's name, for he had never before met a man quite like him. Lane agreed to give him half his name, suggesting that he should be called "Jo." Pleased with his new appellation, the chief asked him also to name his wife and two children. Lane said his wife should be "Sally" and his children "Ben" and "Mary," and the chief's cup was full.

In a lengthy conversation with the captive, Lane was able to persuade him of the folly of further hostility: it would lead only to war and the destruction of his people. If he would let whites settle the valley and mine the surrounding country, the government would pay for the land and send an agent who would live among them, give them annual presents, and look after their interests. By the end of the second day, Chief Jo was ready to accept a treaty. When the other chief (Sam) returned with the warriors, they agreed to accept the terms, and although they had irretrievably dumped the Oregonians' gold dust into the river, thinking it worthless, they turned over some stolen property of little value as a token of good faith. Lane accepted their professions of friendship and, to secure them as much as possible from violations of their treaty rights, wrote his name with a brief warning on slips of paper, which were distributed to each member of the tribe. In this way the name "Jo Lane" became a sort of talisman among the Indians of southern Oregon; for many it was the only English words they knew. In appreciation, Chief Jo presented Lane with a young Modoc slave, dumb, stark naked, and showing unmistakable marks of beatings and malnutrition. Lane took him, bathed and clothed him, named him John, and within a few weeks became quite attached to him.[33]

Sending Quatley and his men back to the Willamette Valley with an escort of whites, Lane proceeded with a small party of

33. The account of Lane's dealings with the Rogue River Indians is told in his "Autobiography," pp. 88–100, and is accepted by Bancroft, *History of Oregon, 2,* 219–20, and Victor, *The Early Indian Wars of Oregon Compiled from the Oregon Archives and Other Original Sources*

Oregonians to the mines of northern California, where he eagerly joined the ranks of the "Forty-Niners." Near Yreka they were the first to find gold in paying quantities, but the Indians were so numerous and hostile that they passed on to the Redding diggings near the present town of Shasta, where they met with less success. At Pitt River they found gold, but again the Indians were so sly and predatory, "as bad looking set of savage cut throats as I had met anywhere," that Lane was forced to keep a constant vigil. While assisting a companion who had fallen into their hands, he found himself surrounded and was rescued only by the approach of some of his own party. "I think I could have shot one as they darted into the thick brush but did not," Lane said later, "and I have been sorry ever since."[34]

Lane continued to work the diggings around Redding until February 1851, when he struck off for Scott River, where rich strikes had been discovered. In March he was back at the flats near Yreka, where—his sharp strictures about the Pitt River Indians notwithstanding—his fair and friendly dealings with the Indians earned him a reputation as "Tyee" (leader) among redmen and whites alike. Whenever an animal strayed from its owner, the Indians would cheerfully retrieve it, and Lane would compensate them for their time with a trinket or an item of clothing. "This

---

*with Muster Rolls* (Salem, Frank C. Baker, State Printer, 1894), pp. 267–70. In the mines some weeks later John saved Lane's life during an Indian raid. When Lane went to Washington, he left John with Nat in Oregon City, where he was well cared for until his death in June 1852.

34. Lane, "Autobiography," pp. 104–05. Some time later he shot one of them during a skirmish. "Autobiography," p. 108. On another occasion when he and Martin Angell camped for the night in some tall grass near the Sacramento River, Angell shot an Indian that was prowling near the camp. "He was dead as a hammer when we got to him," said Lane. "Angel was lucky in killing Indians." "Autobiography," p. 107. Lane, however, distinguished between "good" and "bad" Indians; John was a good one, and the Pitts were bad. Hence the same ambivalence toward the race that he revealed as superintendent of Indian affairs was also evident in the mines.

duty," wrote one of his fellow miners, "was a heavy drawback upon his time and his means, but was performed with a cheerfulness which had endeared him to all the old settlers here."[35]

His fortune in the mines was of the usual kind, respectable wages ($8 to $10 per day) but nothing more. Ignoring the privations, he thoroughly enjoyed the outdoor life. "Felt very comfortable and happy while at it—fully satisfied I would reach a fortune every day," he confessed to Bancroft. Then he added wistfully, with that incorrigible spark of optimism so characteristic of the mining fraternity, "And I think I would have done so if I had held on long enough."[36]

35. [E. Steele] to C. S. Drew [n.d.], cited by Margaret Jean Kelly, *The Career of Joseph Lane, Frontier Politician* (Washington, Catholic University of America Press, 1942), pp. 88–89. On March 14, 1851, the *Sacramento Transcript* described Lane in the mines: "He has long bushy hair, but clean chin; wears a red flannel shirt, and coarse short pea jacket. He is a plain man, but talks well with sound arguments."

36. *Oregon Statesman,* May 2, 1851; Lane, "Autobiography," p. 57.

*Chapter 2*

# BELLE-WEATHER DAYS

"I wish to God Gen. Lane was here and would consent to run," wrote Matthew P. Deady to his crony Nesmith in late February 1851; "I should like to see some man elected whom I had some sort of respect for." Urbane and debonair, the twenty-six-year-old Deady had in the previous spring chaired the meetings in Lafayette that had passed resolutions against the Lansdale letter and Lane's removal. He was not the only one to think of Lane in connection with the coming election of delegate to Congress. In his usual unpredictable orthography, Robert R. Thompson, part owner with Lane of the Island Mills, had already sent a letter to the mines urging his friend to yield to the solicitations of numerous citizens. Lane's reply was characteristically vague: "As to the Delegateship, I will leave the matter entirely to my friends. Oregon is, and shall be my home. Should I be elected, I will try to be useful to the

Territory. I am not ambitious for office. If it is agreed that I am to run, I will perform my part promptly." In political parlance, this meant yes. By special messenger Lane dispatched communications to friends in the Willamette Valley announcing a campaign itinerary that would allow him to work the diggings until the first of April. To enter the canvass was a bold decision, for the odds were against success.[1]

Samuel R. Thurston, Oregon's first delegate, was a man of above-average ability and a large personal following, especially among the influential mission group. In 1850 he had steered through Congress the extraordinarily generous Donation Land Act whereby an eligible settler could obtain legal title to 320 acres of free land—640 acres if married. Admittedly, some people had questioned the clause in the bill that denied McLoughlin his Oregon City claim by ascribing the Island Mills to Abernethy or his legal assigns (now Lane) and the Oregon City lots to the endowment of a university, but Lane could hardly object. "Some few have said that you will endeavour to put the Island and Mills, purchased of Abernethy, in the hands of the old Dr.," he wrote Thurston in January 1850. "Now . . . I know that you will never by any act of yours, take from good *American Citizens* their property and give it to any such foreigner."[2] The only issue that he was prepared to dispute was Thurston's decision to have the rifle

1. Deady to Nesmith, Feb. 23, 1851, MS OrHi; Lane to Thompson, n.d., *Oregon Spectator,* March 6, 1851.

Matthew Paul Deady (1824–93) was born in Maryland, educated in West Virginia and Ohio, and admitted to the bar in Ohio before coming to Oregon in 1849. In 1853 he was appointed associate justice for the southern district of the territorial supreme court and resided in the Umpqua Valley until Oregon achieved statehood. When Buchanan appointed him U.S. district judge for Oregon in 1859, he moved to Portland, where he resided until his death. A brilliant and articulate jurist, he became one of Oregon's most distinguished citizens.

2. Jan. 27, 1850, MS OrHi. Ironically, Thurston labored under the impression that Lane was working through Senator Jesse Bright of Indiana to secure the Oregon City claim to McLoughlin. He must not have known

regiment removed from the territory. In short, in the absence of any party organization, Lane was merely pitting his own popularity against that of the incumbent. He was spared the humiliation of probable defeat,[3] for about the time he reached Oregon City, the newspapers from California arrived bearing the startling news that Thurston, homeward bound, had died at sea.

Thurston's death spared another Oregonian a painful decision. At the instigation of Thurston, who wanted to establish a newspaper to promote his political fortunes, Massachusetts-born Asahel Bush arrived in Oregon City the last day of September 1850 to edit the new organ. Aggressive, calculating, and relentless, Bush had practically secured full control of the *Oregon Statesman* by the spring of 1851, when it began publication, and was determined to make it *the* voice of the Democratic party in Oregon, which he was then attempting to organize. When a group of citizens from Yamhill County unanimously nominated Lane in March 1851, Bush was confronted with the unpleasant prospect of choosing between two prominent Democrats at the very time that he was hoping to unify the party. He chose neither. To Deady he declared he would be neutral and uphold party rather than any individual. Two weeks later the *Statesman* reported the death of Thurston and noted the arrival of Lane, and in the next issue Lane's name ornamented the masthead.[4]

---

of Lane's purchase of the mills from Bryant. George H. Himes, ed., "Diary of Samuel Royal Thurston," *Oregon Historical Quarterly,* 15 (1914), 188–90.

3. In his "Autobiography," p. 57, Lane said Thurston had "acted very handsomely" in Congress. "He made himself so popular that neither I nor anyone else could have beaten him." One reason for contesting the election was that if he were successful he might visit his family and friends, whom he had not seen for nearly three years.

4. Bush to Deady, April 17, 1851, MS OrHi; *Oregon Statesman,* May 2, 9, 1851.

Born in Westfield, Massachusetts, Asahel Bush (1824–1913) in 1851 became territorial printer and in 1859 Oregon's first state printer, the only

Because of events that had transpired during his absence, Lane found that his popularity was even greater than when he had left for the mines. Whig Governor John P. Gaines, who arrived in August, differed from Lane in personality as much as in politics. Vain and pompous, a nonresident of the territory in which his party was in the minority, the hapless Gaines had no easy row to hoe.[5] Besides, he was tactless and overly zealous in the use of executive power. Leading Oregonians were quick to express their resentment. Their opportunity came when the territorial legislature, which three days previously had named a county after Lane, passed a bill locating the capitol at Salem, the university at Marysville (Corvallis), and the penitentiary at Portland. With the support of United States Attorney Amory Holbrook, also a Whig appointee, Gaines attacked the bill as unconstitutional in a message on February 3, 1851, contending that the Organic Act forbade more than one item to be incorporated in any bill. The measure passed over his objections amid cries of unwarranted executive interference. Bush saw in this clash the opportunity to make political capital against the Whigs and, with blithe indifference to the facts of the case, blandly interpreted it along party lines. This identification of the Democracy with Salem and all dissenters with the opposition had ominous overtones, and only time would fully reveal the consequences.[6]

---

elective public office he ever held. Through sheer strength of personality and intellect, he made the *Statesman* the most important newspaper in Oregon in the 1850s and himself the dominant political force in the territory, making and breaking political careers almost at will. He retired as editor in 1862 and subsequently engaged in banking and various other commercial and civic ventures. A very old man at the time of his death, he was regarded around Salem as a minor legendary figure.

5. The resentment of "foreign" appointees was real and deepseated. "If this administration does not colonize Oregon with imported whiggery," wrote Bush (*Oregon Statesman,* May 2, 1851), "it will not be because they do not try, but because they cannot find offices to fill."

6. On the struggle over the location issue, see Charles Henry Carey, *History of Oregon, 1* (Chicago, Pioneer Historical Publishing Company,

For his part Lane was unwilling to alienate votes by a strictly partisan campaign and pledged himself to represent the interests of all Oregonians. In his opening speech at Oregon City, he stated that although he was a Democrat he did not think the territory ought to be "distracted by party politics." Here, where opposition to Salem was most pronounced, he approved even the appointment of Gaines: he knew of no Whig he would rather see in the gubernatorial office. The Whiggish *Spectator,* which reported the event, decided to support Lane because "he would not be the tool of a party," pointing out that he had decided to run before learning of Thurston's demise. The Democratic *Western Star* at Milwaukie, where Lane spoke the following evening, reasoned that no Whig need hesitate to give him his vote since a delegate had no vote in Congress anyway. Even the Portland *Oregonian,* professedly Whig, advocated Lane over Thurston because he was the people's choice "without regard to party."[7]

Lane's only opponent, William H. Willson, nominated by the mission party that had supported Thurston, was also a Democrat, so the campaign was a lack-luster affair. Lane toured the Willamette Valley, visited Astoria, and again ascended the valley as far as Marysville by election day. His speeches consisted of the platitudes common to aspiring politicians. He insisted that Oregon was his home and that he would represent it faithfully. He thought the land law very good but would amend it to make more people eligible. He opposed the recall of the regular troops from the territory and would try to secure a military post for the Umpqua Valley. He would request Congress to pay the expenses of the Cayuse War and allow the volunteers a land bounty similar to

---

1922), 497–501, and Walter Carleton Woodward, *The Rise and Early History of Political Parties in Oregon, 1842–1868* (Portland, J. K. Gill Company, 1913), pp. 40–51.

7. *Oregon Spectator,* May 8, 1851; *Western Star,* May 8, 1851; *Weekly Oregonian,* April 26, 1851.

that given to veterans of other wars. "Leave nothing undone that can be honorably done to help me," he implored Joel Palmer. "See my friends and talk for me all you can. I want to beat Wilson badly. I will do good for this Territory and no mistake."[8]

There was some opposition. A few felt that Lane's property in Oregon City might prejudice him toward that vicinity. More serious was the suspicion that he was too opportunistic. "There is considerable feeling here against Lane," wrote Bush's henchman and Portland correspondent, Reuben P. Boise, "for the reason that he will not commit himself in relation to the Hudson Bay Company, and would say nothing relative to the action of the late legislature. He is entirely noncommittal and trying to shun every question that is asked." Before the campaign was a week old, even Deady harbored second thoughts. His words were to prove strangely prophetic: "I wish Lane could shake off these whig politicians from his skirts. If not, the day will come when he will regret it, and the democratic party also."[9]

The returns tallied 2,375 votes for Lane; for Willson, 543.[10]

Like an indefatigable sentinel overlooking the Rogue River, Table Rock afforded the Indians a commanding sweep of the valley below. From its massive ramparts they could with complete security survey the little bands of travelers passing to and fro on

8. George E. Cole, "A Pioneer's Recollections," Scrapbook 35, p. 1, OrHi; Lane to Palmer, May 26, 1851, MS OrHi. Palmer had chaired the meeting in Yamhill County that first nominated Lane. Cf. Lane to Nesmith, March 27, 1851, MS OrHi.

9. Boise to Bush [ca. May 1851], Bush Papers (Oregon State Library, Salem; photostatic copies in University of Oregon Library, Eugene); Deady to Bush, May 4, 1851, Bush Papers.

10. *Oregon Statesman,* July 4, 1851. Although these figures are given as "official," they include returns that were "reported reliably" from Clatsop County; one precinct in Lane County had not yet reported and was expected to give Lane a majority of about thirty votes. Cf. *Oregon Statesman,* June 23, 1857, which listed the returns for 1851 as 1911–426.

the hot and dusty trail to the California mines. In May 1851, the natives were restless, and their increasing acts of violence were interrupted only by divisions of mounted riflemen marching south at intervals on their return to Missouri. On the first of June, the Indians attacked twenty-six men returning from the mines; two days later they swept down on a party of thirty-two led by James McBride, who fought them off after a four-hour encounter. Word of these hostilities reached Major Philip Kearny, commander of the last division to leave Oregon City, as he was reconnoitering the southern reaches of the Umpqua Valley in search of a better route for a military road through the canyon. With a detachment of twenty-eight men, he immediately set off for Table Rock, where the Indians were said to be congregated. On June 17, about five miles from the Rock, the Indians met a contingent of his men, mortally wounding one and severely injuring another before retreating to their stronghold. Kearny prudently fell back to await reinforcements.

Determined to look after some mining property before leaving for Washington, Lane left Oregon City the morning of June 12 and learned of the outbreak of hostilities along the Rogue when he reached Nesmith's Mills, west of Salem. Hurrying south with about forty men, he received word of the latest battle while passing through the Umpqua Canyon. The next night an express brought word that Kearny had broken camp and was planning to attack the enemy at daybreak. With little chance of success, citizen Lane—for he was now without any official authority—rode hard all the next day, eventually reaching Kearny well after midnight, too late for the showdown with the Indians. After a few minor skirmishes during the mopping-up operations of the next few days, Lane went on to California. In all, about fifty Indians were killed and many injured, while the whites had no losses and only three or four wounded.[11]

11. *Oregon Statesman,* June 13, July 15, 1851. See also Bancroft, *History of Oregon,* 2, 225–31.

With the Indians spurning offers of peace, Kearny was reluctant to surrender his prisoners, mostly women and children, until a treaty was negotiated; but he was anxious to resume his march, and, embarrassed by the absence of any territorial officer, he elected to take his prisoners with him and return them by sea to Oregon City. Meanwhile, Lane took less than three days to settle his business in the Shasta diggings, and, as Kearny had just passed with the prisoners, he offered to relieve him by escorting them back to Oregon. Whereupon Lane, with some twenty other Oregonians to assist him, started north early the next morning. When he reached the Rogue River, several Indians on the other side recognized him and complained bitterly that the whites had invaded every part of their country, that they were afraid to sleep at night lest they be assaulted, and that they were tired of war and wanted peace. He told them he would turn over the prisoners to the governor, who he had heard was waiting for them at the river crossing, and who, he assured them, would make peace if they would honor it. Gaines did conclude an informal treaty and later paid warm tribute to Lane's assistance in settling this unhappy affair.[12]

With her boiler laboring under a full head of steam and her stacks belching great clouds of black smoke, the *Columbia* eased away from the dock at Astoria and pointed her prow toward the treacherous bar that divides river from open sea. On board was Oregon's new delegate, bound for Panama, New York, Indiana, and finally Washington. If he permitted himself a few moments of self-congratulation that July day, 1851, he might be excused, for

12. Lane to ed., July 8, 1851, *Oregon Statesman,* July 22, 1851; *Oregon Spectator,* July 22, 1851; Alban Hoopes, *Indian Affairs and Their Administration with Special Reference to the Far West* (Philadelphia, University of Pennsylvania Press, 1932), p. 88. Addison C. Gibbs, "Notes on the History of Oregon," n.d. (Bancroft Library, University of California, Berkeley), p. 10, also attributes the peace to Lane's efforts.

the felicitations of his friends and neighbors were still ringing in his ears. "Large and enthusiastic" was the *Spectator's* account of his reception in Oregon City the night before. Those present had passed a flattering resolution—Bush was the secretary—commending him for bringing the Whitmans' murderers to justice, recovering the deserters, and rendering assistance in the recent Indian difficulties. "Three hearty cheers for General Lane."[13] And at Astoria, a number of citizens had been waiting at the landing to pay their respects and offer their compliments. It was enough to put any man in high spirits.

Lane could indeed look back with much satisfaction on his brief career in Oregon. The only significant setback had been the Island Mills, but Nat was in charge of them now, and Nat was a good boy. So was Joe, his second oldest son, who had come from Indiana that summer and was improving a land claim in the Umpqua Valley on which Lane had filed under the Donation Land Act. Joe would have a house built by the time Lane returned to Oregon in 1853 with the rest of his family.[14] Now, in a few weeks he would rejoin his family, whom he had not seen for more than three years. Moreover, newspapers in Indiana were talking about running him for president next year.

In San Francisco, Governor John McDougal was on hand to extend the hospitalities of the state during Lane's two-day stopover, giving a reception in his honor at Jones' Hotel. United States Senator William M. Gwin, Lieutenant Governor David C. Broderick, Sheriff John C. Hays, and other dignitaries attended, and the atmosphere was most congenial with "wine and anecdote circulating until the 'small hours' had far advanced." According to one newspaper account, Lane was "the 'bright-particular star'

13. *Oregon Spectator,* July 29, 1851.
14. *Oregon Statesman,* July 29, Sept. 30, 1851. Joseph Samuel Lane came to Oregon in 1851, but precisely when or how is unknown. Scrapbook 11, p. 53, OrHi. He was present when Lane turned the prisoners over to Gaines. *Oregon Statesman,* July 22, 1851.

of the evening" whose sensible remarks and folksy tales found a ready audience. When the reporter left, Lane and his friends were still going strong. "We regret that he has determined on leaving us so soon," the account concluded, "but the General has been always celebrated for rapid movements."[15]

On the steamer *Oregon,* "Queen of the Pacific," Lane found the passengers congenial and arrived at Panama in excellent health and much pleased with the trip. Yet his fine spirits and the pleasant voyage ought not obscure the fact that travel by sea in the mid-nineteenth century was beset with grave dangers. Always present were risks of tropical fevers, unseaworthy vessels, and inclement weather. Just four months before on this same journey, Thurston had contracted a fever that proved fatal—he was only thirty-six—and on this present voyage three passengers expired at sea. With no steamer available at Chagres, the eastern terminal of the Isthmus crossing, Lane preferred to stay at Panama for two additional days. But when he finally reached Chagres, he changed course abruptly, for there he learned that the Venezuelan adventurer, General Narcisco López, had launched a second invasion of Cuba, this time with apparent success, despite the capture and execution of some fifty of his men. Lane's "desire to know the facts" got the better of him, and rather than proceeding to New York as intended, he booked passage on the *Cherokee,* which was bound for New Orleans via Havana, where it would stop for coal. On Sunday, August 31, Lane reached Havana harbor.[16]

15. San Francisco *Daily Star,* cited in *Oregon Spectator,* Aug. 12, 1851, and *Oregon Statesman,* Aug. 19, 1851.

16. Letter from Lane, Aug. 21, 1851, *Oregon Statesman,* Sept. 30, 1851; Lane to Bush, Havana, Sept. 1, 1851, ibid., Oct. 15, 1851; Lane, "Autobiography," p. 112.

A former high-ranking official in Spain and Cuba, López (1798–1851) first attempted to "liberate" Cuba in 1850, after receiving support from American expansionists in the South. The expedition failed to rally the support of the Cuban people, and López himself was arrested and sent back to the U.S. In August 1851 he launched a second expedition from New Orleans.

López and the remainder of his 450 men were captured on Saturday. The general was executed at seven o'clock Monday morning, surrounded by two thousand troops formed in a hollow square to restrain the twenty thousand spectators. "The scene was imposing, although awful," said an eyewitness.[17] In white gown and cap, his hands bound, López ascended the scaffold and spoke a few unrepentant words to the crowd before the iron collar of the garrote was fastened around his neck. His executioner gave one quick turn of the screw, and the metal teeth bit into the flesh, crushing the vertebrae. Death was instantaneous. The episode deeply disturbed Lane, and he lashed out at the apathy of the Cuban people, "who deserve no better government than they now have." "It is greatly to be hoped," he wrote Bush from Havana, "that no further attempt will be made upon Cuba, until it is done in a way that will ensure success."[18]

After leaving Havana, the passengers of the *Cherokee* elected Lane to preside at a meeting called to express their profound indignation at the grisly spectacle and particularly at the apparent indifference of the American consul, A. F. Owens. He spoke feelingly to the group about the barbarity of the Spaniards and chastised Owens for neglecting his trust. A committee drew up resolutions embodying these sentiments and demanding Owens' recall. By the time Lane reached Indiana, his censure of the Cubans had turned to compassion, and he declared that Cuba must soon be free. The problem lay not with the Cuban people but with their Spanish overlords, whose government he pronounced "the most cruel and oppressive on the face of God's earth."[19]

A large number of friends called to pay their respects when Lane arrived at his home, eight miles above Evansville on the Ohio River, and they found him in exceedingly good health and spirits.

17. *Oregon Weekly Times,* Nov. 6, 1851.
18. Lane to Bush, Sept. 1, 1851, *Oregon Statesman,* Oct. 14, 1851.
19. Ibid., Oct. 28, 1851; Lane to Bush, Sept. 23, 1851, ibid., Dec. 23, 1851.

"Indeed," said the *Indiana State Sentinel,* "he seems to improve by age." The next ten weeks were devoted to renewing old acquaintances, attending to personal business matters, and politicking among the people. Some four thousand old friends and neighbors attended a barbecue for him in Vanderburgh County, which he had previously represented in the state legislature. Due to an apparent confusion in scheduling, Lane failed to appear at Logansport, where a gathering of admirers and well-wishers awaited him; some former comrades-in-arms had traveled as far as forty miles just to see him. Wrote one disappointed devotee, "It was said that to look at 'the General' would do the party more service than to hear all the speeches that could be made." Audiences in Ohio, where he also went to campaign, were large and enthusiastic.[20]

Particularly impressive was his reception at Indianapolis, where Indianans assembled en masse to welcome home the man who had led their volunteers at Buena Vista. When he and United States Senator Jesse Bright stepped off the "steam cars" just before one o'clock in the afternoon, they were greeted by a large crowd that had been waiting for more than an hour. Riding with Bright and Governor Joseph A. Wright in an open barouche, Lane made his way to the public square in front of the State House, where the governor delivered a panegyric, recalling Lane's previous legislative accomplishment in thwarting repudiation of the state debt and thereby securing the honor and integrity of the Hoosier State. Lane modestly acknowledged the flattering references to his earlier work but thought that the governor had perhaps attributed more to him than was merited, although he admitted to having been "the artificer of his own fortunes." After lauding the role of the Indiana volunteers in Mexico—"in Old Hickory style," said the

20. *Indiana State Sentinel,* cited in *Oregon Weekly Times,* Dec. 13, 1851; *Oregon Statesman,* Feb. 3, 1852; Mrs. M. V. Fitch to Lane, Sept. 25 [1851]; "Western" [pseud.], *Biography of Joseph Lane; "Not Inappropriately Styled by His Brother Officers and Soldiers, 'the Marion of the War'"* (Washington, Congressional Globe Office, 1852), pp. 34–39.

*Shelby Volunteer*—he commended the Indianans for supporting the measures of the Compromise of 1850, especially the Fugitive Slave Act, the "best measure of all." Slavery, he said, had always been an inflammatory subject, and he had always opposed its agitation; sensible people in the free states should leave it alone as the Constitution had done, because "it could never be agitated without endangering the integrity of the Union." Regarding the talk about himself and the presidency, he hastened to say that he had no aspirations to that office and would support the nominee at Baltimore, whoever he might be; should the choice happen to fall on him, he would do his best to meet his responsibilities. Then, after reviewing the militia, he sat down to dine with the notables of the state.[21]

Since he had been home for less than five months in the past five years, Lane had to become reacquainted with his family. There to greet him was his wife, Polly, a year younger than himself, diminutive, persevering, and long-suffering. Not being able to read or write, she had to rely on his letters to the children for news of his welfare. Of the six boys and four girls that made up the family circle when he left in 1848, Nat and Joe were now in Oregon, and Ratliff, his second oldest boy, had died from cholera during a flatboat trip to New Orleans in December 1848. His eldest girl Melissa, now thirty years old, was married to Andrew Barlow, and seventeen-year-old Emily had recently married Creed Floed, who, like Barlow, spent much of his time on the river. At home were Mary (twenty-one), Simon (nineteen), John (fourteen), Winnifred (eleven), and Lafayette (almost nine).[22] In the warm

21. *Indiana State Sentinel,* cited in *Oregon Weekly Times,* Jan. 31, 1852; Shelbyville *Shelby Volunteer,* cited in *Oregon Statesman,* Jan. 27, 1852; Mary V. Lane to Joseph S. Lane, Nov. 5, 1851, typescript, Lane Papers (University of Oregon Library, Eugene), cited hereafter as Lane Papers, OrU.

22. These ages are approximate, for in most cases only the year of birth is known.

evenings, Lane told them about far-off Oregon, particularly the wonders of the Umpqua Valley, which they tried to visualize as their new home.

The sale of his farm to Judge Bryant settled Lane's indebtedness for the Island Mills and severed the last link that bound him to Indiana. To be sure, the Hoosier State would continue to furnish him a base for national political operation whenever expediency so dictated, but from now on Lane was irrevocably committed to the cause of Oregon. He had been elated by his reception here, he admitted to Bush, perhaps anticipating that his words would be given wider circulation, but somehow Indiana now seemed different. "The people, though as clever as any in the world, don't look healthy as they do in Oregon; nor is the country like Oregon. I long to be there. I would not give my claim in Oregon for twenty miles upon the banks of the Ohio, and be compelled to remain in this country. Oregon is my country—my home."[23]

The first session of the Thirty-second Congress assembled in Washington City on the first day of December 1851, and the new delegate from Oregon set about to familiarize himself with life in the national capital and to assume his necessarily minor role in the legislative process. Without a vote in either house or membership in any congressional committee, a delegate had chiefly to represent the needs and wants of his constituents to Congress and the executive. To do this he might occupy a seat in the House, participate in debates, testify before various committees, expedite business with the departments, and in general inform, persuade, or cajole any person advantageously situated to influence or implement territorial legislation. Because a delegate represented a sparsely populated area more or less remote from urban and commercial centers, he invariably became the chosen agent for any number of

23. Lane to Bush, Sept. 19, 1851, *Oregon Statesman,* Dec. 23, 1851.

constituents, whose continual requests for personal, political, and business favors levied a heavy toll upon his time and energy. The most significant opportunities for aggrandizement and prestige lay in dispensing federal patronage, the "sinews of war" to local party faithful. With the return of the Democracy to the White House in the person of Franklin Pierce, Lane learned to exploit his position as spokesman of party interests in Oregon Territory.[24]

From the first, Lane was overwhelmed by the sheer volume of mail that cascaded over his desk in a veritable avalanche. "The citizens in this section of the country feel, and justly, that they have been neglected, . . . and are growing a little sensitive on the subject, so if you ever expect to solicit their suffrages again, you would do well to show them some little attentions," wrote a settler from Puget Sound. Thurston sent the people documents and papers to secure their favor, stated John Orvis Waterman, editor of the Portland *Times,* advising Lane to do likewise. Six weeks later he reiterated his advice: "Send documents to every man you can think of—it makes no difference what is is." Even Nat added to the admonitions: "I hear a great deal of complaint that your not writing to the Citizens of Oregon. they say you don't seem to think that they are your Constituents. . . . I am sorry you have not written more and hope you will try and make up in the future what you have neglected in the beginning." To Deady, Lane confessed on February 19 that he had never been so busy in his life. "In addition to letters from Oregon, I have received daily an average of more than twenty letters, coming in from every direction and por-

24. John M. Hayden to Lane, Dec. 21, 1851, MS OrHi; Waterman to Lane, Feb. 10, March 25, 1852, MS OrHi.

Waterman (1826–83) was a native of Vermont who came to Oregon in 1850 and began editing the Milwaukie *Western Star.* The next year he acquired full control of the paper, moved it to Portland, and changed its name to the *Oregon Weekly Times.* He sold the *Times* in 1854 but remained as editor until 1857. After practicing law for a time in Portland, he spent the late years of his life as a teacher and public school superintendent in eastern Washington.

tion of this country." Lane estimated that these letters alone now totaled more than two thousand.[25]

Many of the letters were of the kind that plagued most congressmen, then and since, requesting such favors as the latest report from the patent office, a copy of Daniel Webster's speech last March, a sample of the latest variety of wheat, or a subscription to the Washington *Union*—they would pay when he got back, or would pay Nat, and Lane could draw on him. Frequently the requests were for office, often from Mexican War veterans who, more often than not, simply wanted to obtain free transportation to Oregon. One man might have a claim against the government for so many days of military service: could Lane see the War or Treasury Department and find out what the holdup was? Another might have difficulty in securing title to a land claim: could Lane drop by the land office and explain his case to them? Still another needed some equipment for a mill: would Lane get it from a company in New York that traded in these items? Someone even wanted to borrow $300. One correspondent wanted his son appointed to West Point and urged Lane to "make this application direct to the President." Of the several who wanted to go back with him to Oregon, one husband was particularly distraught: "My wife heretofore having been opposed [to the journey], but now willing upon condition that I will go in your *Train* as she believes you will protect her from the Indians from which source she has many fears." Lane conscientiously tried to acknowledge every letter and, whenever possible, accede to the requests.[26]

25. Nat to Lane, June 30, 1852, MS OrHi; Lane to Deady, Feb. 19, 1852, MS OrHi.

26. S. G. Simmons to Lane, Jan. 7, 1852, MS OrHi; H. G. Barkwell to Lane, March 27, 1852, MS OrHi. Lane's willingness to oblige is well illustrated by a reply to his Whig friend, Jesse Applegate, who wanted him to collect some money. "I beg you to remember that it is no trouble to me to attend to any business for you, but on the contrary it is a pleasure. . . . I feel proud of an opertunity of serving you or any other constituent by attending promptly to any business you or any other citizen of Oregon may wish attended to." Oct. 19, 1852, Lane Papers, InU.

Most of the two thousand letters not from Oregon were inquiries about the opportunities there, the nature of the land and climate, or the most feasible route. Before one month had elapsed Lane decided that the only way to cope with the situation was to publish a letter to meet the interests of his correspondents. The circular, which was probably drafted by Lane and then revised by some clerk, described the territory in factual but favorable terms.[27] It circulated widely and won acclaim for its author among those interested in going to Oregon, and for it the author deserves some small notice among the ranks of publicists of the Pacific Northwest.

Lane's first important speech in Washington was delivered not in Congress but at a Jackson Day dinner, January 8, 1852, commemorating the Battle of New Orleans. It was a gala occasion with speeches by Lewis Cass, defeated presidential candidate of 1848, the youthful Stephen A. Douglas, fast-rising "Little Giant" from Illinois, who had contributed substantially to the Compromise of 1850, and the guest of honor, the flaming Hungarian revolutionary, Louis Kossuth. The night was made for oratory, and infected by the effervescence of the evening, Lane delivered a spread-eagle speech in the worst American tradition, clearly identifying himself with the expansionist wing of the Democratic party. Some of the speech was pure buncombe;[28] the remainder was an emotional plea for the extension of American institutions throughout this continent, the Pacific Islands, and ultimately the whole world. Cuba, he said, "is *almost* ours already." Hungary must be free. "Then let any Russian power say these people should not enjoy liberty and equal rights, and the voice of this people, from one end of the nation to the other, would thunder out, in the language of the

27. *Circular of Hon. Joseph Lane, Delegate from Oregon, in Reference to the Settlement, Soil, and Climate of Oregon Territory* (Washington, J. T. Towers, 1852).

28. "I would like to extend to others the principles of our Government; and, after they have become independent and free, I would, by annexation, throw around them our protection." The speech was reprinted in *Oregon Statesman,* March 30, 1852, and *Oregon Weekly Times,* April 3, 1852.

illustrious Jackson, 'By the Eternal, they shall be free.' [Cheers.]" The audience was with him, and he relished their applause. "I have had the honor in my life of voting three times for General Jackson, twice for Mr. Van Buren, and once for Mr. Polk. In 1848 I was not in the country, and things went wrong. [Great laughter.]" Amidst boisterous cheering he concluded with a ringing slogan for Jackson's party: "A UNION OF THE DEMOCRACY FOR THE SAKE OF THE UNION." So elated was he afterwards by the compliments of his friends that he wrote to his son Simon that many thought his speech the best of all.[29]

Unfortunately, his maiden speech in the House was decidedly less successful—in truth, almost a fiasco. One of his first tasks after Congress had convened was to call on President Millard Fillmore, in addition to addressing him by letter, urging him to station troops along the Oregon Trail and the road from Oregon to California in time for the year's emigration. Armed with a memorial from the Oregon legislature, he introduced a resolution on February 9 to ask the President what steps had been taken, if any, to fortify these routes and to "request him to cause" the regiment of mounted riflemen to be garrisoned in the Rogue River Valley and between The Dalles and Fort Hall. The resolution passed without dissent, only to be reconsidered when some members questioned the propriety of instructing the President how to discharge his responsibilities. The resolution simply requested and did not instruct, stated Lane, reminding the House that the regiment had been raised specifically for service in Oregon; would not its removal be a breach of contract with the men who had enlisted? He opposed referring the resolution to committee, because the garrisons would be needed within two months—hardly time enough to recruit and train a new regiment. *He* knew as well as anyone that Congress could not order the President as commander in chief to deploy the troops under his command, and if the resolu-

29. Cited in Simon R. Lane to Joseph S. Lane, Jan. 20, 1852, typescript, Lane Papers, OrU.

tion were not worded correctly, he would like to change it. At this point everyone, it seemed, wanted to get into the act, and the debate ranged from banality to banality: whether the regiment had been recalled from Oregon or California; whether Polk, Taylor, or Fillmore had ordered the regiment so removed; whether infantry or dragoons were better suited for Indian service; whether the Secretary of War or the Ways and Means Committee had authorized the printing of the quartermaster's deficiency estimates. Lane again offered to amend his resolution to make it "merely a request, and not a command," but once more he was ignored. Two days and fifteen pages of the *Congressional Globe* later, the issue was resolved, but not before Lane had slipped out and conferred with the Secretary of War, who gave ready assurances that the troops would be stationed along the route to Oregon in time to protect the emigrants. Lane returned to the half-spent House, apologized for taking so much of its time, and with a little more perseverance managed to obtain a vote to table the resolution.[30]

Despite his lack of experience, Oregon's delegate proved to be very diligent in carrying out his responsibilities. Three items of legislation that he introduced had important consequences for his constituents. He presented a memorial from the majority of representatives in the legislative assembly asking Congress to confirm the removal of the state capital from Oregon City to Salem. It was unanimously accepted by a joint resolution of House and Senate, but of this, more later. Thurston had obtained an appropriation of $100,000 to recompense those who had served or suffered losses

30. Lane to Millard Fillmore, Dec. 12, 1852 [i.e. 1851], *Oregon Weekly Times,* April 10, 1852; *Congressional Globe,* 32 Cong., 1 Sess., pp. 507–10, 512–23. Despite his assurances, the Secretary of War, informed Lane in May that it could not be done. To a prospective emigrant Lane wrote, "The President is, of course, the commander-in-chief of our forces, and being a whig, I do not consider it advisable to rely upon government protection during his official term. A change of administration may correct this evil." Lane to David Adams, May 26, 1852, *Oregon Statesman,* Aug. 14, 1852.

during the Cayuse uprising, but no provision had been made for the disposition of these funds. Lane successfully proposed an amendment, which was adopted, whereby the Secretary of the Treasury was instructed to make payment according to the report submitted by Commissioner Aaron E. Waite. The House defeated a further proposal to make the Oregon volunteers eligible for the usual land bounties and yet another to permit those residents of Oregon entitled to warrants to locate them within the territory.[31] A third measure, which proved to be Lane's greatest personal triumph, was a bill to construct military roads from Fort Walla Walla to Puget Sound, from the Sound to the Columbia River, and from the Umpqua Valley to Camp Stuart on the Rogue River. Unfortunately, none of these routes was surveyed, a fact that critics of the bill were quick to proclaim, and the bill had not been recommended by the Secretary of War because it had been referred to the Committee on Roads and Canals rather than the Committee on Military Affairs. Lane insisted that to wait for a survey would delay construction for three years and that the roads were an immediate military necessity. He admitted that they would also be useful to immigrants and that the proposed appropriation of $50,000 would permit elementary wagon roads to be opened while preparations for the survey were concluded. The House struck out $10,000 for the road from the Columbia to the Sound and sent the bill to the Senate. It arrived too late for action that session, but passage came early in the second session.[32]

A variety of other measures reflected the aspirations of citizens in the new territory and received mixed receptions in Congress. Lane presented a memorial from the legislative assembly to permit Oregonians to elect their own governor and judges, but it was rejected. He introduced bills to extend the benefits of the Donation Land Act, to improve navigation of the Willamette and Yamhill

31. *Congressional Globe,* 32 Cong., 1 Sess., pp. 626–28, 1456.

32. Ibid., pp. 1395–96, 1530; Lane to ed., June 9, 1852, *Oregon Statesman,* Aug. 14, 1852; *Congressional Globe,* 32 Cong., 2 Sess., p. 165.

rivers, to erect customhouses and complete lighthouses under construction, to expand considerably the existing postal facilities, and to amend the Donation Act so that residents could purchase their land for $1.25 an acre before the residence requirement was fulfilled. He relayed petitions from residents of the lower Umpqua and Puget Sound asking for local improvements. He obtained a private bill for the relief of Mrs. Thurston, who had been forced to pay postage on books franked by her husband just prior to his ill-fated return voyage. When Congress agreed to grant the delegate from Oregon the same mileage as members from California, Lane's travel allowance increased from $2,500 to $4,000 a year. Although the actual number of bills that passed was few, Lane prided himself on his effectiveness as a legislator. "No Delegate has ever, at any one session, succeeded in getting more bills thro' the House," he wrote to Bush, confident that he could pry some of the important ones out of the Senate early in the next session. Pratt, in Washington on business for Bush, appraised the situation with more candor. "Congress adjourned without doing much of anything for Oregon," he wrote to Deady, although he added that Lane seemed to be highly regarded by Congress, and "all unite in speaking in terms of great respect & good will for our Delegate."[33]

Oregonians were a vexed and disturbed people in the winter of 1851–52. "The people in this country," complained one of them to Lane, "thinks less and less every day of governor gaines. they say it is to much like being governed by a petticoat to be governed by him." Actually the problem was no longer chiefly one of personality. Thanks to Bush's untiring efforts, party lines were emerging irrepressibly, and the question of where to locate the seat of government had become the touchstone of party regularity, as

33. Elizabeth T. Thurston to Lane, March 17, 1852, MS OrHi; *Oregon Weekly Times,* April 17, 1852; Lane to Bush, Oct. 19, 1852, *Oregon Statesman,* Jan. 1, 1853; Pratt to Deady, Sept. 7, 1852, MS OrHi.

Bush had long since determined it should be—notwithstanding his studied attempts to make the issue appear "simply the support of the laws and opposition to federal usurpation." Immediately following Lane's election, the *Statesman* had issued a call for a convention in Marion County to organize the Democratic party permanently. The minority Whigs insisted that parties were unnecessary inasmuch as territories had no vote in Congress, and positively harmful because they would distract individuals from pursuing the best interests of Oregon. Moreover, they recalled Lane had campaigned on a nonpartisan basis. Bush retorted editorially that Lane had always been an unwavering Democrat and that "his associations, his interests and his sympathies were all with that party." To the great dismay of the Whigs, Lane scotched further debate by sending a strongly worded missive to Bush: *"I am glad to witness your efforts to get a democratic organization. Loose no time in urging the democrats to organize and unite. All local and sectional issues should be dropped.* WITH THE ORGANIZATION AND UNION OF THE DEMOCRACY ALL WILL BE WELL IN OREGON."[34] Bush planted these words on the masthead in March and did not remove them until the day following the territorial election in June 1852. By the time the letter reached Oregon, the Democratic members at Salem had caucused and elected a central committee to coordinate party action. When the legislature, except for Governor Gaines and five northern members, met at Salem in December, Bush declared the location question ended. At Oregon City, Gaines and his supporters daily went through the motions of meeting and adjourning for lack of a quorum until nearly Christmas, when they finally gave up the

34. Thomas C. Shaw to Lane, Dec. 22, 1851, MS OrHi; Bush to Deady, Feb. 25 [1852], MS OrHi; *Oregon Statesman,* Nov. 11, 1852; Lane to Bush, Dec. 22, 1851, *Oregon Statesman,* Feb. 24, 1852. Nat to Lane, Jan. 4, 1852, MS OrHi, suggests that Lane's professed neutrality had not been entirely sincere: "I think when ever an opportunity offers to undeceive the people in reference to your standing with the whig officers it would be well to do so."

struggle. To Lane, Gaines wrote bitterly but with some truth, "If you think this is a controversy between whig and democrat please dismiss that thought. It is a fight between two ways of the Democracy." In fact, several Democrats did favor Oregon City and were incensed at Bush's attempts to read them out of the party. "An old fashioned Iron bound Jackson-democrat," who would soon become a leading Whig, wrote to Lane that "without doubt, the Salem faction intended a deliberate violation of all law, and order; and to reproduce *a Revolution* . . . on these local questions."[35] Yet a Whig like Jesse Applegate endorsed the Salem legislature. Meanwhile two of the three justices of the Oregon Supreme Court, both Whig appointees, upheld the action of the governor. The third, Judge Pratt, Democrat, declared their ruling invalid because they had held court at Oregon City instead of Salem. Pratt immediately became the idol of the legislators meeting at Salem, and they promptly ordered three thousand copies of his opinion printed for distribution. At the instigation of Deady, they also passed and forwarded to Lane a memorial asking Congress not only to ratify their acts but to allow them to elect their own governor, secretary, and judges.

The unresolved debate became more acrimonious with each passing day. Party lines were drawn as Bush persistently paraded the rights of the people's representatives against their "foreign" rulers. "Whatever you do," Nat warned his father, "dont favor Oregon City and the federal officers. They have arrayed themselves against the people and their representatives who met at Salem." The controversy also gave rise to a campaign of journalistic invective that soon gave the press in Oregon a national reputation for vigorous and personal abuse. "We have entered the political arena," announced the *Spectator* in February, castigating Pratt as "a political Judas" and "the biggest toad in the puddle." When Waterman refused to oppose Bush, the *Spectator* dismissed the

35. Gaines to Lane, Jan. 2, 1852, MS OrHi; *Weekly Oregonian,* Jan. 31, 1852; James McBride to Lane [ca. May 1852], Feb. 4, 1852, MS OrHi.

"We(a)kly *Times*" as "only a reprint of the Statesman." Editor Thomas J. Dryer of the *Oregonian* opposed organizing a Whig party but hurled weekly salvos at the "nulifiers" at Salem. Even though he had long since promised his readers not to notice the attacks of "Bush-y" and his "Mormon organ," he eventually reached his saturation point and vented his spleen against "the unholy, ungodly and pusillanimous, semi-official and understrapper attacks, that have for the last six months been poured out like an incessant shower of mud . . . upon the people's officers." Over the signature of "Breakspear" (William L. Adams), the *Oregonian* in February and March featured a series of biting articles entitled "Treason, Strategems and Spoils," a five-act melodrama, which lampooned Democratic leaders without mercy and became the sensation of the day. Pratt, and increasingly Bush—"Ass-a-hell" to his opponents—drew the fire of these attacks, and the implacable editor of the *Statesman* returned in full measure each volley of invective and abuse.[36] Finally Bush's highhanded attempts to read out of the party all who would dispute his stand on the location question aroused the resentment of many Democrats and marked the beginning of long-lasting discord within the ranks of the Democracy. Soon the supremacy of Salem in party councils would engender the appellation "Clique" as a mark of opprobrium by those who protested the centralization of power in the hands of a few.

"All now depends on you and congress," wrote Deady. "Something *must* be done soon. These whigs are getting desperate. . . .

36. Nat to Lane, Jan. 4, 1852, MS OrHi; *Oregon Spectator,* Feb. 10, 24, March 16, 1852; *Weekly Oregonian,* May 1, 1852. For a discussioin of the "Oregon Style" of journalism, see George S. Turnbull, *History of Oregon Newspapers* (Portland, Binfords & Mort, 1939), pp. 81–85.

Thomas Jefferson Dryer (1808–79), a New Yorker who went to California in 1849, came to Portland and began publishing the *Weekly Oregonian* the following year. A passionate and articulate critic of the Oregon Democracy, he was elected to the territorial legislature in 1856 and was appointed U.S. commissioner to the Hawaiian Islands by Lincoln in 1861.

Write them Gen. Speak out." Lane, of course, sided with "the Representatives of the people."[37] When Bush requested his opinions on the issues agitating the public mind, he hastened to comply "with that frankness that should characterize a Representative of the people."

> I have ever acknowledged the right of a constituency to be made acquainted with the views of their Representative, upon questions of public interest, and I have ever regarded it as the duty of the Representative to answer such enquiries freely, fully, and in a spirit of manly candor and frankness. . . .
>
> First, in regard to the memorial of the Legislative Assembly of Oregon, praying the Congress of the United States to give the people of Oregon the privilege of electing their Governor, and Judges, I will say that it meets my cordial approbation and I shall cheerfully comply with the wishes of the people.
>
> As a Democrat I have ever believed in the Democratic doctrine that the people are capable of self Government, and I can see no good reason why the selection of officers to administer laws, in which they alone are interested, and enacted for their protection and happiness, and the protection of their lives and property, should not be entrusted to the intelligent

37. Deady to Lane, March 12, 1852, MS OrHi; Lane to Deady, Feb. 19, 1852, MS OrHi. Lane had also received a memorial, which he referred to as a "very able document," from members of the legislature in Oregon City, and some Salem promoters were afraid he "might be misled by the representatives of the Whig officers of the Territory." Nesmith to Lane, May 30, 1852, MS OrHi. Lane quieted their fears: "There is this difference between Myself and the Oregonian Man. He was deceived in me, and I was not in him. he was weak enough to believe that by making a Show and noise in my favor that he and his whig friends could Use me, did not know me consequently deceived himself. Quite the Contrary with Myself, the first time I seen him I could read him like a book, knew him as well as he knows himself. Consequently, could not trust or have any thing to do with him, further than was my duty as delegate. Such men will find themselves deceived when ever they think that they can use me." Lane to Deady, Dec. 1, 1852, MS OrHi.

> voters of Oregon. In almost every State in the union this system of election by the people prevails.
>
> Are the people of Oregon less capable of exercising this prerogative than other American Citizens? Are they not as intelligent, as patriotic, as law-abiding & as capable of protecting their just rights, as the citizens of any other community? I repeat I can see no good reason why this privilege should be denied them when they desire it. I have accordingly brought it to the notice of Congress. The memorial has been refered to the Committee on Territories in the House and a Bill in accordance with the prayer of the memorial has also been refered to the same Committee.

In a similar vein he went on to explain that he had introduced a joint resolution to approve the proceedings of the legislature at Salem, which he was confident would pass; that he favored organization of the Democratic party; that he opposed a National Bank, monopolies in general, a high protective tariff, and "a grand and magnificent scheme of Internal Improvements by the Genral Government"; and that he supported the present independent treasury system, liquidating the national debt, economy in government, strict construction of the Constitution, and the "careful preservation of the rights of the States as the great bulwark of our liberty." Deady was in the *Statesman* office when the letter arrived. He and Bush were highly pleased.[38]

After some delay, Congress unanimously approved the joint resolution, which Lane forwarded to Salem the following day, expressing the hope that it would finally settle this "most perplexed question." But it was further delayed by the mails—that is, by the Whigs, the Democrats said—so it did not reach Oregon until the morning of June 22, two weeks after the territorial elections. Nevertheless, the newly organized Democrats carried the field by

38. Lane to Bush, March 21, 1852, Bush Papers, reprinted in *Oregon Statesman,* May 18, 1852; Deady to Lane, May 23, 1852, MS OrHi.

a two-to-one margin, and editor Waterman struck an "Extra" within the hour to announce the good news to a grateful Democracy.[39]

Bush had never been happy with his first location—"I get very little patronage in Oregon City," he complained in April 1851—and in October 1852 he made a trip to Salem, the new capital, to see what kind of accommodations he could find there for the *Oregon Statesman.* While there he and his lawyer friend, Benjamin F. Harding, who had a farm not far from Salem, contemplated the state of affairs. Harding previously had been interested in the office of territorial secretary, and now that Lane and Pratt would both be in Washington for the inauguration, perhaps they could wield enough influence with the new president to get some of the federal offices filled by resident Oregonians. Harding was not very optimistic, but he felt that it might be worth a try. Nesmith also had his eye on patronage. "I dont know but what I should make an effort to git the appointment of Marshall of this Territory," he had confided to Deady two weeks earlier. "What do you think?"[40]

The men at Salem were ready to consolidate their ranks.

One of the pleasant features of Indiana by mid-century was that she had become a force to be reckoned with when politicians of every stripe set aside their regular duties to engage in the fascinating business of president making. Politicians in Indiana were as ambitious in this respect as their contemporaries elsewhere, but in 1852 the Hoosiers thought that their chance for success was better than average. They had a candidate, gushed the *Fort Wayne Sentinel,* who possessed "that indomitable energy of character,

39. Lane to Bush, Dec. 31, 1852, Bush Papers; *Oregon Weekly Times,* Sept. 25, 1852; Lane to Waterman, May 5, 1851, *Oregon Weekly Times,* June 26, 1852; Waterman to Lane, June 22, 1852, MS OrHi.

40. Bush to Deady, April 17, 1851, MS OrHi; Harding to Deady, Oct. 1, 1852, MS OrHi; Nesmith to Deady, Oct. 4, 1852, MS OrHi.

purity, strength and singleness of purpose, firmness and good practical sound sense, that so highly distinguished the immortal Jackson." A self-made man of the people, he was free from those "contaminating influences" that attended lengthy residence in Washington City and was preferable to any "mere politician." "We . . . think Gen. Lane's honesty and sound sense, are far better qualifications for the Presidency, than the more showy talents of his competitors."[41]

Lane's reception in the fall of 1851 was not simply for another local-boy-made-good; the Indianans were welcoming a potential candidate for the presidency of the United States. Taylor's defeat of Cass in 1848 had greatly altered the political complexion of the state, for most prominent Indiana Democrats had committed themselves on the question of slavery.[42] Two weeks after the election the *Indiana State Sentinel* pointed to Lane's military reputation and popular appeal, two sure-fire attributes for a possible contender. The following summer Robert Dale Owen, the utopian and reformer, wrote a long letter to Lane in which he tried to persuade him that his chances for the White House were better than those of any other man. The two men had been fast friends since their days together in the Indiana legislature, and in 1846 Owen had procured for Lane the appointment of brigadier general, recommending him for the honor instead of his own brother. In the fall of 1849, Owen agreed to write a short sketch of Lane's life to advertise his availability, and in January 1850 he proposed Lane's name to Democratic members of the state legislature, who responded with wild cheers. We need a man "not loaded down with speeches & votes," wrote another Indianan urging Lane to return from Oregon, but he cautioned, "Make no declaration of

41. Cited in *Oregon Statesman,* Feb. 3, 1852.

42. Ashbel P. Willard to Lane, Jan. 26, 1850, MS OrHi. Cass had taken a proslavery stand in Indiana. Logan Esarey, *A History of Indiana from its Exploration to 1850* (Indianapolis, W. K. Stewart Co., 1915), pp. 483, 486.

opinion on the question of slavery unless you have fully surveyed the ground & formed a deliberate judgement." A year later the state Democratic convention in Indianapolis formally nominated Lane, "the Marion of the Mexican War, and the Andrew Jackson of Indiana." The next months witnessed several mass meetings and much propaganda by Owen and other prominent Democrats, and when Lane, en route to the national capital, finally arrived on the scene, the people accorded him a hero's welcome.[43]

Surrounded by a coterie of advisers, Michael G. Bright, brother of the robust Jesse, masterminded the campaign to bring Lane's name before the national convention at Baltimore. His policy was that of "masterly inactivity" until the opportune moment; at the same time he thought it imperative that Indiana cultivate friendly relations with the delegations from Ohio and Kentucky so that she might count on their support should a bandwagon begin to roll.[44] Lane's promoters were realistic in their aspirations. Even to their candidate they did not pretend that they had a name to sweep the ranks of the convention. Rather, they had soberly calculated the strength of the leading contenders and decided that neither Cass, Douglas, James Buchanan, nor General William O. Butler could gain the time-honored two-thirds majority necessary for victory; each would evoke too much opposition from powerful forces jealous of success. In the event of such a contingency, Bright and his colleagues were convinced that victory would smile upon whoever was best prepared when the front runners had exhausted themselves on the convention floor. With the Whigs hopelessly demoralized, it required little foresight to appreciate that the nominee at Baltimore would likely captain the ship of state. And with a candidate from the West who would offer a creditable war

43. Owen to Lane, cited in Owen to Lane, Feb. 1, 1852, MS OrHi; Ashbel P. Willard to Lane, Jan. 26, 1850, MS OrHi. For an account of Owen's role in the campaign to give Lane the nomination, see Richard William Leopold, *Robert Dale Owen; A Biography* (Cambridge, Harvard University Press, 1940), pp. 293–97.

44. Michael G. Bright to Lane, Dec. 26, 1851, MS OrHi.

record and popular appeal, who possessed a variety of parliamentary experience without once committing himself on the pressing issues of the day, who would represent a Northern state and yet be fully acceptable to the South, the political managers of Indiana believed they might have the winning combination.[45]

The State Democratic Convention met in the Masonic Hall at Indianapolis, February 24, 1852, and the "Ring," as Lane's backers called themselves, closeted themselves in Michael Bright's room to map their strategy. By mail and perhaps through Jesse Bright, Lane had advised them which members in Washington would be most favorable to his interests, so they determined to secure these appointments to the Indiana delegation. As Lane wished, the delegation was uninstructed, although the convention did pass resolutions endorsing Lane, thus giving its representatives in Baltimore a free hand to secure his nomination by all honorable means.[46]

The final plan for the campaign was to publicize their candidate among other state delegations. A proposal to make him the subject of a feature article—complete with engraving—in the March issue of the *Democratic Review* misfired when Douglas interests obtained editorial control in January.[47] Although Owen had twice consented to write a short biography, he apparently had not found the time to do so. Early in May a printer in Washington published a flowery campaign pamphlet by "Western": *Biography of Joseph Lane; "Not Inappropriately Styled by His Brother Officers and*

45. See, for example, Robert Dale Owen et al. to Lane [1850?], MS OrHi. Wrote Edward Cantwell of North Carolina to Lane, Feb. 17, 1852, MS OrHi: "Such is said to be the bitterness of the feeling with which the leading civilians are struggling for the nomination that it is not impossable that Case Buchanan and Douglas will reenact the Kilkenny trajedy, and in that case I regard your election, as the only chance of reuniting their friends and saving the day."

46. Robert W. Dunbar to Lane, Feb. 29, 1852, MS OrHi; Nathaniel Albertson to Lane, Feb. 19, 1852, MS OrHi; E. Dumont to Lane, Feb. 26, 1852, MS OrHi.

47. George P. Buell to Lane, Feb. 9, 1852, MS OrHi. Cf. Allan Nevins, *The Ordeal of the Union, 2* (New York, Charles Scribner's Sons, 1947), 10.

*Soldiers, 'the Marion of the War.'"* Printed at the office of the *Congressional Globe,* the document is curious in several respects. While it referred to Lane's participation in the Mexican War, the work emphasized his experience as governor of Oregon and ignored his career in the Indiana legislature. Its literary qualities surpass the average campaign biography, and its crisp, lucid style and folksy anecdotes were calculated to give it a large audience. The anonymous author referred to himself as a "compiler" and to his writing as "memoirs"; his identity has never been satisfactorily established.[48] Distributed widely, this slim encomium found a favorable reception in most Democratic circles, although it probably arrived too late in many areas to effect its purpose. From Oregon, where the newspapers had followed every move with doting pride, Deady requested a good supply even after the convention was over. "I believe you will be President yet!"[49]

Nearly fifty thousand people converged on Baltimore the first week of June, many of them bivouacking in the streets, to witness

48. The identity of "Western" must remain an open question. Leopold (*Robert Dale Owen,* p. 296) says "there can be little doubt that it was Robert Dale Owen," a judgment accepted by Kelly (*Career of Joseph Lane,* pp. 96–97), but he admits that the evidence is "not conclusive." Based largely upon official government sources and personal acquaintance, the sketch could most easily have been written in Washington—possibly by Lane's secretary, Ethelbert C. Hibben, a young lawyer from Indiana, who was in Washington at this time. One member of the "Ring" in Indiana was so completely in the dark about it that when he first heard of the biography's appearance he suspected it might be a Whig hoax. Robert W. Dunbar to Lane, May 14, 1852, MS OrHi.

49. Deady to Lane, July 16, 1852, MS OrHi. The *Oregon Weekly Times* reprinted large portions of the biography. Bush categorized it as a "succinct history of the prominent events of Gen. Lane's life, but more particularly of his brilliant career in Mexico and popular administration of affairs in Oregon." *Oregon Statesman,* July 10, 1852. The *Weekly Oregonian* (July 24, 1852) protested that it "must have been written for a different latitude than that of Oregon. By looking over it, any one will not fail to discover many new occurrences recorded, which were before unknown in Oregon."

the spectacle of the national convention. The hot weather combined with the "outside pressure" to render every seat in the cavernous convention hall "exciting to profuse perspiration," wrote Lane's private secretary, Ethelbert C. Hibben, to the Portland *Times*. Indiana's John W. Davis was the presiding officer of the convention, and Jesse Bright, who entertained strong hopes for Lane, headed the delegation.[50] When balloting finally began on the third day, Indiana declared for her favorite son seventeen times, hoping to spark a Lane boom, while Douglas, Cass, and Buchanan jockeyed for control. That night the Indiana delegation caucused to review the situation. Bright and several others had by then abandoned hope of success and wanted to throw their thirteen votes to Cass if Lane did not increase his strength on the first ballot the next morning, but the majority was adamant. The next day Lane received the Hoosier votes for another thirteen ballots before Bright shifted their strength to Cass, the second choice of both Indiana and Lane. This shift marked the total collapse of the movement for Lane, and the dogfight went on for another day and a half, when another little-known general from the Mexican War, Franklin Pierce, "Young Hickory of the Granite Hills," emerged the victor on the forty-ninth ballot. Two weeks later the Whigs nominated as their standard-bearer yet another beneficiary of the war with Mexico, General Winfield Scott.

From his vantage point in nearby Washington, Lane accepted the verdict with good grace and without real regret. He immediately sent a letter to Pierce, whom he had met briefly in Mexico, proffering his good wishes and pledging his wholehearted support. The next week he joined Douglas at a ratification meeting in front of the City Hotel, where he delivered himself of some extravagant oratory. Speaking extemporaneously, he scored all Whig administrations of the past, branded Taylor an "accidental Presi-

50. *Oregon Weekly Times,* Aug. 14, 1852; "Some Letters of Jesse D. Bright to William H. English (1842–1863)," *Indiana Magazine of History,* 30 (1934), 377.

dent," said he would quit public life when Pierce was inaugurated, thanked Indiana for her thirty votes of confidence, eulogized the other Democratic candidates—they were all more worthy than himself—although if Douglas had waited ten or fifteen years, "it would have been better."[51] To Bush he declared the ticket the strongest that could have been made, that it would "sweep the country like a whirlwind." Indeed so confident was he that when a Whig from Georgia offered to bet $10,000 on Scott, Lane deposited $250 at Corcoran's bank to secure the wager. Unfortunately for Lane, as it turned out, the Georgian reconsidered and declined. In the House post office a month later, Lane accepted a bet of $300 that Scott would not get even fifty electoral votes—and then promptly offered to put up as much again that he would win the wager.[52]

With both parties pledged to uphold the Compromise, the "finality campaign" of 1852 was without issue and without spirit, one of the dullest in the nation's history. Lane campaigned actively for Pierce but was careful not to endanger his congressional interests and equally careful to inform Oregonians that he had not been absent from Washington "a single day"—except when he was "worn out with constant labor and confinement" and had visited the springs in Virginia. His recuperation did not preclude an appeal to the hustings. At a rally in Winchester he flailed the opposition in a "plain unvarnished speech," accusing Taylor of bringing the nation to the brink of civil war, and urging the preservation of the rights of the states as a necessary alternative. When Congress adjourned the last day of August, Lane took to the stump

51. Lane to Pierce, June 5, 1852, cited in Pierce to Lane, June 22, 1852, MS OrHi; *Oregon Statesman,* Sept. 11, 4, 1852. Lane objected that the Whigs had not developed the nation's resources or "promoted its glory. They have made no acquisition of territory."

52. Lane to ed., June 10, 1852, *Oregon Statesman,* Aug. 14, 1852; *Weekly Oregonian,* Aug. 7, 1852; Lane to John Adair, Dec. 2, 1852, Adair Papers (typescript, University of Oregon Library, Eugene). Cf. Lane to Nesmith, Aug. 17, 1852, MS OrHi.

in earnest, making in all some eighty speeches for Pierce and the Democracy, mostly in Indiana and Ohio. And, he reported to Deady, "every one told."[53]

Democrats in Oregon were surprised by the outcome at Baltimore—"the nominees not having spoken of here"—but they had much at stake in the election and followed the canvass with great interest. "We are looking forward with hope to the Election of Pearce and King," wrote Robert R. Thompson, "as did the prophets of old to the coming of the Messiah with the full assurance that a change in the Administration of the Federal Government will releive us of these Whigs who have no feeling or sympathy in common with us." The election results reached Oregon a few days before Christmas; the demonstration in Portland, where Democrats fired one hundred guns and hoisted a banner with the names of the successful candidates to the top of the liberty pole, was but the first of many throughout the territory. When the clerk announced the news in the legislative assembly, the members allegedly forsook their labors to celebrate, forgetting even the formality of adjournment. Since then, complained an observer, they have not done much of anything "but manufacture candidates for Governmental favor." Lane was equally pleased. "I know Pierce well. He is just the man," he confided to John Adair. And to Deady, that is to say the Salem faction, he promised, "Things will be put right in Oregon, early next March."[54]

In preparation for the coming session, Lane returned to Washington well before Congress reassembled. At a preliminary Demo-

53. Lane to Bush, Oct. 19, 1852, *Oregon Statesman,* Jan. 1, 1853; *Oregon Weekly Times,* Sept. 25, 1852; Lane to Deady, Dec. 1, 1852, MS OrHi.

54. T. P. Powers to Lane, July 23, 1852, MS OrHi; Thompson to Lane, Aug. 20, 1852, MS OrHi; Waterman to Lane, Jan. 5, 1853, MS OrHi; Lane to Adair, Dec. 2, 1852, Adair Papers; Lane to Deady, Dec. 1, 1852, MS OrHi.

cratic festival, he pledged that Oregon would have an electoral vote to cast in the next presidential contest and that it would be Democratic. During his recent sojourn in Indiana, he had sold all of his possessions and made final preparations to take his family to Oregon in the spring. With him at Wirt's boardinghouse this session were his two youngest children, Winnie and Lafayette, to take advantage of greater educational opportunities.[55]

On opening day Lane secured the floor and introduced two measures, one to organize the area north of the Columbia River as the Territory of Columbia, and the other to improve navigational facilities on the Willamette River, a proposal that he had unsuccessfully attempted to attach to the pork-barrel appropriation bill of the previous session. His efforts to improve the Willamette came to nought, but his attempt to establish the new territory met with success. Reading a memorial from settlers north of the Columbia, he effectively squelched objections from the floor of the House. To the charge that population in the proposed territory was inadequate, he replied that it would have as many people as Oregon had when she was organized and further, stretching the truth just a little, that both territories would still be four times larger than the state of Ohio and might in the next generation subsist a population of five million people. The revenues from Puget Sound ports alone, he argued, would very soon equal the entire cost of administering another government. With Oregonians on both sides of the Columbia desiring a division, the bill was accepted with only minor amendments, including one to change the name to "Washington" instead of "Columbia" to avoid confusion, as it was mistakenly supposed, with the district (territory) of the national capital. Isaac I. Stevens, who became the first governor of Washington Territory and also Lane's devoted friend, gave the delegate from Oregon entire credit for the achievement.[56]

55. Rebecca Wirt to Lane, March 21, 1853, MS OrHi.

56. *Congressional Globe,* 32 Cong., 2 Sess., pp. 6–7, 541–42; Stevens to Lane, April 18, 1853 (Oregon State Library, Salem).

The second major piece of legislation that Lane was able to effect was an amendment that extended the operation of the Donation Land Act, due to expire December 1, 1853, for two more years. Jesse Bright rendered invaluable assistance in the Senate, and the act as finally amended also gave settlers an option of gaining clear title to their land by purchasing it for $1.25 an acre after two years' residence.[57] Even today there are few who would spurn the largess of the federal government, especially when they happen to be the beneficiaries.

Twice during the session Lane considered issues unrelated to Oregon important enough to join the debate, thereby revealing something of his own system of values. A confirmed imperialist, Lane had been deeply disturbed by his experience in Cuba, and when discussion turned to the acquisition of Cuba, he declared it a foregone conclusion that she would be acquired—"no power on earth can prevent it"—but that force was unnecessary, as she would come in voluntarily. Exhibiting pronounced moralistic proclivities, he denounced the execution of López' revolutionaries as inhuman and unchristian: "the authorities of Cuba have a heavy sin to answer for, and which will never be wiped out until Cuba is made free." Like most southern planters who wanted compensation for the loss of California, he saw nothing inimical to the peace and harmony of the Union in the acquisition of more territory to the south, because "we have not enough [land] and the area of freedom has not spread wide enough." Soon the Mexican states would also come in, and both Americans and Mexicans would be better off for it.[58]

The other dispute that drew Lane's strenuous objections centered about creating the rank of lieutenant general for Winfield Scott. This was more than merely a partisan move, for Lane had a genuine regard for this man who in Mexico had dubbed him the Marion of the War. Basically he thought the title was "anti-democratic

57. *Congressional Globe,* 32 Cong., 2 Sess., p. 499.
58. Ibid., p. 211.

and smacked of aristocracy," an empty honor more in keeping with monarchical practices than those of the Founding Fathers. And if the title were more than honorary, he argued, the whole army would have to be reorganized, adding another major general and four more brigadiers to accommodate the superior rank. Although he considered his former commander a "great general," entitled to the highest position in the army, there were others like John E. Wool, for example, whose brilliance at Buena Vista had not been recognized at all. When questioned about his own brevet rank he dismissed it as a superfluous honor, professing that he was content to remain "a citizen in peace and a soldier in war." A few days after the squabble Scott wrote to Lane protesting his stand; Lane's reply was courteous but unyielding.[59]

As the day of the inauguration approached, Washington became a political Mecca for the myriads of office seekers who hastened to pay their homage and await their blessing. Lane's personal friendship with Pierce placed Oregonians in a fortuitous position, and on the eve of the inaugural festivities Lane wrote to Deady promising, if possible, to have only Oregonians appointed to territorial posts. As usual there were more seekers than positions, but in two weeks the job was done, and the nominees of the Oregon delegate were promptly accepted by the President and forwarded to the Senate for confirmation. While the precise basis for deciding who was to get a particular office is not always clear, the dispensing of loaves and fishes generally followed traditional machine methods. Aspirants often appealed directly to the delegate, but the usual procedure was to submit a petition signed by the Democratic members of the legislature in caucus. In this manner a handful of prominent members, Bush and his friends, secured virtual control of territorial patronage by merely bestowing or withholding their favor; already they were refining their art to a high degree of

59. Ibid., pp. 211–12, 217–18; Scott to Lane, Jan. 11, 1853, and Lane to Scott, Jan. 17, 1853, MS OrHi. Cf. Wool to Lane, Jan. 26, 1853, MS OrHi.

perfection, as was demonstrated by the case of Asa L. Lovejoy, who wanted very much to be governor. Lovejoy requested several members of the legislature to give him their endorsement and got a special letter from Bush to forward to Lane. This letter, the wily editor confided to Lane in a confidential communication under separate cover, was "purposely ambiguous" for the very good reason that Lovejoy's appointment would be a "sad misfortune" because he was simply "not competent to fill the office."

> Your own appointment [Bush continued] will give *entire* satisfaction to the Democracy of the Territory, and no one would be more pleased than your humble servant. But if you are unalterably fixed against receiving it, I am decidedly of the opinion that it will be better for our party to send some good man from the States than to appoint such a man as Lovejoy, and I do not hear that any one else in Oregon applies for it. And I know that this is the opinion of most if not all the members of the Legislature who signed his "Jack-at-a-pinch" letter. They want you should receive the appointment but if you will not they do not desire Lovejoy to be appointed under *any circumstances.* I have talked with a number who signed that circular and I know their views coincide with mine. They signed his circular to get rid of his importunity, but would not have it if they had expected him to be appointed. But all this is unnecessary as you know Gen. Lovejoy and his unfitness for the office of Governor, and the motives which have prompted this letter.[60]

General Lovejoy did not get the appointment; he was made postal agent instead, and Waterman, who had requested that position, was left wanting.

60. Bush to Lane (confidential), Dec. 29, 1852, MS OrHi. Cf. Deady to Lane, Jan. 21, 1853, Bush Papers.

To repay the Whigs and salve his own ego, Lane had Gaines removed and himself reappointed governor of Oregon. Although Hibben and Lane both reported that the appointment was unsolicited, Lane had in his possession a recommendation from the territorial legislature and personal letters from Oregon, and at least one prominent Democrat, General Wool, interceded for him in the White House.[61] To complete the rout of the "pensioned Aristocracy," as the Whig officeholders were called, Judges Nelson and Strong were removed from the supreme court, Pratt was named chief justice, and Deady and Cyrus Olney associate justices; Curry became territorial secretary, Harding district attorney, Palmer superintendent of Indian affairs, and Nesmith marshal in place of Joe Meek, removed. John Adair, who had been replaced by the Whigs as collector of customs at Astoria, was reinstated, as was William M. King, surveyor of the port of Portland, in place of Dryer of the *Oregonian;* in addition, Lane's neighbor in Indiana, Robert W. Dunbar, was appointed surveyor at Milwaukie and Addison C. Gibbs, collector at the mouth of the Umpqua. Together these individuals constituted an imposing set of politicians who were, with a few additions, to dominate Oregon politics for some time. To be sure, the appointments were not universally satisfactory, but for the most part complaints were minor. "I am d - - - - d sorry that Boise does not occupy the place of Olney," Deady wrote Nesmith, still uncertain whether he should accept his own commission. Harding had desired the position of secretary but was satisfied with the commission he received. Most bitterly disappointed was Waterman of the *Times,* who had silently watched Bush finagle the public printing, had supported the location of the capital in Salem, had then declined Whig support to run for printer to avoid splitting the party, and had written glowing

61. *Oregon Weekly Times,* April 30, May 21, 1853; Wool to Lane Jan. 26, 1853, MS OrHi. To Bancroft, Lane declared, "I took care to have Mr. Gaines removed as a kind of complement to me." "Autobiography," p. 58.

letters to Lane hoping to receive the postal agency to offset some of the expense of publishing the *Times*.[62]

On March 1 Lane was invited to a dinner at the White House given by Fillmore for Pierce, incoming and outgoing cabinet members, and a few members from both houses of Congress—an eloquent testimony to his standing in Washington. The past session had witnessed a more mature and effective delegate from Oregon, a man of more determined and vigorous action who was acquiring a reputation for getting things done. Pushing through the bill to establish Washington Territory had been a singular achievement, augmented by the amended land act, the $40,000 appropriation for military roads, further implementation of the Cayuse War claims, and several lesser favors. Besides all this was the control of patronage, the crowning triumph. And this in a short, lame-duck session of Congress when Congressmen are traditionally concerned about the transfer of power to the new regime. These facts were not permitted to pass unnoticed in Oregon. An unnamed correspondent from Washington reviewed these accomplishments in the columns of the *Statesman:* "Your popular Delegate, Gen. Lane, seems to be devoted to the interests of his Territory. He is always on the alert, and has accomplished more than all the other Territorial Delegates put together. . . . They all complain that Gen. Lane can get anything through Congress he wishes, while they can get nothing." With a reception like this awaiting him, it would be good to get home.[63]

62. Waterman to Lane, April 10, 1853, MS OrHi; *Oregon Weekly Times,* April 30, 1853; Deady to Nesmith, April 29, 1853, MS OrHi; Waterman to Lane, Nov. 30, 1852, MS OrHi. On April 4, 1853 (MS OrHi), Bush wrote to Deady that Boise was "due to be" one of the judges, along with Deady and Olney.

63. *Oregon Weekly Times,* May 7, 1853; *Oregon Statesman,* April 9, 1853.

*Chapter 3*

# HIGH NOON

On the northern branch of the Umpqua River, five miles above the forks, lay the town of Winchester, a striving hamlet with a store, saloon, sawmill, and blacksmith shop that gave a sense of purpose and meaning to the small, single-storied homes. The site had been fully platted, and although the town proper occupied only the southern bank, some lots had spilled across to the opposite shore. By the summer of 1851 few lots remained unclaimed, and the early proprietors, eager to command the resources of this large undeveloped hinterland, were sanguine that their location at the head of the valley would soon become the seat of a new and prosperous county. As yet the valley could boast of few residents, but travelers crossing between the Rogue and Willamette rarely failed to appreciate its natural beauty. "The Switzerland of Oregon," Deady pronounced it upon his arrival to take up residence in the southern judicial district in the fall of 1853, "the finest scenery in the world." An impressionable New Englander, seeing it for the first time in 1852, observed little sign of human habitation except "now and then a straggling band of Indians seeking game or packing cammas, or the lonely cabin of a settler who with his gun and dog were waiting for civilization." Nonetheless the placid countryside gave him the impression of an old, well-settled region where "the sloping hillsides sending out their clear rivulets of sparkling spring water, the pasture, oaks, and green grass interspersed with flowers, all seemed to speak of nature once subdued."[1]

Those few persons who had made the Umpqua their home were as friendly as any on the frontier. On Christmas Day 1851, for example, they had cleared the saloon, and their community supper and ball lasted until sunup next day. "I've got the rink-a-tink of the music in my ears yet," chirruped one of them the following day, "and can't help balancing to the woodpile, chasseeing to the pig trough, and resolving to get up a petition to Congress to make Christmas come about once a month or oftener if possible." Two years later the Lane family would take part in such community festivities, for it was to this valley and to these people that the delegate from Oregon would bring his clan; his donation claim bordered the southern limits of the town. The valley with its abundant grass and plentiful streams had struck his fancy when he first passed through on the way to the mines in 1850. "It just suited my taste, so I went out there, instead of investing here [in Portland], & making my fortune," he later told Bancroft, with overtones of regret.[2]

Before Lane's family exchanged their home on the Ohio for one on the Umpqua, political considerations once more altered the

1. *Oregon Statesman,* July 4, Sept. 30, 1851; Deady to Nesmith, Nov. 13, 1853, MS OrHi; "The Diary of Lafayette Grover," typescript (University of Oregon Library, Eugene), Jan. 1, 1853.

2. "One of them Hoosiers" to ed., Dec. 26, 1851, *Oregon Statesman,* Feb. 10, 1852; Lane, "Autobiography," p. 63.

course of their lives. For reasons best known to himself, Lane had consistently rejected suggestions that he run again for delegate in 1853. "I shall not be a candidate for re-election," he explained to Deady as early as February 1852, "for the reason first I dont want the office and second because, I shall at the Close of this Congress, take my family over land to Oregon, there to spend the ballance of my days in peace and quiet, except holding myself ready to defend our frontiers against Indian depredations. I shall not be able to reach Oregon untill the fall of 53." Lane was undoubtedly sincere in this profession, for so he wrote to numerous constituents. He might have thought he really had a chance for the presidency or some other post in Washington. Perhaps he decided it would be impossible to return in time to campaign because he and his sons were planning to drive a large herd of livestock across the plains. But possibly he was simply playing coy, waiting for "the people" to commandeer his services. In any event, he soon had misgivings about the anomalous course he was pursuing and began to trim his sails. By mid-September he intimated to Waterman that he might be willing to reconsider his position.[3] A month later he informed Bush he would return to Oregon the next summer or "perhaps next spring"; in November he wrote again advising that if necessary Bush might use his name in connection with the delegateship. To this Bush "hardly [knew] what to say," and explained he had delayed answering—for nearly a month—so that he might sound out various members of the legislature. "My own opinion is that you are the strongest man we can run," he replied. "But as the matter now stands—the impression having long existed that you would not run again—I am inclined to think that you would not be presented with that entire unanimity which you should have in case you run." Thereupon, Lane dropped further pretense and stated his case as clearly as he could under the cir-

3. Lane to Deady, Feb. 19, 1852, MS OrHi; Aaron D. Shelby to Lane, Feb. 13, 1853, MS OrHi; Lane to Waterman, cited in Waterman to Lane, Nov. 30, 1852, MS OrHi.

cumstances: "You are aware that I do not wish it, but am willing and always will be to promptly comply with the wishes of the Democratic party, and obey their orders or requisitions." The whole episode was a political mistake and a humiliating lesson. Never again did Lane fail to make his availability crystal clear to the politicos in Oregon.[4]

By this time the damage was done, and several hopefuls had been encouraged to play the field, for politics, like nature, abhors a vacuum. One of the leading contenders was Deady, who found it difficult to conceal his annoyance when rumors warned that Lane would run again after all.

> In relation to the delegateship [wrote Deady], I have but a few words to say. If you desire it I shall not throw anything in your way. Shortly after you left here the impression became general that you would not accept the office again *under* any circumstances. This was the purport of your letters. Upon this suggestion the democracy of the Ter. have been casting about for a suitable person for your successor. In this way several names are before the country for nomination. Among these by the partiality of friends my name has been used, with as many think a fair prospect for success. But with me the great question is unanimity and success. Although under the circumstances I could not in justice to my friends without their consent go for your nomination; I could if you were nominated and would do my utmost for your success. I have spoken freely to you in this letter, thinking it better to speak the truth with you at all hazards.[5]

Lane said nothing further about the matter.

4. Lane to Bush, Oct. 19, 1852, *Oregon Statesman,* Jan. 1, 1853; Lane to Bush, cited in Bush to Lane, Dec. 29, 1852, MS OrHi; Lane to Bush, Feb. 2, 1853, Bush Papers. Bush apparently delayed publication of Lane's letter of Oct. 19—unless it was delayed in the mails—until he received another letter from Lane.

5. Deady to Lane, Dec. 28, 1852, MS OrHi.

Before Lane reached Oregon the nominating convention met at Salem, April 11 and 12, so there was little that he could do to affect the outcome. His popularity with the voters, especially after it became known that he would accept a second term, was an important factor in his favor. So was the realization that the opposition candidate would likely be Alonzo A. Skinner, whose popularity in the southern mines could best be offset by the incumbent. On the other hand, Lane's name had clearly become anathema to most Whigs since his espousal of the legislature at Salem, although their continual opposition to party organization left them with no alternative save a nondescript "no-party" or "people's" ticket.

Within the Democracy the fires of potential discord smoldered as the Salem group increasingly called the tune in the territorial legislature, offending a minority of their own party—branded as "Softs"—who professed to base party principles upon national rather than local issues. Before the end of the session Deady complained that the Whigs had tampered with "a sufficient number of our soft democrats to frequently command a majority in the house." In February a group of Softs calling themselves "national Democrats" attempted to establish a broader base for their movement. Bush was alarmed enough to editorialize about the "sudden and remarkable" affection between Whigs and disenchanted Democrats, and to warn about the dangers of a party split. Not unrelated was his concern that the Whigs might try to give Dryer the public printing, or that the Softs might demand it be divided between Waterman and himself. On February 11, Bush confided to Deady his "suspicions that the *tender footed democracy* have assurances or think they have that Peter [Waterman] will become their organ"; on February 12, Waterman raised Lane's name to the masthead of the *Times*.[6]

6. Deady to Lane, Jan. 21, 1853, Bush Papers; *Oregon Statesman,* Feb. 19, 1853; Bush to Deady, Dec. 29 [1852], Feb. 11, 1853, MS OrHi. The terms "Soft" and "Hard" were a part of the national political and religious vocabulary at that time. As early as Oct. 1, 1852, Nat referred

All these factors influenced the selection of a candidate. None of the Salemites—the "Hards"—preferred Lane to Deady, but Lane was strong in the areas where opposition to their favorite was most pronounced. A week before the convention Bush was still not convinced that Lane wanted the position but thought his renomination on the first ballot a "foregone conclusion." "I'll do my utmost for you if you say you are a candidate," Bush promised Deady. "I at least will not desert. But as a friend . . . I would advise you to withdraw this heat. I believe your defeat in the Convention is certain, and to run against Lane & be beaten would injure you. . . . Pratt says that under the circumstances you ought not to allow your name to be used against Lane." Although Deady determined to stand firm, many of his friends decided that party success rested with Lane. The convention voted Lane thirty-eight, Deady eleven, and Olney five. Perhaps Deady was consoled by assurances of a place on the supreme court, and to Nesmith, that "best of fellows and the prince of blackguards," he expressed satisfaction with the decision and promised to work for Lane's election. Applauding the convention's choice, the *Statesman* predicted that Lane would return with the commission of governor but would doubtless "consult their wishes instead of those of the President" and return to Washington if they so desired.[7]

On Saturday, May 14, twenty-nine members of the Lane family —"near and remote," said the *Statesman*—arrived in Portland on the mail steamer *Fremont.* A committee headed by Waterman received Lane at the wharf and, with the Vancouver Brass Band,

---

to Joe Meek as a "soft shelled democrat." An early hint of factionalism within Democratic ranks can be seen on a measure in the House, sponsored by the Salemites, not to consider Gaines' message to the legislature; the motion passed after long controversy, but only by a vote of 12–10.

7. Bush to Deady, April 4, 1853, MS OrHi; Addison C. Gibbs to Deady, April 16, 1853, MS OrHi; Deady to Lane, Jan. 21, 1853, Bush Papers; Deady to Nesmith, April 15, 1853, MS OrHi; *Oregon Statesman,* April 9, 1853.

escorted him to the Columbia Hotel where another Soft, William M. King, welcomed him back to Oregon, promising that Lane would be returned to Washington for a second term. Lane responded to this handsome demonstration, stating that he had but "yielded to the wishes of the President" in regard to the governorship but would gladly comply with their wishes. After reviewing his recent legislative accomplishments, he sought to refute Whig charges that he was a resident of Indiana, that his trip to Oregon in 1849 had cost the government some $12,000—"it never cost the Government one half cent"—and that he had deceived the people in the previous canvass. "*He* had deceived no one; but if *some* persons had deceived *themselves,* it was their fault, not his. His politics were well known, and he was never ashamed to avow them." He spent the day walking about the city admiring the wondrous changes that had occurred during the past two years. That evening he was guest of honor at a dinner and ball, and the next morning, escorted by the band and several well-wishers, he rejoined his family in Oregon City. That Bush was not among those assembled to greet him was of no great significance, although it was noted and remembered by a few.[8]

Just three weeks remained before the election. On Monday, Lane boarded the boat for Salem, where he took the oath of office and replaced Gaines; on Wednesday he resigned the governorship and opened his campaign for the delegateship with a speech in Legislative Hall; and on successive days he debated Skinner, the "no-party" candidate, in Lafayette, Albany, and Marysville, returning to Oregon City the following Sunday. At Albany he first met Delazon Smith, a recent immigrant from Iowa, who was destined to play an important role in Oregon Democratic politics and who had been much prejudiced against him, presumably by Whigs like Dryer. "As an orator, though he is not *brilliant,* he is pleasing, argumentative and agreeable," testified Smith after their

8. *Oregon Statesman,* May 21, 1853; *Oregon Weekly Times,* May 21, June 11, 1853; *Oregon Statesman,* June 21, 1853.

brief encounter. "He has a very happy, and, apparently perfectly natural faculty of going 'from grave to gay, from lively to severe.' All he says is said earnestly and candidly, but courteously and good naturedly. His auditors are either convulsed with laughter or silently nodding assent to either his statement of facts or the conclusions drawn from them." After the meeting Lane conversed with Smith for nearly two hours, and the next day the former Iowan joined Nesmith at Marysville in Lane's behalf.[9]

If the campaign was short, it was nonetheless spirited. Prematurely bald and inclined to corpulence, Skinner became the butt of many a cruel witticism. "It is an old Scotch saw," taunted the *Statesman,* "that 'an empty barn needs no thatch'!" Caricaturing "his rotund self. . . . *waddling* about the Territory begging votes for Delegate," Bush usually dismissed him as "Granny Skinner" or "*the lazy man's candidate.*"[10] Bush commonly referred to the *Oregonian* as "the Sewer" and to Dryer as "the Sewer-man." Even Waterman fell victim to Bush's acid-dipped pen for "cow-towing" to Whigs and "Softs" and "tailing on" to Lane, who "knowing that it pleases the boy, with his usual good nature, lets him *bob*

9. Smith to Bush, May 23, 1853, Bush Papers. Cf. Smith to Bush, July 16, 1853, *Oregon Statesman,* Aug. 2, 1853.

Born in New York, Smith (1816–60) experienced a turbulent career as a student at Oberlin College, Ohio, served as a newspaper editor, U.S. commissioner to Ecuador, and Methodist minister in Iowa. In 1852 he emigrated to Oregon and in 1853 became a member of the territorial legislature and six years later one of Oregon's first U.S. senators. Denied re-election to the Senate in 1859 by a split in the party, he established the Albany *Oregon Democrat* in an attempt to win re-election and secure vindication. He died suddenly the following year, a spent and broken man.

10. *Oregon Statesman,* May 14, 21, 28, 1853. Bush characterized Skinner (ibid., May 21) as "a negative character, so far as he has any, which makes neither warm enemies or friends . . . His mental capacity is, to say the most, *extremely moderate;* and his mind, like his body, having for a lifetime remained dormant, has in a great degree become torpid, and to some extent ceased its functions. He is an embodiment of idleness, inertness, and inefficiency. . . . He is destitute of *resolution, life,* or *energy,* as men 'ever get to be.' "

*away.*" "The little fellow of the Times, imagines that he is an object of rivalry," mused Bush after Waterman charged him with "straining every nerve" to defeat Lane in the convention. The *Times,* rejoined Bush, was a "flippant" sheet circulating about 200 copies—Waterman claimed 1,100—"one-third of which are taken by democrats who think they must support it because it is nominally democratic; one-third by whigs and softs, who alone feel an interest in its continuance, and one-third by old women of *both sexes,* who want a *mild, moderate* paper."[11]

Lane employed the last two weeks of the campaign touring southern Oregon, spending election day at the remote community of Althouse so that he might bring the election returns to the Willamette Valley. Skinner was much abler than the columns of the *Statesman* might suggest and advocated an essentially Whiggish platform despite his lip service to a nonpartisan cause, but he was no match for the more popular Lane. Apart from the usual charges and countercharges, the only legitimate issue related to establishing Indian reservations in areas settled by whites. Such a policy, Lane argued, would menace the growth of the country and needlessly plague the settlers with an eternal nuisance; he advocated relocating them beyond the settlements and supplying them with blankets and food as necessary for their comfort. Although the opposition was much more vigorous than in 1851, Lane's margin of victory was 4,516 to 2,951, a substantial majority of about 60 per cent of the total vote.[12]

The successful termination of the campaign did nothing to diminish the feud between the *Statesman,* now relocated in Salem, and the *Times,* both of which had been stumbling over themselves in support of Lane. "'Asahel' has not the least idea but that he can annihilate every one that will not be dipped at *his* baptismal fount,"

11. *Oregon Statesman,* March 5, May 28, June 4, 1853.

12. Ibid., May 28, 1853; *Congressional Globe,* 32 Cong., 1 Sess., p. 891; *Oregon Statesman,* July 19, 1853. Ibid., June 23, 1857, lists the returns for 1853 as 4,529–2,969.

charged Waterman, who declared he had tried to avoid a collision between the two Democratic presses. In his opinion the nub of the matter was clear, and all else was mere pretext: "We brought Gen. Lane before the people." "*You havn't offended whiggery!*" roared Bush in reply, railing at Waterman's "mortifying mental weakness, and namby-pamby non-commital course." As for the *Times* carrying Lane through, " 'What a tremendous dust we kick up,' said the fly to the coach wheel."[13]

And what of Lane's position in this festering row between party factions? He was probably trying to conciliate both sides but too busy to devote much attention to either, for he was at this time getting his family settled in their new home on the Umpqua.[14] Late in August, Waterman received the postmastership of Portland, undoubtedly on Lane's recommendation. But within the Salem camp two miscues threatened to cause trouble. After Lane left Washington, Senator Douglas had blocked Pratt's appointment as chief justice on the grounds that Pratt had previously represented the Hudson's Bay Company and might be corrupted by British gold. George H. Williams of New York was appointed in his stead. Although somewhat miffed by the incident, Pratt had not especially desired the position and allegedly was content to let it pass. The second appointment to go awry was Deady's, which provoked a more serious crisis because some people suspected that Lane had obtained his original appointment to the bench to remove him from the race for delegate. Due to a clerical error of which Lane was as innocent as he had been in the Pratt affair, Deady's name was incorrectly listed on the commission as "Mordecai" instead of "Matthew." Deady was clearly unhappy; "How the hell Lane made Such a botch of it is surprising to me," he exclaimed privately to Bush. "A d - - - - d unfortunate *botch,*" agreed Bush, "a legitimate subject of ridicule for the opposition." Yet under the

13. *Oregon Weekly Times,* June 11, 1853; *Oregon Statesman,* June 21, 1853.

14. *Oregon Statesman,* June 28, 1853.

circumstances what could be done? Silence, he counseled, was their best defense.[15]

At one o'clock in the morning, August 17, 1853, an express messenger reached Lane's house in Winchester with news that, after several clashes with the whites, the Klamath, Shasta, and Rogue River Indians had united to wipe out the white settlements of southern Oregon. Prospects were grim, the messenger reported, and companies were being formed to repulse the attackers. Already the well-armed marauders had killed several whites and destroyed much property. Within five minutes Lane was making preparations to leave for Rogue River with as many volunteers as could be found.[16]

At sunrise, Sunday, August 21, Lane reached the headquarters on Stuart Creek, where some two hundred volunteers and a handful of regulars were mobilizing under the leadership of Captain Bradford R. Alden, who promptly tendered the command to the more experienced Lane.[17] Lane divided the troops into two battalions, the first under Alden to pursue the Indians hiding out beyond Table Rock, where they had fled after earlier engagements, and the second under Colonel John Ross to ascend Evans Creek, which empties into Rogue River from the north, to prevent the Indians from slipping back into the valley. If either group picked up the trail before a designated rendezvous point on Evans Creek, it should give chase while the other came up to reinforce it. They broke camp at four o'clock Monday morning.

Lane accompanied Alden's battalion, which located the trail

15. Deady to Bush, May 29, 1853, MS OrHi; Bush to Deady, July 24, 1853, MS OrHi.

16. Lane to Bush, Aug. 17, 1853, Bush Papers.

17. Lane to E. A. Hitchcock [Sept. 16, 1853], U.S. House *Executive Document* No. 1, Pt. 2 (33 Cong., 1 Sess.), pp. 37–41. A few days later Lane received the commission of brigadier general from Acting Governor Curry.

about noon and followed it until evening to an abandoned encampment on Evans Creek. They renewed their march at daybreak, slashing their way up an almost impenetrable canyon that the Indians had partially fired to cover their tracks and discourage pursuit. After crossing a high summit Wednesday morning, Lane discovered the enemy encamped in a ravine and immediately ordered the men to dismount and prepare for battle. He directed Alden to attack from the front while part of one company skirted a ridge to the left in a flanking maneuver. Lane was delayed for a time while his pack train came up from the rear; when he rejoined his troops, Alden had already been dangerously wounded and his men pinned down by a withering fire from the Indians well-posted behind logs and underbrush. With both sides digging in, Lane determined to take the offensive. He was leading the charge when a bullet struck his right shoulder—the same one splintered at Buena Vista—the ball passing through the shoulder blade and narrowly missing his backbone. Before withdrawing to have his injury dressed, he ordered his men to extend their line. Three hours later the Indians were willing to talk peace, and when the chiefs Jo—Lane's namesake—Sam, and Jim learned that Joe Lane was the white commander, they asked to see him. They agreed to assemble their people at Table Rock in one week's time, when they would surrender their arms and place themselves under the protection of the whites. As evidence of their good faith, Chief Jo offered his son as a hostage. The battle proved costly. Lane and his little army lost three men, and four besides Lane were badly wounded, one dying later, while their adversaries lost eight and had twenty wounded, of whom at least seven died shortly thereafter. On the advice of the surgeon, Lane had his men camp on the battlefield for two nights after which they slowly departed for the valley, the Indians bearing the litters of the wounded whites.[18]

"Your presence is imperatively required," Lane informed Joel

18. Ibid.; W. G. T'Vault to Bush, Aug. 26, 1853, *Oregon Statesman,* Sept. 6, 1853.

Palmer, superintendent of Indian affairs, as he settled back to wait out the uneasy truce.[19] But the situation worsened. Irresponsible whites, seeking total extermination of the native population, incited sporadic armed clashes in which more Indians were killed. When the Indians failed to assemble at the designated time—Palmer had not arrived either—and asked for more time to round up their braves, many of the whites demanded war. However, Lane had promised peace to the Indians and extended the deadline to September 4, at which time the parley began. The "waw-waw" was in its fourth day when Nesmith arrived with a company of volunteers from the Willamette Valley, bringing a large supply of ammunition and a twelve-pound howitzer from Fort Vancouver; on the same day a company of dragoons from Port Orford provided further reinforcement, and the entire command was eager for battle. Had Lane wanted a war of extermination—and the glory of leading a popular crusade—he might well have capitalized on his situation that September day. But negotiations with the Indians had progressed favorably, and he determined to treat with the enemy in another two days.

A quarter century later Nesmith recalled the dramatic climax of this Rogue River War. He agreed to act as interpreter but protested that Lane's promise to go unarmed with ten men into the heart of the Indian encampment was sheer folly. To Lane's suggestion that he need not participate, he replied that he was as little acquainted with fear as Lane and would go along to what he laconically termed "our slaughter." Thereupon they mounted their horses, rode as far as they could up the edge of Table Rock, scrambled up the last half mile on foot, and stood surrounded by a large contingent of well-armed warriors in full battle regalia. The speech making was long and burdensome, all remarks having to be translated into Chinook jargon and then into the language of the recipient. In the middle of the afternoon a young Indian runner, stark

19. Lane to Palmer, Aug. 23, 1853, *Oregon Statesman,* Sept. 6, 1853.

naked and exhausted, flung himself into the camp, announcing that one Captain Owens and a body of whites had seized an Indian that morning on Applegate Creek, tied him to a tree, and used his body for target practice. "I thought my time had come," said Nesmith, "and hurriedly thought of wife and children." Clad in a red hunting shirt, his right arm cradled helplessly in a sling, Lane slowly rose to his feet and delivered a deliberate but straight-from-the-shoulder speech that awed friend and foe alike. Owens, said Lane, was not one of his men but a bad white, whom he would punish as soon as he could lay hands on him. We came here unarmed in good faith, he spat out defiantly, and could be murdered in a minute, but what good would that do? Only cowardly dogs would resort to such action, he concluded, urging them to proceed with the treaty and promising compensation of shirts and blankets for their murdered brave. Impressed as much by his courage as his logic, the Indians placed their mark on the treaty, thereby ending officially a war that had cost the lives of more than one hundred whites and several hundred Indians.[20]

The treaty marked a turning point in relations between the two races and became a model for future negotiations with the Indians of the Pacific Northwest. But it was not so regarded by the "exterminators." "Ten dollars reward to the ladies of Jacksonville if they will present Jo Lane with a petticoat," bawled a drunken rabble rouser riding through the southern Oregon town two days after the treaty was signed. That night some residents attempted to organize an indignation meeting.[21] Against such sentiment Lane

20. Nesmith, "A Reminiscence: A Recollection of the Rogue River War of 1853," *Transactions of the Seventh Annual Reunion of the Oregon Pioneer Association; for 1879* (Salem, E. M. Waite, 1880), pp. 45–47; Lafayette Grover, "Notable Things in a Public Life in Oregon" (Bancroft Library, University of California, Berkeley, microfilm in University of Oregon Library, Eugene), pp. 30–31, 38. Although the treaty formally ended the war, further armed clashes frequently occurred.

21. *Oregon Statesman,* Sept. 27, 1853. As early as August, the *Yreka Herald* (cited ibid., Aug. 30, 1853) proclaimed, "Let our motto be EXTERMINATION *and death to all opposition, white men or Indians!"*

remained adamant, and his conduct in handling both redmen and white brought forth his best qualities as leader and statesman. Notwithstanding his recent campaign for Indian removal, he became convinced that the only solution lay in guaranteeing the Indians a portion of their historic domain, and he had the courage to resist popular clamor to institute a bloodbath.

Before Lane resigned his commission, the people of Jacksonville expressed their approval of his treaty at a public meeting, September 24. He might also have derived great satisfaction from the course of the *Statesman.* The day before Lane left Winchester, Bush had called for the extermination of a Rogue River band; with word of the battle on August 24 and Lane's decision to treat, the *Statesman* was "more willing to trust his [Lane's] judgment in the matter . . . than our own"; and by the end of September, Bush was ridiculing those opposing the Table Rock Treaty, "who have not participated in the battles, but declare themselves 'exterminators!'" Meanwhile, a mile below the Rock on the south side of Rogue River, the dragoons from Port Orford were constructing a fort to discourage future hostilities. Lane urged the army's Department of the Pacific to establish a permanent post there and sought assurances that troops were being requested specifically for this service. "If I have the naming of it," promised the officer in charge, "it will be called Fort Lane as you are particularly identified with this rogue river war."[22]

While the people of Jacksonville were resisting demonstrations, an unidentified caller decided to visit the general and satisfy his curiosity.

> Having seen Generals in the States togged out in epauletts, gold lace, cocked hats and long shining swords, I expected to find something of the kind at "Head Quarters." But fancy my

22. *Oregon Statesman,* Oct. 11, Aug. 16, Sept. 13, 27, 1853; E. A. Hitchcock to Lane, Sept. 30, 1853, Lane Papers, InU; Andrew Jackson Smith to Lane, Sept. 24, 1853, Lane Papers, InU. The post was named Fort Lane.

> surprise on being introduced to a robust good looking middle aged man, with his right arm in a sling, the shirt sleeve slit open and dangling bloody from his shoulder, his nether extremities cased in an old pair of grey breeches that looked as though they were the identical ones worn by Gen. Scott when he was "exposed to the fire in the rear." One end of them was supported by a buckskin strap in the place of a suspender, while one of the legs rested upon the top of the remeins of an old boot. His hair so twisted, tangled and matted . . . was surmounted by the remains of an old forage cap, which judging from its appearance, might have been worn at Braddock's defeat.

The quarters of the "old hero" were in keeping with his person: a rough log cabin about sixteen feet square, its dirt floor piled high in one corner with sacks of provisions for the troops; in another corner were stacked guns of every description; in the third, an old kettle, frying pan, coffee pot—minus the spout—a dozen tin cups, a dirty shirt, one old shoe, and a moccasin; a pair of blankets in the remaining corner served as the general's bed, on top of which lay a chunk of raw beef and some dirty dough.[23] From such republican simplicity, reminiscent of campaigns in Mexico, political fortunes grew.

In the Willamette Valley, reports circulated that Lane had left for San Francisco and Washington directly from Rogue River. He was indeed concerned that he might miss the opening of Congress but finally decided he had ample time to return via Portland and bid farewell to family and friends. To Nesmith he entrusted the guard-

23. "Socks" to ed., Sept. 13, 1853, *Oregon Statesman,* Sept. 27, 1853. For a general account of the Rogue River War of 1853, see Victor, *Indian Wars of Oregon,* pp. 307–18. Lane ("Autobiography," pp. 113–28) gives a detailed account of his role in effecting a peace treaty with Tipsey, a Shasta chief.

ianship of sons John and Lafayette, whom he enrolled in Salem's Willamette Institute, the best preparatory school in the territory. To Joel Palmer he turned over the young Indian hostage, whom he had earlier considered taking to Washington for exhibition. And to William H. Farrar, a Portland attorney, and James Guthrie, Jr., nephew of Pierce's Secretary of the Treasury, he and Nat sold their interest in the Island Mills "for less than half its value."[24]

Toward the politicos at Salem, his actions remained overly solicitous, suggesting a perceptible want of confidence and intimacy. In the Marysville post office, he left Samuel B. Garrett, a young acquaintance from Indiana, to keep him reliably informed about local political currents; when the next legislature convened Garrett became chief clerk of the Council and directed confidential missives to Lane until spring, when homesickness induced him to return east. To squelch speculation about a rift between them, Lane sent Bush a curious note on October 1 containing extravagant assurances that he had never "at any time or under any circumstances" been displeased by his acts; "my confidence in you as a gentleman friend, and Editor remains unshaken and I have not the slightest reason to believe I shall ever have good reason to regret the friendship and confidence I entertain for you." But three days later the *Statesman* noted the appointment of one Obediah B. McFadden of Pennsylvania to the judgeship intended for Deady and issued a veiled warning to Lane by announcing that this must be erroneous, because there was "no vacancy" in Oregon. From bustling San Francisco, Lane sent an effusive letter to Nesmith, with whom Lane had remained on the most friendly terms. "How easy we might have been worth a half million or more . . . if we had set our stakes here," he philosophized, but "heaven directed otherwise and I am content." The marshal had prospered where he was, and

24. *Oregon Statesman,* Oct. 11, 1853; *Oregon Spectator,* Oct. 29, 1853; Lane to Nesmith, Jan. 18, 1854, MS OrHi. A year earlier Thompson had sold his quarter interest in the mill for $11,000. Nat to Lane, Dec. 12, 1852, MS OrHi.

"bye and by," Lane concluded patronizingly, "it will be your turn to go to Washington, to look after the interests of Oregon." Deady continued to sulk and suspected Lane of gross duplicity, even after Lane had seen him in Portland and sworn to have his appointment corrected. "Of one thing I am certain," the judge confided to Bush, "that the election of Lane under the circumstances last summer was a misfortune to the party from which it will not soon recover. Since he returned from the Rogue River country and before his departure for Washington he done more to strengthen the hands of the Softs and whigs than anything that has happened Since they have had a name."[25]

The unwanted McFadden arrived on the steamer that bore Lane away, and only then did the new judge learn the awkward truth regarding his appointment. His reception was courteous enough, but when he ignored pointed suggestions in the *Statesman* that he resign for the peace of the party, Bush opened a barrage of criticism designed to drive him from the territory. The Softs, on the contrary, were delighted by the embarrassment of the Hards, and Waterman pronounced the new appointee "a prince of good fellows." "Upon your suggestion [I] do justice to both men," he wrote Lane in December, warning that Bush was determined to rule or ruin the party. Garrett, more ambitious for Lane than Lane was for himself, entertained similar views but felt Bush had so aroused the public mind that Lane ought to acquiesce and thereby gain the credit of having Deady reinstated. "You certainly can have no love for [Bush] or Deady, but of course you will keep on

25. Garrett to Lane, Sept. 20, 1853, Lane Papers, InU, and Dec. 20, 1853, MS OrHi; Lane to Bush, Oct. 1, 1853, Bush Papers; *Oregon Statesman,* Oct. 4, 1853; Lane to Nesmith, Oct. 31, 1853, MS OrHi; Deady to Bush, Nov. 27, 1853, Bush Papers. Replying to Lane (Nov. 22, 1853, MS OrHi), Nesmith chortled: "I am inclined to think that you laid on the 'soap' tolerably thick in your Sanfrancisco letter. However you should perhaps be pardoned for dispensing with a bountiful hand the article which nature has so abundantly supplied you with."

good terms with them until your elevation to the U.S. Senate or the Presidential Chair."[26]

Although of paramount importance, the reinstatement of Deady would not remove all squalls from the horizon. The appointment of Samuel Parker, a notorious Soft, to a minor postmastership "goes down with some like castor oil," wrote Curry. Oregon's new governor, John W. Davis, an ardent Democrat from Indiana, received a warm reception and assumed his duties early in December. Despite his subservience to the Bush faction and his national reputation—he had served as House speaker in Congress, commissioner to China, and president of the last national Democratic Convention—his vanity and "foreign" residence soon evoked discontent. Not even his democracy was sacrosanct to the Salemites: "I like Gov Davis verry well," confided Nesmith to Lane, "but suspect that he is a little on the 'soft' order. How is it?" Finally, the case of the new surveyor general, Charles K. Gardiner of Washington, D.C., aroused greater dissatisfaction. Decidedly relieved to be rid of the Whig incumbent, John B. Preston, leading Democrats were appalled by Gardiner's refusal to fill out certificates of application, thereby forcing applicants to the additional expense of procuring an attorney—or Preston himself, who set up an office for this very purpose across the street from the surveyor's office. "Christ," groaned Nesmith, "I begin to tremble for my own morals when I see what a proclivity public men have for 'Stealings.' " Whether or not Lane was actually responsible for these appointments, he was blamed nonetheless by local party members who regarded patronage as their personal prerogative.[27] The only appointee to give general satisfaction was Judge Williams, whose location in the central district facilitated his rapid admission to the Salem machine.

26. McFadden to Lane, Oct. 27, 1853, MS OrHi; *Oregon Statesman,* Nov. 22, 1853, ff.; Waterman to Lane, Nov. 14, Dec. 11, 1853, MS OrHi; Garrett to Lane, Nov. 8, Dec. 20, 21, 1853, MS OrHi.

27. Curry to Lane, Aug. 16, 1853, MS OrHi; Nesmith to Lane, Feb. 20, 1854, Dec. 3, 1853, MS OrHi. Correspondence does not reveal the extent of Lane's responsibility for these appointments, but a Washington

Ironically, within a few years it would be Williams' own articulate views about slavery that would contribute substantially to the division of the party and the downfall of Lane.

The national Democracy, ostensibly unified by its great triumph of 1852, actually functioned as an uneasy coalition of local factions united quadrennially by the spoils of office. Unfortunately, Franklin Pierce had not the ruthlessness to dispense favors with the efficiency and precision demanded of a party leader. Upon reaching Washington, his arm still in a sling, Lane was alarmed by the internecine squabbles in some of the states, notably New York, where Pierce's manipulation of patronage had set Hard against Soft and handed the Whigs a plurality. To Bush he expressed the hope that principle would prevail "at least on the Pacific side of the Rocky Mountains"; in confidence he added, "The Administration has made some d - - - - d, bad blunders and unless they right up, (and speedily) they are gone to the devil or in other words we will be badly used up by & bye. It will not do to try to conciliate extremes; heart and soul of the party must not be lost sight of."[28]

Lane's first move after Congress organized and after he paid his respects to the various department heads was to investigate the cause of Deady's removal. "Deady shall be put right, or I shall have a row," he promised Nesmith but cautioned that it might take some time. When Lane saw Pierce, the President explained that while he had been forced to withdraw Pratt's name because of the accusations made against him in the Senate, he did not recall any

---

correspondent to the *Times* (Feb. 18, 1854) absolved Lane of all blame. Lane, however, wrote Nesmith (Oct. 31, 1853, MS OrHi), "Tell me how you like my old friend Col Gardner. He is a first rate man and will make a good Surveyor Genl."

28. Roy Franklin Nichols, *Franklin Pierce: Young Hickory of the Granite Hills* (Philadelphia, University of Pennsylvania Press, 1958), pp. 381–82; Lane to Bush, Dec. 2, 1853, Bush Papers.

charges against Deady; however, he had left judicial appointments to his Attorney General, so Lane might inquire further of him. This Lane did and, after a thorough search of the records, learned that the pressure for offices was simply so great that when Deady's name was incorrectly listed, his commission was offered to the Pennsylvania delegation to appease their importunity. Associate Justice Olney had offered to resign so that his colleague might be reinstated, and Lane showed this letter to Pierce but immediately withdrew it when the President solemnly pledged to reappoint Deady and find a place elsewhere for McFadden.[29] The Senate confirmed the nomination, and Lane "followed it to the white house" to insure it went out by the next mail, in time for Deady to hold the spring term court in southern Oregon. "Thank God it is over," he sighed, "and you are again on the bench." Deady was not entirely convinced. Three months later he requested Bush, who had gone east to purchase a new power press for the *Statesman,* to ascertain what had really happened and to get certified copies of any correspondence submitted to the department. The answers Bush got were the same as those given Lane, and Deady was finally satisfied.[30]

By the time Bush reached Washington in April 1854, Lane had requested congressional action on several important measures: to raise two or more army regiments for frontier service; to pay the cost of the recent Rogue River War; to extend the military road from Myrtle Creek to Scottsburg; to increase the salaries of executive and judicial officers in Oregon; to appropriate another $75,000 to cover the remaining Cayuse War claims; and to establish customhouses at Port Orford and Coos Bay. Except for the last

29. Lane to Nesmith, Dec. 13, 1853, MS OrHi; Lane to Deady, June 18, 1854, MS OrHi; Olney to Lane, Oct. 18, 1853, MS OrHi; Lane to Nesmith, Jan. 18, 1854, MS OrHi. McFadden was reassigned to the supreme court of Washington Territory.

30. Lane to Deady, Feb. 3, 1854, MS OrHi; Deady to Bush, May 12, 1854, Bush Papers; letter from Bush, April 18, 1854, *Oregon Statesman,* June 6, 1854; Deady to Nesmith, Aug. 21, 1854, MS OrHi.

item, jettisoned for lack of time, Congress obliged on all counts, but only after some timely efforts by Oregon's delegate.[31]

Three days after Bush's arrival, Lane presented a memorial from the Oregon legislature to enable the territory to draft a constitution and organize a state government. Three weeks later he presented to his colleagues Columbia Lancaster, delegate from the new Territory of Washington. Lancaster had been one of the five members to support Gaines in the struggle over locating the capital in 1851–52, so there was no great affection between the two delegates. They soon clashed during a debate on the Oregon land bill, which Lane succeeded in amending so that the owners could obtain warrants and sell surplus portions of their unwieldy tracts. Lancaster referred to the exclusion of foreign born from the original act whereby McLoughlin was deprived of his claim at Oregon City. Understandably sensitive to such a charge, Lane responded with a eulogistic defense of his predecessor and some carping criticism of McLoughlin, "a perfect aristocrat British gentleman." Minimizing the doctor's aid to immigrants, he grossly exaggerated the Briton's wealth at "a quarter of a million at least," and perhaps "more than $500,000 in cash besides his property." "I should be sorry to see Congress deprive him of one particle of his property, but it is absurd to say that the Government of the United States shall not make what disposition they please of their own property because it is occupied by British subjects."[32]

Lane pressed Congress to authorize Oregon to organize a state government, vaguely estimating her population at "some sixty thousand inhabitants"—it was hard to tell with so many miners and immigrants arriving.[33] The measure, like the customhouse pro-

31. *Congressional Globe,* 33 Cong., 1 Sess., pp. 46, 140, 182, 371–72, 492.

32. Ibid., pp. 1080–82. For McLoughlin's reply, see his letters of July 17 and Aug. 12, 1854, *Oregon Spectator,* July 21, Aug. 18, 1854.

33. *Congressional Globe,* 33 Cong., 1 Sess., pp. 1117–18. In the *Statesman* (Feb. 21, 1854), Lafayette Grover estimated the population of Oregon at 45,000.

posals, languished in committee, for the Thirty-third Congress had more urgent matters to consider: a Pacific railroad, including ratification of the purchase of Mexican territory for a southern route; a homestead bill designed to encourage the settlement of Western states; the perennial hassle over tariff policy; and a bill, destined to shake the very foundations of the Union, to organize the territories of Kansas and Nebraska upon the principles of popular sovereignty. In one of the most fateful decisions in White House history, Pierce agreed to a proposal by Stephen A. Douglas that virtually repealed that part of the Missouri Compromise that since 1820 had restricted slavery to lands south of Missouri's southern boundary. Overnight national attention focused on Nebraska. "The papers are full of it, men everywhere talk about it, even the ladies, (God bless them!) gossip about it; Ministers of the Gospel have dropped the Bible, and preach of it—the very air around us is full of it," reported the Washington correspondent (Hibben) to the *Statesman.* In Oregon popular sovereignty was hailed as a measure of greater local autonomy. Lafayette Grover, an aspiring young politician whom Bush had chosen to edit the *Statesman* during his absence, proclaimed it "western not southern" in character, merely "another term for democracy." Debate raged in the House through most of May, and although the delegate from Oregon supported the measure he remained silent throughout the controversy.[34]

On another issue Lane committed himself in bold and unequivocal terms. In southern Oregon there was a movement afoot to combine with northern California and form the Territory of

34. *Oregon Statesman,* June 30, Aug. 15, July 25, 1854. Cf. *Congressional Globe,* 33 Cong., 1 Sess., pp. 575–76.

A native of Maine, Grover (1823–1911) attended Bowdoin College and was admitted to the bar in Pennsylvania. Like Bush, he was a protégé of Thurston, who encouraged him to come to Oregon as his law partner. Upon Thurston's death, Grover instead entered a partnership with B. F. Harding and also became a successful businessman. He served as Oregon's first representative in Congress (1859), as governor (1870–77), and as U.S. senator (1877–83).

Jackson. Backers of the scheme, including Lafayette Mosher, an ardent supporter of Lane, forwarded petitions to Salem and Washington, but in both places they were received coolly. Lane objected that further division of Oregon would seriously retard statehood, but if a division were effected it should be along the Cascade Mountains; besides, the California delegation looked askance at any proposal to reduce the size of their state. Earlier Grover had cautioned that it would "turn out to be a purely *whig lead,*" and that many farmers in southern Oregon, fearing domination by the miners, opposed division. As it was, "the south will present your name as one of our first senators, provided we are so fortunate as to be borne into the Union, in the due course of human events."[35]

Whatever else transpired during Bush's four-month visit, it is evident that the energetic editor gained a new appreciation of Lane's role in Congress. The two got along famously, and after witnessing Lane in action for several days Bush wrote back to Oregon with unrestrained enthusiasm. "He labors unceasingly for the territory, and with more success than all the delegates from the other territories here. He enjoys (and deserves to) the confidence and esteem of the members, President, and heads of departments, in a degree second to no member of either House." As time passed, the editor gained fresh insights into the problems of a territorial delegate. "It is very difficult here to make people understand the state of things on the Pacific coast," he testified two months later, applauding Lane's "incredible influence" and deservedly enviable reputation. Bush returned early in September, and the next *Statesman* announced in a most matter-of-fact manner, "We make no doubt that Gen. Lane will be the next delegate from Oregon." Another issue featured an unabashedly sentimental poem, "To the Gen. Jos. Lane, on receiving a Gift of his Daguerreotype," by a Washington matron, Mrs. A. L. Ruter Dufour.

35. *Oregon Weekly Times,* Feb. 18, 1854; Mosher to Lane, Feb. 12, 1853 [i.e. 1854], MS OrHi; letters from Lane, n.d., *Oregon Statesman,* May 30, July 11, 1854; Grover to Lane, Feb. 7, 1854, MS OrHi.

How shall I thank thee for this charming gift?
How tell thee what a prize I deem it, too?

. . .

God bless thee, *patriot, soldier, statesman, friend,*
Heaven's choicest gifts be thine, whate'er thy way;
May life immortal be thy sure reward,
When earthly glories to thee pass away.[36]

During the last week of the session, Lane was stricken with a high fever and serious intestinal infection. For the first time in his life he was dangerously ill and for ten days lay prostrate with two physicians hovering over him day and night. President Pierce visited him daily, and on the sixth day he was moved from his room at Willard's boardinghouse to the White House, the coolest building in Washington, where the President and his "good kind Lady" waited upon him as they would "their own brother." After a period of recuperation and a few days of relaxation at nearby mineral springs, he was fully restored.[37]

A visit to his former home in the "Pocket" of Indiana awakened old memories and kindled fresh hopes among friends and well-wishers. Stumping the state with Senator Jesse Bright and Representative John L. Robinson, Lane campaigned with good effect before responsive audiences, including one of 17,000 at Indianapolis that must have brought back reminiscences of 1851. The *Evansville Enquirer* soon raised Lane's name for President in 1856, and determined supporters attempted to have State Librarian Gordon Tanner or the poetess, Mrs. Sarah Bolton, write a biography of him. In response to a proposal to nominate him, Lane gave what by this time had become his classic reply: he did not wish the honor, but as the immortal Jackson had said, the presidency was "a position not to be sought or declined." "No individual," he

36. Letters from Bush, April 19, June 23, 1854, *Oregon Statesman*, June 6, Aug. 15, 1854; ibid., Sept. 5, Oct. 10, 1854.
37. Lane to Bush, Aug. 3, 12, 1854, Bush Papers.

continued, "ever has had the hardihood to set his will in opposition to that of an entire party, seeking to bestow on him the highest honors on earth. I therefore shall acquiesce in whatever the democratic party may do."[38]

With Deady appeased and Bush apparently committed to support him—Bush was dependent on Lane to get his territorial printing account approved—Lane's relations with Nesmith were now threatened with subtle deterioration. Nesmith, who had named his eldest son after Lane, had desired to be made a visitor to West Point and accompany Bush to Washington, but Lane had been unable to procure the appointment because Pierce feared there was no precedent for such action. Nesmith would have come anyway but was temporarily out of funds, partly because he had loaned Nat some $1,300 to operate the Island Mills, and when the mills were sold the debt had been turned over to the new owners, who were reluctant or unable to pay. Nesmith appealed to Lane to exert influence on his behalf, and Lane assured him that he would not lose one dime. Yet shortly before Bush left, Nesmith was still without funds and contemplating a lawsuit against Nat. "I shall come to Washington as soon as Farar & Guthrie pay me the funds necessary to pay my passage, which I think probably will be somewhere between the day of Judgement and the time when Hell freazes over." At least with Nesmith, one knew where he stood. By October he had mellowed considerably, although he still had not recovered the debt. Asking Lane to submit his resignation as marshal, he explained that he had bought some land and was going farming.[39]

38. *Oregon Statesman,* Nov. 21, 1854; *Evansville Enquirer,* cited in *Oregon Spectator,* Jan. 20, 1855; William C. Larrabee to Lane, Oct. 17, Nov. 11, 22, 1854, MS OrHi; Lane to Albin P. Hovey, Nov. 24, 1854, Lane Papers, InU.

39. Nesmith to Lane, Feb. 7, 1854, MS OrHi; Lane to Nesmith, Jan. 18, 1854, MS OrHi; Nesmith to Lane, Feb. 7, Oct. 20. 1854, MS OrHi. Nesmith was also wearied of operating without sufficient funds and was generally disillusioned with the Pierce administration. Lawrence Dean

Throughout this session, as always, Lane was compelled to keep a sharp eye on territorial patronage, the master key to good relations with local party members. When Waterman resigned as postmaster of Portland, his position was given to his former assistant, Alonzo Leland—a reassuring gesture to the supporters of the *Times.* The Postmaster General removed Lovejoy from the more important office of postal agent for dereliction of duty, in spite of Lane's disposition to retain him; to the displeasure of the Softs, he was replaced by John C. Avery, who was as yet within the good graces of the Salemites. Not a few deplored the appointment of young Guthrie as receiver in the land office and believed it a sinecure to insure payment for the Island Mills, but at least some, including Nesmith, were charitable enough to attribute it as much to the Secretary of the Treasury, Guthrie's uncle, as to Lane. A disillusioned Governor Davis left the territory for Indiana in August, and Secretary Curry, whose previous service as acting governor had been acceptable to the Hard faction, got the nod. Ben Harding assumed the vacated secretaryship, an office he had always coveted, and Farrar stepped into Harding's old post of district attorney. "How do you like the appointments?" Lane confidently inquired of Bush. "Who will set up a howl about any of them?"[40]

The "howl" about Surveyor General Gardiner, on the contrary, showed no signs of abating. The charge was incompetence; he was embarrassing the party. "Besides," Bush told Deady, "he is a damn soft-whig, and a perfect d - - n fool." Lane realized that removing one Democrat simply to reappoint another alienated supporters

---

Williams, "James W. Nesmith and Oregon Frontier Community, 1845–1860" (unpublished master's thesis, University of Oregon, 1963), pp. 89–92.

40. Waterman to Lane, Dec. 11, 1853, MS OrHi; *Oregon Weekly Times,* Feb. 11, 1854; Lane to Deady, July 17, 1854, MS OrHi; Nesmith to Lane, Sept. 14, 1854, MS OrHi; Lane to Bush, Nov. 2, 1854, Bush Papers.

and subjected the Administration to the charge of "fickelness," but he promised to secure the desired removal. The delegate soon learned that it was easier to promise than to deliver. When Bush arrived, Lane reiterated his pledge but requested petitions from Oregon to aid him in his task. The matter dragged on, and when Bush got back to Oregon he again implored Lane, "General—are you not going to get old Gardiner turned out *forthwith?*" Lane laid the facts before Pierce, who promised to make the change as soon as the Secretary of the Interior returned to Washington. His must have been an extended absence—Lane was still waiting for action the following spring.[41]

"What does Mrs. Pierce charge for acting as nurse to [a] Congressman?" Deady wanted to know as he reviewed the state of affairs with his friend Bush. "Did you *steal* Madam *Rooters* lines on Genl Lane or did he partly by accident and partly by design leave them where he knew you would find them?" Two weeks earlier, Deady asserted, a friend had written to inquire why Bush had rendered himself so ridiculous by giving "Old Joe" such "foolish puffs." "Everybody knows that Lane is no favorite of Bushs, the result is every one is saying whats up?" Bush shrugged off the matter without comment; his eye was on the next election. "Pratt was here a day or two ago," he replied. "Says he is a candidate for delegate. . . . How does Pratt feel towards me?"[42]

41. Bush to Deady, April 17, 1854, MS OrHi; Lane to Deady, July 17, 1854, MS OrHi; Bush to Lane, Sept. 23, 1854, MS OrHi; Lane to Bush, Oct. 18, 1854, Bush Papers.

42. Deady to Bush, Oct. 15, Sept. 30, 1854, Bush Papers; Bush to Deady, Oct. 7, 1854, MS OrHi. The appellation "Old" was commonly applied to married men in the nineteenth century. It had been applied to Lane in his first election campaign, when he was referred to (*Oregon Spectator,* June 5, 1851) as "Old Jo.—the *Lane* that has no *turn* in him." Moreover, Lane was then fifty, and most of the other leading Democrats—Bush, Deady, Nesmith, Grover, Harding—were still in their twenties.

Oregon politics had undergone basic modifications since Lane's re-election in 1853. Conceding the realities of political operation, the *Oregonian* did an abrupt about-face the week following the June election and advocated the immediate organization of the Whig party on a platform of internal improvements and a Pacific railroad.[43] Organization was not fully complete by the 1854 elections, but the party achieved noteworthy success, particularly in the northern counties.

In addition to this Whig activity was the rise of a temperance movement that sought to prohibit the sale of intoxicating beverages within the territory and to elect a slate of temperance candidates. In 1844, in the days of the provisional government, prohibition advocates in Oregon had succeeded in banning liquor sales. Two years later Maine became the first state to legislate against the sale of alcoholic stimulants, inspiring a dozen other states to follow suit in the next decade. Supporters of the "Maine Law" met in Salem in the spring of 1852, and in April 1854 they called a convention to urge the nomination of county candidates on a temperance platform.[44]

Federal appointments by the Whig Fillmore administration had first induced Democrats in Oregon to consider statehood as early as the spring of 1852, but their enthusiasm diminished in proportion to the increasing prospects of a solid Democratic victory in the national elections. After Pierce's subsequent fumbling of Oregon patronage, most recently in the appointments of Gardiner and Davis, the old arguments re-emerged. Less than two months after Governor Davis took his oath of office, the legislature memorialized

43. *Weekly Oregonian,* June 18, 1853. Bush responded with characteristic scorn in the *Statesman,* July 4, 1853: "The Sewer man is in favor of organizing the whig party. Greely, of the New York Tribune, says that the Whig party is dead in the states. But, like all animals of the reptile order, it dies in the extremities last; and him of the Sewer is the last agonizing knot of the tail."

44. Woodward, *History of Political Parties in Oregon,* pp. 61–62.

Congress for permission to draft a state constitution and ordered a referendum to be taken at the next territorial elections.[45]

Neither individually nor by tacit collusion, as happened in some counties, could the imperfectly organized Whig and Maine Law forces shake the grip of the more efficient Salem machine, although for the first time the Democrats were obliged to recognize a tangible opposition. The Whigs won only eight of the thirty-four seats in the legislature, but Democratic losses in Benton and Marion counties were especially heavy, prompting Grover to editorialize on the need for unity and harmony within party ranks. The vote to hold a constitutional convention was defeated 4,079 to 3,210, but even before the results were fully known the *Statesman* promised, if the referendum were defeated, to make statehood party policy until Oregon was admitted to the Union.[46] With this stand Lane heartily concurred. From the vantage point of 1854, it was impossible to anticipate how rocky the road to statehood would be.

Following the election, adherents to the Native American or Know-Nothing party began organizing their "wigwams" in the Willamette Valley for the alleged purpose of mobilizing opinion against foreign influence in government. Actually, except for a lingering hostility to the British Hudson's Bay Company and "un-American" Roman Catholics, there was little antiforeign sentiment in the territory, and the new movement seemed to have been directed as much against the dictatorship of Salem as anything else. When Bush returned from the East where he had witnessed the Know-Nothings in action, he immediately launched a campaign against the mushrooming local order. His tour de force was a caustic exposé of the membership of the secret organization after a printer in his employ infiltrated the Salem wigwam and obtained access to

45. *Journal of the House, 1853–1854* (Salem, Asahel Bush, 1854), p. 139.

46. *Oregon Statesman,* June 20, July 11, 1854.

its membership rolls and constitution. In a letter to Lane shortly thereafter, Nesmith referred with contempt to future prospects of the new movement.[47] Before many weeks passed, however, it became obvious that the wigwams were providing the kind of machinery that the Whigs had hitherto lacked and were ready to challenge the ascendant Democracy. By January 1855, Nesmith admitted that they had underestimated the strength of the new order and that it might even carry the next election. "They avow in their Lodges that their real object is to break down and disorganize the democratic party. As a matter of cource they sweep all the Whigs softs, tenderfootted, and disaffected." "These things can readily be accounted for with such Democrats who are 'Out,'" he continued candidly, "but why the treason Should extend to the 'Ins' is more than I can account for." One of the "ins" he referred to in particular was Joel Palmer, "*once* our mutual friend," who had reportedly defected to the enemy. Another was Waterman of the *Times,* whom Nesmith would never have considered an "in," but with whom Lane had always sought to maintain friendly relations.[48]

When the territorial legislature convened at Salem, the Democratic rulers determined to revitalize party machinery and discipline. On December 11, Delazon Smith introduced a bill in the House "to substitute the *viva voce* for the ballot method of voting" in territorial elections. On December 12 an editorial in the *Statesman* warned vacillating Democrats to "Beware." "There is not a man of prominence or influence belonging to the damning conspiracy in Oregon whose connection with it will not be known in less than six months. They are doomed men." Three days later, with some Democrats voting with the Whig opposition, the House

47. Ibid., Nov. 1, 8, 1854; Woodward, *History of Political Parties in Oregon,* p. 67; Nesmith to Lane, Nov. 29, 1854, MS OrHi; Priscilla Knuth, "Oregon Know Nothing Pamphlet Illustrates Early Politics," *Oregon Historical Quarterly, 54* (1953), 40, 47–48.

48. Nesmith to Lane, Jan. 1, 1855, MS OrHi.

accepted the bill, fourteen to twelve, and the following week the Council voiced its approval, five to three.[49]

The *viva voce* bill, wrote Curry, was a "trump card" designed to make "these midnight politicians come out in the open sunshine." Bush publicly lauded it as an effective "know-nothing antidote" and sought to equate nativism with Whiggery—"the most of them are *natural know-nothings,* and ought to have been admitted without initiation"—although he was forced to concede that "three or four" Democrats had also joined their ranks. What no one said but was nonetheless apparent was that the *viva voce* law might also serve effectively to keep recalcitrant Democrats in line. Among the voices raised in opposition was that of the Portland *Times,* which decried it as "rather a retrograde movement for progressive Democracy" and "about as antiquated as the 'blue-laws' of Connecticut, and quite as applicable to the wants and wishes of the Territory." James F. Gazley, a Soft member of the legislature from Douglas County, opposed the new dictum and was promptly read out of the party. Alarmed by the course of events, Nat warned his father against being party to proscriptive measures: "My impression is that most of your influential friends will be called Know Nothings."[50]

Two rather minor incidents further illustrate the tenor of party politics at this time. In August 1854 the Snake Indians near Fort Boise massacred all but two boys in a party of twenty-one immigrants on the Oregon Trail, raising once again the prospects of a full-scale Indian war. When regulars from Fort Dalles failed to apprehend the Snakes, Curry issued a proclamation for two volunteer companies to march against the Indians. Militia Brigadier

49. *Journal of the House, 1854–1855* (Corvallis, Asahel Bush, 1855), pp. 17, 32–33; *Journal of the Council, 1854–1855* (Corvallis, Asahel Bush, 1855), p. 34; Knuth, *Oregon Historical Quarterly, 54,* 51.

50. Curry to Lane, Dec. 19, 1854, MS OrHi; *Oregon Statesman,* Dec. 19, Nov. 21, 1854; *Oregon Weekly Times,* Dec. 23, 1854; *Weekly Oregonian,* Jan. 13, 1855; Nat to Lane, Dec. 31, 1854, MS OrHi.

General Nesmith doubted their ability to procure the necessary supplies and conduct a succesful campaign so late in the season. When he refused to take the field Bush supported him in the columns of the *Statesman,* and Curry was obliged to countermand his proclamation. There was something decidedly juvenile about their delight at Curry's distress, "I wish you had of been here to witness all the Farce," bantered Nesmith to Deady. "Chicopee [Bush] and I have had many a harty laugh." The second incident, totally unrelated at first glance, occurred when the legislature voted seventeen to twelve in the House and five to four in the Council to move the capital from Salem to Corvallis, a decision fraught with overtones of revolt. It was no accident that the label "Salem Clique" became common currency for the Democratic leadership at this time.[51]

All this was fodder for the next election campaign, which promised to be the most critical to date. Lane's relations with the Clique were not all that he might have desired, and he was noticeably concerned about the coming canvass. Moreover, he was optimistic that Congress would approve Oregon's statehood, so stakes would be high with all the new offices to be filled. With local politics in a state of flux and Lane removed four thousand miles, it was not easy for him to keep abreast of developments. Bush had no sooner arrived in April than Lane's good friend Dunbar of Milwaukie wrote him, warning that "Political wire workers," apparently Hards, were seeking underhandedly to defeat him. "Can this be possible?" Lane confidentially asked Palmer. "What say you?" The warnings kept coming, and Pratt's name was increasingly mentioned. "So many good men have written me the same thing that there must be something in it," Lane insisted to Bush late that summer. "They say I am strong with the people but the politicians are determined to put me down."

51. Nesmith to Deady, Sept. 25, 1854, MS OrHi; *Journal of the House, 1854–1855,* pp. 54–55, 81; *Journal of the Council, 1854–1855,* p. 81.

> Why is this? in what have I failed to do my duty? God knows that no man living has a stronger desire to do his whole duty. . . beg the members for God's sake to put off the Election and we will see whether I dont come back. I have no fears, if you will only give me a chance to see the people. at all events I am a candidate for nomination, and it is the only occasion that perhaps may occure in my life when I shall be anxious for Election, and hope that democrats will not abandon me at the comeing nomination. Who is it that is deceiveing me. Who is guilty of dissimulation. Please find out and write me, and let my friends know at once that I am a candidate for nomination, and am anxious to receive it. I have been as successful as any delegate in Congress, and can and will do as much for Oregon as any one can do. What I ask again for heaven sake is the cause of complaint.
>
> I can scarcely think of this matter with anything like pleasure. dont allow me [to be] beaten. One time more and I am if my friends wish it out of the way.[52]

Nesmith undertook to quiet Lane's fears, although he could not refrain from chiding him a little for not trusting his "real friends" and for paying so much attention to "corrospondants who would like to frighten you with Bug bears, and magnify their own consequence by continual representations of their own devotion to your interests." Except for Guthrie's appointment, Nesmith thought Lane's conduct had given *"eminant satisfaction"* to most Oregonians. True, some settlers in Umpqua were unhappy about his giving Jesse Applegate, an avowed Whig, the appointment of surveyor on the military road to Scottsburg; Jesse was now posing as his confidential adviser and openly taunting Democrats to try to destroy Lane's confidence in him. But the masses were with Lane,

52. Lane to Deady, June 18, 1854, MS OrHi; Dunbar to Lane, April 29, 1854, MS OrHi; Lane to [Palmer], June 1, 1854, Lane Papers, InU; Lane to Bush, n.d. [ca. end of Aug.], 1854, Bush Papers.

and so were most of the politicians "who have influence." From Deady came reassurance that he would not again be a candidate, and Bush replied that Lane's nomination was certain.[53]

All this was very comforting, but how could Lane know that they were not all conspiring to bring him down? About this time letters from Palmer reported that Pratt was covertly a candidate, and Nesmith's name was frequently mentioned; Deady would not be a candidate, but he was friendly to neither Pratt nor Lane; Waterman was still his friend and champion; and Bush's support appeared to be sincere. Waterman, however, warned that a secret caucus had been held in Portland that summer to bring Deady to the fore. The most trustworthy appraisal came from Nat, who was no politician but had long since served as one of Lane's most reliable sources of information. "You know your business," Nat wrote, "but I would suggest to be careful who you correspond with and what you say." In his opinion Bush was "all right so far," as was Nesmith, and both Palmer and Curry were friendly. The Know-Nothings were strong and would beat a man like Pratt, so instead of seeking the nomination, Lane ought to "lay back and look at the race."

> You may say this is not very democratic in me, but I do assure you I am tired of all such party organizations as those that have to use so much intrigue lying and rascality as our would be leaders and rulers out here have to, to secure there own aggrandisement. I do think the democratic party in Oregon is made of the poorest hacknied rotten hearted set of Office Seeking Sons of Bitches I ever knew. You know that I dont seek nor would not have an office, and therefore these intrigues look worse to me perhaps than they do to Office hunters. I am satisfied that every effort will be made to secure Pratt the nomination by his (Pratts) proselites. I wish you

53. Nesmith to Lane, Oct. 2, 1854, MS OrHi; Deady to Lane, Sept. 30, 1854, MS OrHi; Bush to Lane, Sept. 23, 1854, MS OrHi.

> were in a condition to retire from Public life. I would then suggest that we all emigrated to some quiet little valley in a pleasent part of California where we might Cultivate the soil and have our little herd of Cattle horses and sheep and live a quiet happy life, and be free and far away from this Oregon democracy.[54]

No, Nat was no politician. Politicians are made of much sterner stuff.

Bush, Deady, and Nesmith did not renege on their commitment to Lane, even though Deady at one point supposed Nesmith might support Pratt. Pratt's candidacy did not impose so difficult a choice for the Clique as it might appear, for as Ben Harding said to Lane, "There is no other man [than you] on whom the party can so readily unite." The Clique had opposition enough; it needed the strongest man it could put in the field, and Lane had done nothing to violate its trust.[55]

Pratt had been one of Lane's most prolific correspondents, writing every mail and sometimes twice. Although he had not actively sought the appointment of chief justice of the supreme court, he had played a dominant role in forming the Democratic party and was deeply offended by the Senate's refusal of his commission; it soon became apparent that he expected Lane to secure redress from the "reproach & stigma of a fatal & secret stab made by professedly honorable men at a time & in a place where I was without the means of self defence." When such redress was not forthcoming, he sought to effect it by returning to Washington in Lane's stead. About the time Lane was recuperating in the White House, Pratt had visited a Salem saloon, and as the night wore on, Nesmith told Deady, he became "wonderfully communicative" and boasted that nobody could be elected delegate without his influence, further

54. Palmer to Lane, Sept. 22, Oct. 18, 1854, MS OrHi; Waterman to Lane, Oct. 9, 1854, MS OrHi; Nat to Lane, Sept. 28, 1854, MS OrHi.

55. Deady to Bush, Oct. 15, 1854, Bush Papers; Harding to Lane, Oct. 16, 1854, MS OrHi.

declaring that Lane did not desire renomination. The following month he sounded out friends and courted support, and early in September advised Lane that he had consented to having his name used in connection with the delegateship—although three days earlier he had told Deady his preference for delegate was Lane. By this time Lane had already made it unmistakably clear that he desired the renomination himself. Pratt wrote again, asking him to reconsider his "supposed wishes for a renomination" so that he might vindicate his honor by an appeal to the voters. Picking up the gauntlet, Lane responded so as to preclude further doubt. *"Your reply to me is certainly frank,"* retorted Pratt dourly; "& *no one will misunderstand it.* All who inquire of me shall be correctly informed of our true positions."[56]

Deady, irrepressible as ever, had anticipated the inevitable clash. "I suppose you have learned that Pratt . . . has written to Genl Lane to withdraw which he will not do of course," he gossiped to Bush, adding that in this contest he would remain aloof—"You recollect the story of the disinterested wife when the husband and bear fought." And to Nesmith he predicted a battle royal: "There is going to be a fight between these two distinguished individuals who have heretofore loved one another so devotedly. Some rich developments will come out of it."[57]

The congressional elections of 1854 went badly for the national Democracy; in fact, Lane confided to Nat, they were disastrous, although he was confident that the results would spur Democrats everywhere to unity and victory in 1856. Throughout the North popular reaction was decidedly hostile to opening further territory

56. Pratt to Lane, Feb. 16, 1854, MS OrHi; Nesmith to Deady, Aug. 10, 1854, MS OrHi; Pratt to Lane, Sept. 6, 1854, MS OrHi; Pratt to Deady, Sept. 3, 1854, MS OrHi; Pratt to Lane, Dec. 9, 1854, MS OrHi.

57. Deady to Bush, Sept. 26, 1854, Bush Papers; Deady to Nesmith, Nov. 2, 1854, MS OrHi.

to slavery in keeping with the principles of popular sovereignty embodied in Douglas' Kansas-Nebraska policy. Anti-Nebraska Whigs, Free-Soilers, and disenchanted Democrats spontaneously rallied to support fusion tickets; a new party calling itself "Republican" sprang up in a half-dozen places at the same time; and in the Northeast especially, the Know-Nothings abetted the conspiracy to rout the party of Jackson. The October elections in Indiana, Ohio, and Pennsylvania resulted in the net loss of thirty-one representatives—half the Democratic majority in the House—and by the time the final returns were tallied in November, the Democracy had lost every free state except California and New Hampshire, Pierce's home state. The Republicans elected 15 senators and 108 representatives—25 more than the Democrats; the Know-Nothings sent 5 members to the Senate and 43 to the House. Lane blamed these unfortunate developments on patronage rather than on popular sovereignty. "The General policy of the Administration is good such as any democrat can cheerfully approve," he declared to Nat. "Many of the appointments, have been very unfortunate, consequently much grumbling and dissatisfaction, has been manifested throughout the country."[58]

While the anti-Nebraska forces were taking their toll, the delegate from Oregon was unusually busy with territorial business and had little time for national prognostications. From the middle of October until Congress reconvened in December, Lane concentrated his efforts on processing and expediting payment of some $175,000 worth of Rogue River War claims. This tedious job dragged on until Christmas, and he was glad to be rid of this "most troublesome affair."

On the opening day of the second session of the Thirty-third Congress, the delegate from Oregon introduced bills to permit the completion of public buildings in Oregon, to locate bounty land warrants within the territory, to construct a military road from

58. Lane to [Nat], Dec. 17, 1854, Lane Papers, InU; Nichols, *Franklin Pierce,* pp. 364–65.

Salem to Astoria—a polite fiction, but any road had to be justified as a military road—and to grant pensions to certain volunteers of past Indian wars. Lane further sought legislation to create a second territorial land office, to establish military posts and mounted troops along the Oregon Trail, and to regulate further the custom service in Oregon, including a special measure to settle the accounts of John Adair, collector at Astoria, who had been obliged to employ his private purse in the execution of his public duties. Considering the fact that this was a short session, Lane's efforts met with more than moderate success. Congress responded with legislation establishing the two new collection districts as well as a new land office in the Umpqua Valley for the southern part of the territory. No longer would settlers of the Rogue and Umpqua have to travel to Salem to register their claims. In addition to the regular operational expenditures of the territorial government, some $100,000 was appropriated, of which $30,000 was allocated for the Salem-Astoria road and $67,000 for the final completion of the statehouse and penitentiary. Lane himself was reimbursed more than $1,400 for expenses he had incurred as governor in 1849.

Charges by an Ohio newspaper that the delegate from Oregon was advocating a policy of extermination of the Indians drew a prompt and vigorous denial, in which Lane reviewed his dealings with the native race and read into the record a gory description of the recent Ward massacre on the Oregon Trail.[59] Of greater import was his brief speech supporting a Pacific railroad or more properly, railroads, for he thought that at least two transcontinental routes

59. In part, the newspaper quoted Lane as saying: "Mr. Speaker, 'Taint no use trying to civilize the Indians of Oregon. They care nothing about treaties. They'll rob and murder whenever they get a chance. The only way to treat the critters is to *sculp* 'em.' " Lane apparently did express ideas similar to this to the chairman of the Ways and Means Committee one day in the lobby of the House but claimed that he was speaking only against Indians who were openly hostile to emigration and settlement. *Congressional Globe,* 33 Cong., 2 Sess., pp. 415–16. Cf. his speech in the House, July 27, 1854, ibid., 33 Cong., 1 Sess., pp. 1953–54.

could be justified in the national interest; were they not essential for the military defense of the Pacific Coast? The southern route, he felt, was superior to all, and having personally traversed that part of the country he could testify to its suitability. With scant regard for reality, Lane proceeded to transform the barren Southwest into a veritable Eden, where fertile soil and ample rainfall combined to render large portions of its superior agricultural and grazing land, the best he had ever seen. Defying even the rudiments of logic, he then endorsed a central route as most suitable for the construction of a transcontinental railway. Finally, he argued, why not a northern road too? "Is their anything in the Constitution furnishing a reason why Congress should not appropriate land for this purpose? Can Congress make a better disposition of the public lands . . . which would more promote the interests of the whole country. . . ?" he asked rhetorically. In his opinion Congress could not "better dispose of the public domain."[60]

Because this was a short session, the pressure of various legislative issues was so great as to jeopardize territorial business, and during the three days traditionally devoted to territorial affairs, Lane's customary affability deserted him for a moment as he crossed swords with Representative E. Wilder Farley of Maine. When Farley introduced a bill to construct a telegraph line to the Pacific, Lane was quick to insist that the House get on with the business at hand; he had no objection to the bill, but they had already frittered away nearly half of the designated three days, and he had a bill pending to establish a new land office in Oregon. Farley objected:

> MR. FARLEY—I rise to a point of order.
>
> MR. LANE—I do not yield for the gentleman's point of order.
>
> MR. FARLEY—The gentleman refuses me the courtesy which I extended him a short time since.

60. *Congressional Globe,* 33 Cong., 2 Sess., p. 332.

MR. LANE—I did not call the gentleman to order; and if he says I did, he is a liar.

MR. FARLEY—You are a d - - - - d liar.

"At this point MR. LANE advanced towards MR. FARLEY with threatening gestures, but was arrested in his progress, by several members, who interposed to prevent difficulty," reported the House clerk. "The greatest confusion prevailed in the Hall. Members left their seats and crowded around the two gentlemen. The Chair called loudly to order, and directed the Sergeant-at-Arms to restore order. The Sergeant-at-Arms proceeded, as directed, to that part of the Hall where the difficulty had occurred, and, after some minutes, order was restored." A few minutes later Lane regained the floor and resumed doing "what I had intended to do when that fellow called me to order." This provoked another outburst and loud cries of "Order!" The chairman cautioned the delegate from Oregon against further "disrespectful remarks," and Lane submitted with good grace. The last day of the session Lane publicly apologized if, "under circumstances of excitement," he had offended the Representative from Maine or the dignity and decorum of the House. Farley reciprocated in kind, and the incident was closed.[61]

With scarcely a murmur, the House passed the bill introduced in the last session to enable Oregon to frame a constitution and apply for statehood, but the Senate subjected the measure to greater scrutiny. To get it out of committee, Chairman Stephen A. Douglas added the proviso that Oregon's population must be 60,000 before she could be admitted. This amendment failed to satisfy Southern critics, who by a strictly sectional vote on the final day of the session dashed all hopes of immediate action. Actually, the population issue was merely an excuse for further deliberation; the real issue was slavery, once again pre-eminent in national affairs. Southern senators were understandably reluctant to admit addi-

61. Ibid., pp. 474, 1191–92. Cf. Farley to Lane, March 8, 1855, *Oregon Statesman,* May 26, 1855.

tional colleagues from free states. Kansas and Nebraska had seen to that.[62]

News from Oregon proved somewhat disconcerting. The territorial legislature restirred old animosities by moving the capital from Salem to Corvallis and the putative university to Jacksonville. Leading members of the Clique were circulating a petition calling for the removal of Joel Palmer as superintendent of Indian affairs. And from Palmer and at least one other source came word—later proved erroneous—that Pratt, Deady, and Joseph W. Drew had been electioneering for Pratt in southern Oregon. Leland's *Standard* had capitulated for Pratt, body and soul. Undoubtedly Lane determined to capitalize in the forthcoming campaign on his newly won congressional measures as well as on the patronage opportunities afforded by them. To the collectorship of Port Orford, he named his old friend Dunbar, whose confidence he both enjoyed and trusted. Lafayette Mosher and George W. Lawson were named register and receiver, respectively, in the new land office that was to be located in Winchester. Lawson had visited Washington after Christmas and had written a glowing report of Lane's effectiveness as a legislator, which Bush had featured prominently in the *Statesman.* Mosher, it will be recalled, had accompanied the Lane family to Oregon in 1853 and had served as Lane's aide-de-camp in the Rogue River War that fall.[63]

Making no effort to disguise his anxiety, Lane again admonished Bush not to let him be defeated for the nomination. Subsequent issues of the *Statesman* allayed his fears as did private communications from the editor. "The Delegate contest is waxing warm, and I suspect it will get d - - - - d hot before the nomination comes off,"

62. *Congressional Globe,* 33 Cong., 2 Sess., pp. 991, 1149–51. For the best analysis of the opposition in Congress to Oregon's statehood, see Henry L. Simms, "The Controversy Over the Admission of the State of Oregon," *Mississippi Valley Historical Review,* 32 (1945), 355–74.

63. Nesmith to Deady, April 20, 1855, MS OrHi; Lane to [Nat], Dec. 17, 1854, Lane Papers, InU; *Oregon Statesman,* March 20, 1855.

replied Bush, cautioning him not to be misled by stories about Pratt's strength. "You will most certainly be nominated, so *make no compromises with Pratt.*" "If the d--n seat of government question is broached," he continued, "I would acquiesce in the action of the Assembly, and go for having the second appropriation of Congress placed within their control. Pratt can make no capital on that then."[64]

When Lane departed from Washington, it was impossible to predict the outcome of the contest; by the time he arrived in Oregon, it would be all but over. As the delegate took his leave of the national capital, President Pierce presented him with a cane in token of the respect of the Administration. It was a fine cane with a gold head, the shaft carved from the keel of the old *Constitution,* whose prow had borne the figurehead of Jackson. Congress adjourned about midnight of March 3, and Lane, cane in hand, left for New York and the 6,000 mile voyage home.[65]

64. Lane to Bush, Jan. 17, 1855, Bush Papers; Bush to Lane, March 3, 1855, MS OrHi.
65. *Oregon Weekly Times,* April 21, 1855.

*Chapter 4*

# GATHERING CLOUDS

Bushrod W. Wilson was in a sour mood in January 1855. Times were bad in Oregon, he wrote his brother in Minnesota Territory; money was scarce, trade bad, and farming unprofitable. "Politics at a low ebb, all a one sided question in this country," he continued, explaining that Independents, Whigs, and even Democrats were "rated as apostates, renegades, turn coats, softs and Now Nothings, unless they will meekly bow to the yoke of a clique of Political aspirants usurping the name Democrat, but falsifying its principles to their own interests." A Whig couldn't get anything through the territorial legislature, he complained, while whatever the Clique proposed, "no matter how ridiculous," won ready approval.[1]

1. Wilson to Lane, Jan. 6, 1855, Wilson Papers (University of Oregon Library, Eugene).

The politicians at Salem, on the other hand, were less concerned about what people thought than they were about losing their privileged position. The "Clique" label, Nesmith informed Lane, was merely a ruse of Pratt's to cover his own pretensions, but Pratt would find that "the 'Clique' will give him some trouble yet." "They all have the *clique* story," Bush reiterated to Deady, declaring that Pratt had "doctored up" most of the Softs for his service.[2]

Pratt, moreover, was determined to have his day. Charging that Lane had forgotten his constituents and had set his sights on the presidency instead, the judge began a campaign to pack the nominating convention with disaffected supporters. The Portland *Democratic Standard* came out unreservedly for Pratt and published a series of unsigned letters heavily scoring Lane and the Clique. Although Bush had previously refrained from endorsing candidates for the Democratic nomination, he now hoisted Lane's name to the masthead and charged that Pratt was the author of the offending letters. "The fight opens rich," wrote Deady the following day, expressing some disappointment that Bush had followed Waterman so closely in endorsing Lane: "The vexed question of which of you is the generals best friend will still remain unsettled, and be the source of interminable altercation." Yet, as Deady knew, Bush had good reason to stick with Lane; if the Pratt men were successful, the public printing, worth $5,000 annually, would go to the *Standard*. Under the circumstances Deady promised to do what he could in the campaign—"a good deal that otherwise I might leave undone."[3]

Bush's efforts paid handsome dividends, and the boom for Pratt was checked rapidly and decisively. So completely had the tide changed by the time Lane arrived two days before the convention

2. Nesmith to Lane, Dec. 19, 1854, MS OrHi; Bush to Deady, March 17, 1855, MS OrHi.

3. Dunbar to Lane, Nov. 18, 1854, MS OrHi; *Democratic Standard*, cited in *Oregon Statesman*, March 6, 1855; Deady to Bush, March 7, 1855, Bush Papers. Cf. Bush to Deady, Jan. 21, 1855, MS OrHi.

that the result of the voting was a foregone conclusion.[4] When the *Columbia* docked at Portland, Lane received the usual salutes and was in high spirits as he departed for Salem that afternoon. The convention on April 11 nominated Lane over Pratt, fifty-three to six, after which the winner responded with a short speech. One of the five resolutions passed commended the candidate's record; another strongly supported statehood.[5]

Pratt's defeat represented only the first hurdle; the main campaign lay ahead, but before Lane could leave Salem another thunderstorm appeared out of the blue. "What in Hell does the Old Genl. mean by practicing duplicity towards his friends," Nesmith exploded to Bush after learning of Dunbar's appointment to the collectorship at Port Orford, Mosher's and Lawson's to the land office in Winchester. "He certainly told us at Curreys that the place at Port Orford was open and that Drew should have it, but now it turns up that that damned Indiana friend of his Dunbar is already appointed. God Damn all such appointments as this last batch. they would sink any body to Hell but Old Jo." That afternoon Nesmith worked off his aggression at "such damned folley" by planting potatoes. "Bush growls like the Devil about those appointments," replied Joe Drew, who had carried the letter to him, "but I think we had better keep quiet." Bush apparently thought so too, although his understanding had been the same as Nesmith's. When Deady received the news at "Fair Oaks," his home in the Umpqua, he was almost livid with rage. Two days later he was still fuming:

> I am at a loss whether to curse myself or Somebody else [he wrote to Nesmith], and in the mean time I am giving vent to to my indignation by a little miscellaneous damning. Here

4. Deady to Nesmith, March 20, 1855, MS OrHi; Deady to Bush, March 15, 1855, Bush Papers; Curry to Bush, March 20, 1855, Bush Papers; Bush to Deady, March 29, 1855, MS OrHi.

5. *Oregon Statesman,* April 14, 1855; *Oregon Weekly Times,* April 14, 1855.

> after the test of a mans standing in the party and political worth, will not be fealty to Democratic principles and the party which maintains them, but fidelity to the personal interest of Old Jo, or some other nine days wonder, whom a sun of good luck or something else has chanced to make a hero of. If he only maintains the interest of his Chief whether right or wrong, he may with impunity combine with the Know Nothings, to destroy the party and its principles. . . . To say the least . . . it is a d - - - - d shabby conclusion for a campaign conducted and won by the Statesman.
>
> If this once vaunted democratic party is to sink into a mere *personal* party, where the soulless Flunkey who sings old Jo's praise loudest and longest, is alone to be elevated and honored, I think the institution had better be abolished, to make room for the divine rights of Kings.

"I shall probably see Lane before he starts back to Washington," he concluded, promising to express himself "in the plain vernacular. Then let him procure my removal if he dares and be d - - - - d."[6]

On his way home from Salem, Lane stopped at Corvallis to give Bush his campaign itinerary and vigorously denied Nesmith's charges. A few days later the Whigs nominated one of Lane's old antagonists and announced the vague slogan, "John P. Gaines against the world." The following week the *Statesman* extravagantly eulogized Lane. "We question if any man was ever more widely known and highly esteemed at the National capital," wrote Bush defiantly; unlike Gaines, the incumbent has "a happy faculty of getting along peaceably, and making friends, in his intercourse with mankind." Gaines accepted Lane's challenge to debate him in a series of engagements through the territory, beginning in the Umpqua community of Deer Creek. "I should like to be on the ground to witness the commencement of the campaign, and see the

6. Nesmith to Bush, April 13, 1855, MS OrHi; Drew to Nesmith, April 14, 1855, MS OrHi; Deady to Nesmith, April 18, 1855, MS OrHi.

Skirmishes and light troops thrown forward," Nesmith prattled to Deady. "What a fine opportunity to hit *Hard Licks* [Gaines], but I am afraid that Old Jo aint the man to do it. It is not a contest which calls for the exebition of any *amiable* qualities. And the people arn't a gowing to assemble to listen to egotistical desertations from Spiritless Old 'Fogeys.' "[7]

Pert and irascible, Deady was there and described the encounter to Nesmith and Bush. Lane had spoken first: "The Same old story about the Oregonians being the bravest handsomest most generous, most intelligent, most patriotic, people in the world. How he loved them all and every part of them. What he had done for them and what he intended to do for them." Comparing himself to David before Goliath, Gaines replied with a few derogatory remarks about Lane's "cabin and potato patch" nearby, his no-party campaign in 1851, and his general ineffectiveness in Congress. Each man kept up the appearance of good humor while accusing the other of all sorts of questionable conduct. "I never felt as sick at heart about politics Since I've been in the Territory," moaned Deady, still smarting from the recent appointments. "Of course I shall do my duty to Old Jo in the Canvas and I think he will be elected by at least five hundred majority. But the seed is now sewn for future trouble for years to come."[8]

It took the candidates nearly two weeks to complete their circuit through southern Oregon. Judging from the final returns—Lane carried Jackson County 819 to 677—the campaign went reasonably well for him, but both Drew and Deady, who were in the area at the time, sent back alarmist reports to Bush. "The *Clique* must not rely upon this county to secure old Jo's election," warned Drew. Deady offered "a small share of my interest in heaven to have Nes out here," because Gaines was continually bullying and abusing Lane.

7. Lane to Nesmith, April 14, 1855, MS OrHi; *Oregon Statesman*, April 28, 1855; Nesmith to Deady, April 22, 1855, MS OrHi.

8. Deady to Bush, April 24, 1855, MS OrHi. Cf. Deady to Nesmith, April 29, 1855, MS OrHi.

"L. has taken it all so far as meekly and mildly as ever Skinner did his abuse in '53. . . . For Gods sake do something in the Wallamette valley or we are beaten."[9]

Bush, who had already done more to ensure Lane's re-election than anyone else, told Lane before the debate in Corvallis that he had heard Gaines had him bullied. Unloosing a mouthful of profanity, Lane swore that if Gaines had said anything that could even have been construed as an insult, he would have "cut his heart out." That afternoon Lane flayed Gaines mercilessly from the rostrum, charging him with penury, arrogance, and deceit. "Gaines was d - - n mad, but took it," Bush told Deady, adding that some persons present thought Gaines was afraid of Lane. What effect Bush's prodding had on Lane can never be known, but a few days later in Dallas, the two contestants literally came to blows, each calling the other a liar, and each being restrained by his friends before any real damage could be done. Should they fight again, observed Bush, "I am confident Lane can lick him, and if he gets the advantage of him he'll pound him like hell, for he hates him most cordially."[10]

The campaign terminated without further incident. In Whiggish Portland, Lane found it necessary to vindicate himself of the McLoughlin claims, and he issued a general invitation to old national Whigs and "honest well-meaning Know-nothings" to sustain him at the polls.[11] Whigs and Democrats in Oregon differed sharply over the principle of popular sovereignty embodied in the Kansas-Nebraska Act, but the contest centered around personalities rather than issues. The *Statesman* attempted to portray Lane as Oregon's most effective champion of a Pacific railroad, although

9. Drew to Bush, May 7, 1855, Bush Papers; Deady to Bush, May 7, 1855, Bush Papers.

10. Bush to Deady, May 22, 1855, MS OrHi. See also *Oregon Statesman,* May 26, 1855, and *Oregon Weekly Times,* May 26, 1855, for accounts of the scuffle.

11. *Oregon Weekly Times,* June 2, 1855.

Lane does not appear to have made much of the issue. He did, on the other hand, request Bush to republish a testimonial from Senator Gwin of California, which vigorously denied that Lane had been guilty of intoxication or dissipation while in the national capital.[12] As the campaign progressed, the weekly invective and abuse exchanged between the *Statesman* and the *Oregonian* supplanted all other aspects of the canvass, and the clamor was further abetted by Waterman of the *Times* and by "Parson Billy" Adams—of "Breakspear" fame—whose newly established Oregon City *Oregon Argus* endorsed Gaines.

The hysteria of the press reflected both the critical nature of the struggle and the closeness of the race. For the first time ascendant Democracy was fighting for its political life. Both sides exuded confidence in public, although privately the Clique expressed misgivings. "My own opinion is that the contest is to be a close one, and should not be surprised if we had a 'fusion' legislature," Nesmith confided to Deady. Bush was also apprehensive. "The Whigs and Know Nothings appear confident of Old Gaines' election," he told Deady. "God preserve us from the infliction."[13]

The results at the polls were little short of sensational. Although the constitutional convention referendum failed by 415 votes, Lane defeated Gaines 6,178 to 3,943, an impressive 61 per cent of the total vote; in the legislature the Democrats retained control of the Council 7 to 2 and of the House by an overwhelming majority of 28 to 2. Besides being a personal triumph for Lane, the election thoroughly demonstrated the effectiveness of the *viva voce* method of voting as well as the lack of organization and cohesion

12. Lane to Bush, May 7, 1855, Bush Papers. Cf. *Oregon Statesman,* April 28 and May 12, 1855. Most frontiersmen were hard drinkers, but there is no evidence, apart from the partisan press, to suggest that Lane ever drank immoderately. Bush, Deady, and Nesmith made innumerable references to the drinking habits of themselves and others, but they never referred to Lane's use of alcohol.

13. Nesmith to Deady, May 5, 1855, MS OrHi; Bush to Deady, May 13 [1855], cited in Woodward, *History of Political Parties in Oregon,* p. 73.

within the ranks of the disparate opposition: Whigs, Know Nothings, temperance men, and Softs. The defeat left the Whigs totally demoralized, and their Know Nothing and prohibitionist allies utterly shorn of future hope.[14]

The election was particularly a personal triumph for Lane, whose strength at the polls was again convincingly demonstrated. Of course, he had much in his favor. The *Statesman* was the most influential newspaper in the territory. His last term in Congress had been singularly successful, procuring for Oregon, as the *Times* pointed out, more than one million dollars. And even as the campaign got under way, nearly two hundred thousand dollars in government drafts, payment for the recent Rogue River War, began arriving in the mails. Moreover, the political appeal of his opponent was limited, his war record uncertain, and his personality uninspiring. Nevertheless, the opposition to the Clique was considerable, and the Clique itself had exhibited no great enthusiasm for its candidate but had no one who could take his place. Following the election the *Statesman* raised Lane's name for the presidency in 1856, the editor confident that the nation would respond "with an enthusiasm, ardor, and devotion, equalled only by that which followed ANDREW JACKSON. Like him, Gen. Lane is invincible, in war or in peace, upon the 'tented field,' or in the political arena."

> JO LANE is the very man for the crisis; just the man to reunite and lead to victory the scattered, but now gathering hosts of democracy. . . . Make JO LANE the Democratic Standard bearer for 1856, and the battle is already half fought and won. . . .
>
> As a soldier or civilian, America holds not a truer patriot than JO LANE; as a statesman, she has none of more national, liberal, and correct principles, and none truer to the Consti-

14. *Oregon Statesman,* Aug. 18, 1855; Woodward, *History of Political Parties in Oregon,* p. 75.

tution and the Union; as a man, as "Old Joe," a warmer-hearted, whole-souled, generous gentleman never breathed the breath of life. He is one of nature's noblemen. . . . He has come up, unaided by wealth or rank, from humble life, through force of native talent, unconquerable energy, and an indomitable will. He is emphatically a self-made man, and made not amiss.[15]

The week following the election, Lane accompanied Waterman and others on a leisurely river excursion to Astoria, where he renewed acquaintances, made a few speeches, and generally relaxed and enjoyed himself. Upon his return he instructed Major Benjamin Alvord, the army paymaster at Fort Vancouver, to turn over to Governor Curry the nearly $400 in wages due him from the Rogue River War to be placed in trust for the two boys whose families were killed by the Indians during the Ward massacre the previous year.[16] About the same time, word came from the Treasury Department in Washington announcing that a new revenue cutter for Oregon would be named the *Joseph Lane.* On his way south to rejoin his family, he honored the Linn County militia by presenting them Santa Anna's gold-mounted sword, which he had taken during the Mexican War.[17]

Yet all was not well with the general-turned-politician. Delazon Smith had puffed him lavishly for the presidency in the *Statesman,* and, not to be outdone, the *Times* had also raised his name to the masthead, along with several papers in "the States." But problems of patronage continued to trouble his relations with the Clique.

15. *Oregon Weekly Times,* June 2, May 5, 1855; *Oregon Statesman,* June 9, 1855.

16. *Oregon Weekly Times,* June 16, 23, 1855; *Oregon Statesman,* June 16, 1855.

17. *Oregon Statesman,* June 16, 1855; *Oregon Weekly Times,* July 30, 1855.

Shortly after Lane reached Winchester, Deady dropped by one afternoon to ask about certain letters Lane said he had received purporting to show that Deady had used dishonorable means to oppose his nomination. It was all very cordial, Deady told Nesmith, but Lane, "with that humbugging smile of his," was unable to produce any incriminating evidence. He did, however, show the judge a letter from Jesse Applegate, warning him that Bush and the Clique had sought to "kill Lane and Pratt off" and give the nomination to Deady.[18]

When Lane defended Dunbar's appointment to the collectorship at Port Orford, he offered instead to give Drew a secretaryship there or at Gardiner at the mouth of the Umpqua, which naturally Drew rejected. Stephen F. Chadwick then accepted the position at Gardiner only to learn that Washington would not grant the appointment on the grounds that it was unnecessary. Chadwick was bitter, and so was Deady. Lashing out at Lane's "humbug dynasty," he explained to Bush how Chadwick had "called on Ancient Joseph, and the latter went on coining new lies on the subject, but its no use," he concluded. "I think it would now be a matter of difficulty to get a politician in this community to believe Joseph on oath. We are not only of little faith, but absolutely without that essential ingredient." When Bush got the letter he relayed its contents to Nesmith:

> In short the Southern wing of our honored *Cli*que is damn mad, and in a "fine phrenzy." . . . [Surveyor General] Gardner is *not* to be removed. . . . What shall we do? I swore once that I would never do or say another d - - n thing about it. But I'll recall that. When Lane comes here I intend to have a *free* talk with him about that matter, Palmer, and those d - - n Southern appointments. Will you help me about that Gd d - - n Surveyor Generalship, and try to impress upon Lane's mind,

18. *Oregon Statesman,* June 16, 1855; *Oregon Weekly Times,* June 16, 1855; Deady to Nesmith, July 17, 1855, MS OrHi.

when he passes *through your residence* that something has got to be *did?*

And to Deady he expressed himself in the same unequivocal vein:

I shall have a *free* talk with Lane . . . when he passes through here. I'll be d - - - - d if I am not going to know *what* screw is loose in the surveyor general matter. It is well enough for Lane to "humbug" you Umpqua chaps a little, but the article shouldn't be brought this side of the Calipooiah. Nesmith says Lane don't intend to have Gardner removed. But you know Nes. is a d - - n poor authority.

"I think that 'Chicopee' [Bush] is getting sick of his candidate for the Presidency in '56," Nesmith chortled to Deady upon receipt of this latest missive. "In reply I gave him my views generally in pretty plain terms about the damned humbuging course which Old Jo has thought propper to persue since his return, and advised a call of the Cli-que to throw him overboard. . . . I am in hopes to see Lane before he leaves for Washington, and intend to tell him plainly what I think!"[19]

Presumably Lane heard enough "plain talk" to last him all the way to Washington that September as he made his way down the valley to Portland, where he departed for the East. But it is unlikely that Bush handled Lane as roughly as he professed to his friends, for on the very day he was putting up such a bold front to Nesmith, he also addressed Lane. The tone of the second communication was markedly subdued:

I have never supposed, General, that you had any dislike to urging Gardner's removal, and do not now suppose you have. But if such shall be the case, I desire you to be governed by your own preferences in the matter. I never asked you whether

19. Deady to Bush, Sept. 5, 1855, Bush Papers; Bush to Nesmith, Sept. 9, 1855, MS OrHi; Nesmith to Deady, Sept. 14, 1855, MS OrHi.

> or not there was any reason why you disliked to urge Gardner's removal. Perhaps we should have done it before. Yet I am confident there is none, and that you prefer that he should be evicted. It is certainly due the democratic party that for the short remainder of the term of Mr. Pierce, the *only* office in Oregon that has any patronage attached should be practically in democratic hands.[20]

Bush could be infuriatingly compromising at times.

The reason for Bush's double talk, for his extravagant editorializing, for his soft-pedaling the trouble between Lane and the Clique is not too difficult to divine. Bush appreciated the obvious advantages to himself in particular and to the Oregon Democracy in general of having a man like Lane in Washington, but he had a special need to curry favor with the delegate at this time. The new power press he had ordered in 1854, along with five hundred copies of the territorial statutes for 1853–54, were on the steamer *Southerner* when she was lost at sea. The legislature released Bush from delivery of the statutes, allowing him no pay, and authorized him instead to reprint five hundred copies of all the laws in force in Oregon, in addition to the statutes of 1854–55, but the Secretary of the Treasury disallowed payment for the reprints, amounting to almost $5,000, on the grounds that they had not been authorized by Congress.[21] With times already bad, this triple loss of press, statutes, and reprints taxed the editor severely. Bush did talk to Lane about removing Gardiner and Palmer, but he also importuned Lane about his printing claim. Bush was probably quite right and undoubtedly sincere in his professions that Lane was the man most likely to be able to secure an appropriation if, in fact, an appropriation could be obtained at all. "General, for God's sake (more particularly for mine however)," he wrote two weeks after Lane's

20. Bush to Lane, Sept. 9, 1855, Lane Papers, InU.

21. Bush to Lane, April 15, 1856, Lane Papers, InU; James Guthrie to Elisha Whittlesey, Feb. 20, 1856, Lane Papers, InU.

departure, "get an appropriation for me for the statutes of 1855. . . . If I lose that it will d - - n near break me up."[22]

The Table Rock Treaty of 1853 had departed from traditional American policy by permitting the Indians to remain on a small portion of their land instead of ordering them transported beyond settled areas to some nondescript region unwanted by the whites. During the latter part of 1854 and throughout the summer of 1855, Indian superintendents Palmer in Oregon and Stevens in Washington had negotiated treaties with most of the main bands in the Pacific Northwest, reserving for each a fragment of land in exchange for stipulated gifts and annuities. Tribes east of the Cascades were generally less disposed to part with their lands than their more sedentary neighbors to the west, but in neither area did the formal treaties mark any significant improvement in the relations between Indian and white. West of the Cascades, especially in southern Oregon, the proximity of Indians to the white settlements evoked periodic demands for extermination of the Indians nearby; to the east, hundreds of whites flooded across the beckoning land before the Indians were even fully established upon their reservations.

During the summer of 1855, gold strikes near Fort Colville on the upper Columbia led to violent exchanges between prospector and native, while in the Rogue River country friendly Indians warned that further clashes there would touch off another major conflict.[23] These fears were justified. A scant two weeks after Lane's departure for Washington, the Yakimas, Walla Wallas, and their allies went on the warpath, and simultaneously the Indians of southern Oregon swept down upon the settlements of the upper Rogue Valley. A culmination of lesser brutalities by both sides,

22. Bush to Deady, Sept. 30, 1855, MS OrHi; Bush to Lane, Oct. 7, 14, 1855, Lane Papers, InU.

23. Stephen F. Chadwick to Lane, Dec. 26, 1855, Lane Papers, InU.

the Rogue River outbreak was provoked by the wanton massacre of a small party of Indians, including women and children, who were encamped outside of the reservation. Fearing that all tribes in the Northwest were acting in concert, Governor Curry hastily called for volunteers to put down the uprisings, north and south.

From the beginning, the prosecution of the war degenerated into a bitter partisan squabble. Although the Clique was inclined to minimize the seriousness of the threat at first—Bush warned Lane to beware of false rumors, saying that "the *immediate* cause of the outbreak South, was a massacre *by the whites*"—it became fatuously delirious over the appointment of Whigs to positions of leadership. The Clique arranged the "decapitation" of several political opponents by having Curry disband all militia units that had been organized before his proclamation,[24] but the governor further incurred the wrath of Salem by ordering an extensive punitive expedition to the north in which Whigs again won minor appointments. Nesmith, in command of the northern regiment, reported to Bush that Curry was "almost crazy" in mobilizing for war, and that Dryer was making a "d - - n fool" of him. "I am afraid Indian wars are the *rocks* on which Curry will split," Bush scrawled to Deady. "He seems to have a weakness for them and a G - d d - - n weakness concerning them." Subsequent issues of the *Statesman* made it quite plain that no office in the territorial army was available to anyone who had voted for Gaines.[25]

In mid-December, Curry complained to Lane about having had

24. Bush to Lane, Oct. 21, 1855, Lane Papers, InU; Bancroft, *History of Oregon, 2,* 385.

25. Nesmith, cited in Bush to Deady, Oct. 21, 1855, MS OrHi; cf. Drew to Bush, Oct. 30, 1855, Bush Papers; *Oregon Statesman,* Nov. 3, 10, 1855. Drew blamed the Whigs and Know Nothings in Jackson County for inciting the war "for political purposes and a speculation in wheat & cattle," but accepted his own appointment as adjutant general, saying, "I have no good excuse for refusing to take part in the muss and displaying a little of what they call *patriotism.*" Drew to Bush, Nov. 16, Oct. 30, 1855, Bush Papers.

"a most mean and despicable 'fire in the rear' "; but since Bush had recently "dried up," Curry had decided to support him again for the territorial printing—"for the good of the party." In truth, both governor and printer found they had a bigger war on their hands than their feud with each other: a conflict between the regular officers of the army and the territorial volunteers that was becoming so intense that it threatened to supplant even the struggle against the Indians, which was going badly enough. A major offensive against the Yakimas in November failed dismally after posing nearly insurmountable problems of logistics and supply to the hapless territorial administration. When the volunteers finally mounted the offensive, the elusive Indians simply melted away into the hills, and after several such encounters, the men from the Willamette began to tire of playing soldier. Besides, winter was coming, and the men were poorly equipped. Nesmith attempted to have the volunteers mustered into the regular army, but he was not successful and shortly thereafter submitted his resignation. "Ill health in his family is assigned as the cause," Curry told Lane, "although others have attributed it to other reasons. Be this as it may the regiment appears to be doing good service without him."[26]

General John Ellis Wool arrived at Fort Vancouver late in November. Like many regular officers, he believed that the whites were usually to blame for trouble with the natives. And he said so publicly. He harbored grave misgivings about the effectiveness of the three- and six-month volunteers, to say nothing about their motives, and he sincerely believed that the treaties recently concluded had not adequately safeguarded the rights of the Indians. When Nesmith's request arrived, he dismissed it out of hand. He had neither the authority to accept volunteers nor the animals and supplies necessary for a prolonged operation. These expeditions against the Indians, he added, had been made "in too much of a

26. Curry to Lane, Dec. 15, 1855, Lane Papers, InU. Cf. Nesmith to Curry, Nov. 30, 1855, *Correspondence and Official Proceedings Relating to the Expeditions against the Indians* (Salem, Asahel Bush, 1855), p. 60.

hurry" and by men "unable to act efficiently, and without supplies to keep the field." With that, Wool returned to California, and although he requisitioned Washington for another regiment of reinforcements,[27] he also obliged the California press with views highly uncomplimentary to the citizens of Oregon. Superintendent Palmer also took the side of the Indians and supported Wool in many of his charges.

The volunteers had one brief moment of glory when the Walla Walla chief Peu-peu-mox-mox agreed under flag of truce to sue for peace. The volunteers being vastly outnumbered, Lieutenant Colonel James K. Kelly held the chief hostage during the negotiations, but when fighting broke out and he tried to escape, a volunteer clubbed him to death, taking his scalp and ears as trophies of war. The four-day battle fortuitously permitted Governor Stevens of Washington to return from the Blackfeet country, where he had been trapped by the outbreak of the recent hostilities. Stevens was even more critical of Wool than was Curry and credited the volunteers with saving his life.[28]

The winter of 1855–56 was one of the coldest on record. Thermometers at Winchester registered twelve degrees below zero, Lane was told; at Portland the Willamette froze so solidly that horses were able to cross.[29] With the regulars firmly ensconced in winter quarters at Fort Vancouver and The Dalles and with the volunteers still in the field, Oregonians showed little charity toward Wool's alleged obstructions to their war effort and for his general reluctance to engage the enemy. With wondrous unanimity, the territorial press leapt to the defense of their maligned volunteers, although Leland of the *Standard* could not refrain from

27. Wool to Nesmith, Nov. 24, 1855, *Correspondence and Official Proceedings Relating to the Expeditions against the Indians,* p. 56; Wool to Lane, Dec. 11, 1855, Lane Papers, InU.

28. Stevens to Lane, March 9, 1856, Lane Papers, InU.

29. Chadwick to Lane, Dec. 26, 1855, Lane Papers, InU; Harding to Lane, Dec. 31, 1855, Lane Papers, InU. Hiram Richardson (Jan. 7, 1855, Lane Papers, InU) also reported a temperature of twelve below at Siuslaw.

twitting Bush for his recent attempts to "dethrone" the governor.[30] The legislative assemblies of both Oregon and Washington passed resolutions petitioning Congress to recall Wool and assume the expenses incurred by the volunteers.

Wool retaliated with a long, forthright letter to the *National Intelligencer,* expressing utter disdain for the citizenry of the Pacific Northwest. The "alarm pervading the country," he declared, had been stirred up by "political demagogues" who were grasping for war at any price. "Something had to be done," he said, in reference to the northern campaign against Pep-peu-mox-mox, whose barbarous "murder" he found totally reprehensible. "A fight with the Indians, no matter whether friends or enemies, was indispensable to excite the sympathy of the nation, and especially Congress, or the propriety of paying contributions, so profusely levied on the people of Oregon, might be questioned." This campaign, he asserted, was one of the most extravagant ever undertaken in the United States, a "crusade" undertaken with the sole motive of plundering the federal treasury for the enrichment of the territory. In southern Oregon the situation was no better, he declared, although the war there would have been long since over had it not been for the "indiscriminate warfare" and "massacre" of friendly Indians by the volunteers. The war would end if the volunteers were withdrawn and private warfare prevented, but Oregonians were determined to exterminate the Indians. Should Congress assume the costs of war, which he estimated at from two to four million dollars, it would only encourage larger wars. "As long as Governors of the Territories make war and exercise powers, as I believe, unknown to the President of the United States, and individuals raise volunteers and make war on the Indians whenever they please, and Congress will pay the expenses, so long will we have war in Washington and Oregon Territories."[31] And similar letters followed.

30. *Democratic Standard,* Dec. 20, 1855.

31. Wool to eds., April 2, 1856, *National Intelligencer,* cited in *Congressional Globe,* 34 Cong., 1 Sess., pp. 1135–36.

Spring again brought the regulars into the field, once the grass proved sufficient for full-scale campaigns. It also saw the return of many volunteers to their farms, but the recriminations between civilian and military showed no sign of abating. Curry had issued scrip to finance the war, which had been another bone of contention between him and Bush—Dryer had approved—but local merchants had been obliged to sell at inflated prices because of the uncertainty that the federal government would honor scrip at par value. Indeed, as the war progressed and the reports by Wool and Palmer were given national circulation, it became increasingly questionable if Congress would honor the scrip at all. Worried Oregonians appealed to their delegate for Congressional action. "Almost every man has turned over to [the] Government, his horses, mules, oxen, and grain," wrote one, warning that a delay in payment "would be equal to bancruptcy." "Oregons whole Salvation depends upon your efforts in having this war paid," asserted another. But the price of scrip continued to falter until by the spring of 1856 it was selling in Portland for as little as thirty cents on the dollar. Even then few were buying.[32]

In January, Oregonians received word that Lane was being appointed brigadier general and would, presumably, proceed to set matters right in Oregon. Deady got the rumor from Pratt in San Francisco and relayed it to Bush, who in turn printed it in the next *Statesman,* along with an item from an Eastern newspaper announcing the appointment. Deady was puzzled. "Is Pierce putting him out of the way for the succession?" he asked. "For Lane it will be a short and easy way out [of] a troublesome future in this Territory," he concluded, "and he had better accept it—if he can get it."[33] Other members of the Clique were equally anxious to believe the report, undoubtedly because Lane's appointment would

32. Chadwick to Lane, Dec. 26, 1855, Lane Papers, InU; John E. Ross to Lane, March 21, 1856, Lane Papers, InU; Aaron D. Shelby to Lane, March 1, 1856, Lane Papers, InU. See also A. P. Dennison to Lane, April 11, 1856, Lane Papers, InU.

33. Deady to Bush, Jan. 21, 1856, Bush Papers. Cf. Pratt to Deady, Jan. 5, 1856, MS OrHi.

have removed him from the political arena, but the next mail brought a letter from Lane categorically denying there was any truth to it. And there the matter ended.[34] Lane did contemplate returning to Oregon to volunteer against the Indians, or so he professed, but that he would have accepted such an appointment is most unlikely. For Lane, military adventures were important for their political appeal, but he was not prepared then, or ever, to sacrifice a political career for a mess of military pottage.

Two legislatures convened on the first Monday in December 1855, one territorial and the other national, and the task of providing liaison between them fell to the territory's delegate. Lane arrived in Washington a full two weeks before the session began, in plenty of time to get settled at Brown's Hotel, a haunt of several Southern representatives, and to enroll his son John, who had accompanied him east, in one of the better schools in nearby Alexandria. When Congress assembled, Lane was ready.[35]

Disaffected members of the territorial legislature, led by Joseph C. Avery, had mustered enough anti-Clique votes to remove the capital from Salem to Corvallis in 1855. After falling out with Bush, Avery had gone to Corvallis and from there joined the *Standard* in hurling scathing denunciations at the Salem machine. With the Clique securely back in control after the election, the new legislature promptly voted to return to Salem permanently after the Christmas recess; and during the bitter cold spell between Christmas and New Year's, the partially completed capitol building in Corvallis inexplicably burned to the ground.

The legislature of 1855–56 was not "over-modest in its memorials," wrote the chronicler Bancroft, who listed twenty petitions

34. See Nesmith to Deady, Jan. 28, 1856, and Drew to Deady, March 1, 1856, MS OrHi; Lane to Bush, Dec. 5, 1855, *Oregon Statesman,* Jan. 29, 1856.

35. Lane to Lafayette Lane, Nov. 17, 1855, Lane Papers, InU.

that it forwarded to Congress. Among them, the petitioners urged the recall of Wool, the payment of military expenses, and the disallowance of a treaty negotiated by Palmer, locating an Indian reservation within the Willamette Valley. In addition, a Democratic caucus called for the removal of Gardiner, Palmer, and Avery and the appointment in their stead of Grover, Edward R. Geary, and Drew. Members from the Umpqua further requested that Lawson be replaced in the southern land office by Riley E. Stratton, a move heartily approved by Bush. "The Legislative Guillotine seems to be working bravely this winter," said Deady when apprised of the news.[36]

The Thirty-fourth Congress was likewise dominated by intense partisanship. Born of anti-Kansas sentiment, the new Republican party entered its first Congress with a plurality in the House, firmly determined to check any further advance of the slavocracy. With equal determination, the Democrats caucused the Saturday before Congress convened and nominated for the speakership an ardent champion of the Kansas-Nebraska Act. When the balloting began, the minority Know Nothings pursued an independent course, and the Democrats, without sufficient strength for their own success, managed to prevent a Republican majority for an unprecedented 122 ballots. For two months the House was paralyzed, unable to organize. The dogfight ended on February 2 when the Republicans won a suspension of the rules requiring a majority decision, and a former Democrat and Know Nothing, Nathaniel P. Banks of Massachusetts, received a plurality of three votes. As early as mid-November, Lane had predicted a contest over organization and advocated a hard party line in defense of the "great principle asserted in the Kansas Nebraska bill," but as the struggle wore on he became increasingly apprehensive about getting his own legislation through. Over the signature "Democrat," he wrote to

36. Bancroft, *History of Oregon, 2,* 414–15; Waterman to Lane, Jan. 22, 1856, Lane Papers, InU; Bush to Lane, Feb. 6, 1856, Lane Papers, InU; Deady to Nesmith, Jan. 21, 1856, MS OrHi.

the *Statesman,* completely absolving the Democracy from any blame in the spectacle and charging the Know Nothings and "black republicans" with obstructing the nation's business. The outcome of the contest displeased him. "The struggle is over, the child is born & named Banks, Black republican, know nothing," he wrote dejectedly after the final ballot.[37]

The week following, Lane joined other friends of the Administration at a state Democratic convention in Concord, New Hampshire, the President's home state, where the party faced an uphill battle. There he met several neighbors and acquaintances of Joe Drew's father and learned from them that the old man was a Whig, as Joe had been before he left for Oregon. When Lane confronted Drew with the information, Nesmith snorted, but Bush was annoyed. "I think you do Drew injustice General, in suspecting his democracy," he countered. "Whatever he may have been in New Hampshire, there has been no more consistent democrat in Oregon than he." Lane's reply was not very conciliatory; Drew's antecedents smacked of abolitionism.

> I said in my letter to Drew that it was honorable to change & I am glad that he has changed and trust that he may continue true to National democratic principles & he will while he remains in Oregon, but I would not trust him in N. H. among his old associates. I understand quite well & too well [the] workings sayings & doings of democrats tinctured with abolition (as too many are in the nothern states) to place implicit confidence in them. . . . I only have to say that I trust that Drew may prove himself a true man—I am or at least think I am a great judge of men.[38]

37. Lane to Bush, Nov. 15, 1855, Bush Papers; Lane to Bush, Jan. 2, 1856, *Oregon Statesman,* Feb. 26, 1856; "Democrat" to Bush, Jan. 22, 1856, Bush Papers, reprinted ibid., March 11, 1856; Lane to Bush, Feb. 2, 1856, Bush Papers.

38. Lane to Drew, March 2, 1856, Lane Papers, OrU; Nesmith to Deady, April 1, 1856, MS OrHi ("Aint that Rich!!"); Lane to Bush, May 30, 1856, Bush Papers.

Upon his return to Washington, Lane introduced several bills, including one to pay the expenses of the Indian war and another to enable Oregon to draft a state constitution, but he did not get the floor to speak until the end of March, when he made an impassioned plea for an appropriation of $300,000 to suppress Indian hostilities in Oregon and Washington. The Indians, he stated, were waging a war of extermination against the whites. The regulars had "utterly failed" to afford protection, and only quick action by the volunteers had prevented greater disaster. Wool was a competent officer but when confronted by Indians, totally "unequal to the task of coping with them in their mode of warfare." Lane thought himself "a good Indian fighter" and expressed "a great inclination to go out to Oregon and assist its people in their defense." Should the hostilities continue for another mail, he thought he might do just that. The speech was widely circulated and enthusiastically received in Oregon, the *Statesman, Times,* and *Standard* all reprinting it. "We Oregon men think it equal if not superior to any effort made in either House for the last thirty years," gushed Waterman, who was in dire need of some patronage to save him from imminent bankruptcy. Then he nearly spoiled it: "They used to think, many of them, that you couldn't make a speech. I always insisted that you could—and now they all tell me that *I* was right and *they* wrong."[39]

Lane achieved only part of his goal, but his conduct on the floor of the House exhibited new levels of sophistication. Instead of referring the bill to the Ways and Means Committee, the usual channel, or the Committee of the Whole House, he asked the House for unanimous consent to suspend the rules and pass it immediately so that the warrants could be issued before the mails to Oregon closed next Thursday. When the chairman of the Ways and Means Committee objected to this "extraordinary" procedure for considering an appropriation bill, a third member suggested

39. *Congressional Globe,* 34 Cong., 1 Sess., pp. 766–67; Waterman to Lane, May 27, 1856, Lane Papers, InU.

a compromise: let the Ways and Means Committee consider the bill at their next meeting, at which Lane could present all his evidence, and if the committee were convinced of the emergency, it could report to the House for immediate action. The committee chairman offered to call a special Saturday meeting to consider the bill, and Lane was satisfied. The committee thought the bill too "warlike" in design and so amended it by earmarking the funds for "restoring and maintaining the peaceable disposition" of the Indians rather than for "suppressing hostilities," which would have implied tacit recognition of the territorial war debt. In short, it became simply another Indian appropriation bill to be administered by the superintendent of Indian affairs. Lane decided to accept it nonetheless. The committee reported the bill on Monday, and in the debate he refuted the official reports of Wool and Palmer. The House passed the bill the following day.[40]

During the debate on deficiency estimates, Lane again responded in considerable detail to Wool's charges, especially to his letter in the *National Intelligencer*, which had been read into the *Congressional Globe.* While disclaiming any desire to "pluck one laurel" from his former commander, Lane regretted to see a brilliant career marred by this last campaign, which "impartial history" would judge "unfortunate for the reputation of this honored veteran." The general was a West Pointer, a "tactician after the fashion of the military fogies of Europe," who had become "thoroughly imbued with the faults of the old system, so far as its utter inadaptation to Indian warfare is concerned." Wool was "mistaken" in his information, Lane argued, and cited a letter from Stevens to Wool to set the record straight. He would prefer to see the deficiency bill defeated if any part of it were to be used for "supporting troops to remain in their barracks, and to pay officers for writing defamatory letters."[41]

No single issue preoccupied Congress more than Kansas, whose specter intruded at every level of consideration. The violence of

40. *Congressional Globe,* 34 Cong., 1 Sess., pp. 766–77, 789.
41. Ibid., pp. 1144–45.

that troubled territory was suddenly translated to the highest councils of the land when a representative from South Carolina strode into the senate chamber, a gutta percha cane in his hand, and beat a senator from Massachusetts until he sank senseless and bloody to the floor. The assault transfixed the nation. Preston S. Brooks was infuriated by Charles Sumner's extravagant tirade, "The Crime against Kansas," delivered in the Senate two days earlier, in which the Northerner had made disparaging remarks about the Palmetto state and its senator, Brooks' uncle, who was out of town and unable to reply for himself. Party and personal feelings, already intense, reached fever pitch as Northerners joined ranks behind their martyred colleague, and Southerners lauded the outrage as a manly vindication of their wounded honor. Sumner bore the effects of the attack the rest of his life; not for three-and-one-half years was he able to resume his seat in the Senate.

Like most Democrats within his constituency, Lane sided with the young Carolinian, minimizing the severity of Sumner's injury. "He is not badly hurt, and is now able if he would to go about and attend to his duties," he informed Bush a few days after the affair; several weeks later he dismissed it as "a small matter," Sumner having received "only two cuts and one bruise on the head." The *Statesman* gave the incident scant notice—only eight lines—as did the *Times,* but the *Oregonian* and *Argus* reacted with garish condemnation, particularly after Lane publicly implicated himself in the affair by serving as Brooks' second in abortive duels with Sumner's congressional colleagues from Massachusetts, Senator Henry Wilson and Representative Anson W. Burlingame. But from William J. Martin, Lane's devotee and neighbor in Winchester, came glowing commendation: "Thare is afiew of us out heare having a cane made to Send to the Hon. Brooks of South Carolina to replace the one he broke over Sumner."[42]

Lane continued to placate Bush in matters of patronage and by

42. Lane to Bush, May 29, July 18, 1856, Bush Papers; *Oregon Statesman,* July 22, 1856; *Oregon Weekly Times,* July 12, 1856; *Weekly Oregonian,* Sept. 13, 20, 1856; Martin to Lane, Oct. 28, 1856, Lane Papers, InU.

seeking to procure his disallowed printing claim. Before Lane left Oregon, Bush had expressed an interest in having his father-in-law, John S. Zieber, appointed surveyor general, and when the territorial caucus called for the appointment of Grover, Zieber's name was already before the President. Similarly, Lane had Robert Thompson named postal agent, replacing Avery, before he received the recommendation for Drew, whom he most certainly would not have appointed anyhow.[43] Voicing misgivings to Bush, Lane wondered if he would "catch the devil" for ignoring the wishes of the caucus, but the editor reassured him that under the circumstances all would be well. Zieber would be acceptable to all who recommended Grover, Bush replied; Thompson was "deficient in the clerical requisites," and should have had "a little more education" but would probably make a good officer. On the other hand, Waterman hailed Thompson's appointment as excellent—"just the man to straighten things out." Lane had independently decided to dismiss Lawson from the land office and appoint his illiterate friend, Bill Martin, instead of Stratton. This occasioned "a good deal of hard swearing" in the Umpqua, reported Deady, because the nominee was patently unfit for the position. Instead of the recommended Geary, Absalom F. Hedges finally replaced Joel Palmer as superintendent of Indian affairs, and Waterman received a minor appointment in Portland.[44]

Bush's printing claim was another matter. Despite his best efforts, apparently, Lane was unable to obtain satisfaction from the Treasury Department. Each time he wrote, Bush fervently implored Lane to get the bill allowed, and as time passed the matter threatened to upset relations between the two men. Bush neglected to write for some time, and Lane nervously inquired about the reason.

43. Bush to Lane, Sept. 9, 1855, Lane Papers, InU; Lane to Bush, Jan. 22, March 17, 1856, Bush Papers; Lane to Drew, March 2, 1856, Lane Papers, OrU.

44. Lane to Bush, cited in Bush to Lane, April 17, 1856, Lane Papers, InU; *Oregon Weekly Times,* March 15, 1856; Deady to Bush, March 4, 1856, Bush Papers.

Bush apologized for his negligence, pleading both lack of time and news, but he was also visibly annoyed.

> I discover from the tone and general character of yours [Lane's letter] that you are of the opinion that something is wrong with me, or that I am unfriendly. It is not unlikely that some G-d d----d *go-between* has written you that such is the case. It is not so General, there is not a word of truth in any intimation of the kind that some two-cent toady may have furnished you, and not a particle of ground for any such impression on your part. If you were on the ground where you could see for yourself, I should never have written this. It is more than I ever took the trouble to say before, if I mistake not. But as you are liable to be deceived, so far off, and as there never has been, and never will be any lack of coat-tail danglers to attempt to deceive, perhaps the above is not amiss. But I reckon this once will have to answer for all.

Thereafter the matter was dropped, and the correspondence resumed as usual, although Lane was forced to reply that he had made little headway in getting a special appropriation bill through the House; the Black Republicans had blocked it. Bush continued his solicitations, but his heart was no longer in them. "Likely, I reckon he thinks it best to keep that suspended over my head to 'hold the wretch in order,'" he confided to Deady. "Well, let it hang. 'Who's afeard.'"[45]

Lane's efforts to win congressional approval for Oregon's war debt and her aspirations for statehood also proved elusive. The bill to authorize a state constitution provoked a spirited debate in which Lane attempted to answer objections, real or imagined, that were voiced in the House. The measure failed to come to a vote for want of time. He tried to attach a rider to the army appropriation bill to

45. Lane to Bush, July 18, 1856, Bush Papers; Bush to Lane, Aug. 30, 1856, Lane Papers, InU; Lane to Bush, cited in Bush to Deady, Oct. 11, 1856, MS OrHi.

pay the expenses of the Indian war; when that failed he made a last-minute attempt to get the civil appropriations bill amended in the Senate to authorize the Secretary of War to appoint a commission to adjust, audit, and pay the war debts. The provision authorizing payment was struck out, but Lane was consoled by the establishment of a three-man commission headed by Lafayette Grover. The appointment of a commission might not seem very important, he wrote to Waterman, but in fact it represented "Congressional recognition of the justice of our claims upon the Government."[46]

Anti-Negro sentiment was part of the intellectual baggage most Oregonians brought with them from "the States."[47] The anti-slavery provision of the Ordinance of 1787 was incorporated into the organic acts of both the provisional and territorial governments, and one of the first acts of the provisional government, which the first territorial legislature reaffirmed, was to exclude free Negroes and mulattoes from Oregon Territory. With that the matter might have rested had not the Kansas-Nebraska Act injected its ambivalent doctrine of popular sovereignty into the political arena. Slavery was not an economic issue in the Pacific Northwest, although many of the arguments about it were couched in economic language; it was the far-reaching social and political implications of the subject that stirred Oregonians to renewed activity.

The trouble with the Kansas-Nebraska Act was its ambiguity. What was particularly unclear was the precise time at which a territory might rule for or against the "peculiar institution." Northern Democrats like Douglas saw the act as a means of re-

46. *Congressional Globe,* 34 Cong., 1 Sess., pp. 1143 ff., 1494 ff., 1994, 2150; Lane to Waterman, Aug. 19, 1856, *Oregon Weekly Times,* Sept. 27, 1856.

47. For a good discussion of the effect of slavery on the Pacific Northwest, see Robert W. Johannsen, *Frontier Politics and the Sectional Conflict: The Pacific Northwest on the Eve of the Civil War* (Seattle, University of Washington Press, 1955), pp. 15–50.

moving slavery forever from the halls of Congress by letting the territories themselves decide the issue. Other Northerners regarded it as the opening wedge of an aggressive slavocracy, while Southerners could view it as a theoretical victory for Calhoun's doctrine of nonintervention by the federal government. Most Oregonians, like frontiersmen everywhere, hailed the measure as a substantial advance in territorial self-government.

In December 1854, Delazon Smith introduced a series of resolutions in the Oregon legislature endorsing the Kansas-Nebraska Act for extending the *"constitutional right"* of the territories to adopt slavery, although he assumed that "nature" and the "convictions and will of a large majority of the people" would doubtless prevent the establishment of the institution in Oregon. The resolutions produced a lively response by certain members who were reluctant to renounce congressional control over slavery in the territories.[48]

The controversy over Kansas-Nebraska begot a new national political party and led to the mobilization of antislavery sentiment in Oregon. Opponents of slavery met at Albany in June 1855 and urged their fellow citizens to support only free-soil candidates and newspapers. The *Statesman* refused to "lumber its columns" with the proceedings of this "collection *of old grannies"* and thought it "decidedly *icy* in these nigger-struck *dames* to ask the *Statesman* to publish their stale fanaticism." "If anything could make the people of Oregon desire slavery," wrote the implacable Bush, "it would be the agitation of the subject by such fanatics as these."[49] Nevertheless the agitation continued, and by the end of the year, Adams of the *Argus,* the "Parson Brownlow of the West," emerged as the leading antislavery editor in the territory.

Meanwhile, events in Kansas reached a critical stage as New England abolitionists vied with Missouri slave owners to determine the status of slavery in the new territory. When Missourians

48. *Journal of the House, 1854–1855,* pp. 28–29. Cf. *Oregon Statesman,* Dec. 26, 1854.

49. *Oregon Statesman,* July 14, 1855.

crossed over to vote in the Kansas elections to ensure a proslavery legislature, free-state men retaliated with elections of their own and organized a rival antislavery legislature, which the Pierce administration refused to acknowledge. Extremists on both sides appealed to force. In May 1856 violence erupted anew when a party of Missouri "border ruffians" raided the free-soil town of Lawrence, and a few days later the abolitionist fanatic, John Brown, wrought unholy vengeance upon a handful of proslavery settlers along Potawattomie Creek.

"Bleeding Kansas" arrested the public mind as the national parties named their candidates for the coming presidential election, but it should be observed that Kansas "bled" more profusely in the partisan press than it ever did on its native soil. The status of slavery in the territories became the chief issue in the campaign of 1856. The Republicans, pledged to arrest the spread of slavery, named as their standard bearer the one-time explorer and military hero, John C. Frémont. The Democrats selected a "doughface" from Pennsylvania, James Buchanan, and wrote a nebulous platform upholding the Kansas-Nebraska Act and the principle of popular sovereignty. The Know Nothings, divided over slavery, nominated former Whig President, Millard Fillmore.

Lane expressed himself most fully on Kansas a few months before the Potawattomie massacre when he addressed a state Democratic convention in New Hampshire. His speech was important not only as an example of his rhetoric but also for the strong states' rights position that it espoused.

> I come from a Territory that had imposed upon her, in her organic law, the Wilmot Proviso [prohibiting slavery]. I went out under the law of Congress as the first governor of Oregon, & the only word I heard uttered against this law was that Congress should [not] have interfered in any of our affairs. "Why," it was said, "should Congress prohibit us from exercising our judgment in relation to slavery, or any other ques-

tion?" The question of slavery is safe with the people; & it is no more safe with the Wilmot Proviso than it would be without it; for slavery is a thing that will regulate itself. Climate, soil, products, commerce, business, profit on investments—these are the things that must settle the question of slavery or no slavery. Leave it to Kansas & Nebraska to look after their own affairs: & if there is a man among you who would join an Emigrant Aid Society, set him down as an unfortunate man.

Fellow-citizens, there are not two dozen sensible men in the country who ever believed that Kansas would become a slave State. All the South asked of the whole country was that the people of that territory should be left perfectly free to settle the matter for themselves, without the interference of New Hampshire or of any other State. That is the true doctrine; and if there is a man among you who would encourage emigration to that country, with the idea that force is necessary for the establishment of freedom or a free State there, he will be, in fact, guilty of murder, if blood is shed in that Territory—guilty of the slaughter of American citizens, & of disturbing the peace & quiet of the whole country.

Gentlemen, this country of ours is the most beautiful the sun of heaven ever shone upon; & the wisdom of man never before created such a government as that under which we live. . . . The . . . States, at the formation of the Constitution, yielded to the general government all the powers necessary for the management of the general and external policy of the nation, reserving to themselves the right to manage their domestic affairs each and every one according to their convictions of justice and expediency, independent of the General Government, & each State independent of every other. . . . It is a beautiful Confederacy.

Bush thought the speech the best Lane had ever made. By the "true doctrine," however, it soon became apparent that Lane meant territories could decide about slavery only when ready for admission to the Union. When Douglas suggested that the people might act earlier through their territorial legislature, Lane lashed out at "that heresy" and "fundamental error."[50]

The demand for statehood in Oregon proved to be both cause and result of the mounting agitation about slavery. Oregonians increasingly became aware that their stand on slavery might influence their chances of admission and even the future of the nation, while at the same time they became convinced that only through admission could they settle the question. The presidential election likewise suggested the advantages of statehood because if no candidate won a clear majority—a likely possibility with three candidates in the field—the House would decide the election, each state having one vote. Curry proposed another plebiscite on framing a state constitution. "The people may fail to elect," he advised Bush. "In that case if Oregon be organised she will be on an equality in the Electoral College with either of the other States. What think you?" The Clique apparently agreed, for the next legislature called a special election for April 1856, well before the national conventions. When Leland raised a questioning voice, Bush imperiously denounced the "Iscariotism of the Standard on the Convention Question."[51] But a majority of Oregonians had yet to be convinced, and the proposition was defeated, 4,346 to 4,097.

Concern about the presidential election was widespread. Lane wrote from Washington in July that many "sensible good Democrats" were apprehensive, that the northern states were "decidedly unfavorable," and that things were generally "out of joint," but he believed that Buchanan must and would be elected because the

50. Lane's speech, Feb. 7, 1856, Lane Papers, InU, is reprinted ibid., April 29, 1856; Bush to Lane, April 17, 1856, Lane Papers, InU; Lane to Lafayette Lane, May 15 [?], 1856, Lane Papers, InU.

51. Curry to Bush, Sept. 15, 1855, Bush Papers; *Oregon Statesman*, April 22, 1856.

existence of the Union depended on it. As the campaign progressed, Lane became more confident of victory than many Oregonians. "I firmly believe that Buchanan will be elected," asserted Bush, yet he expressed a "lingering *fear* that Fremont may slip in." Then in September, Maine gave the Republicans a landslide, and Bush's hopes were shattered. "The game is up," he wrote to Lane; it seemed to him that "hell itself had been let loose to tear down the democratic party." "Lane says Buchanan will be elected," he declared to Deady. "But he isn't good at guessing." In its next issues, the *Statesman* despaired of Buchanan's election.[52]

Despite Democratic fears, Buchanan was elected by a substantial majority, and Oregonians, especially those who opposed slavery, decided they now had more to gain than to lose by admission. "Let us have a state government and make the issue at once," cried the *Oregonian* in an abrupt about-face on November 1, obviously fearful of another proslavery Democratic administration. "If we are to have slavery forced upon us, let it be by the people here and not by the slavery propagandists at Washington City." The following June the voters called for a constitutional convention by a majority of 7,617 to 1,679.

The prospects of statehood immeasurably intensified the controversy over slavery. Proslavery sentiment was increasing daily, and everyone was talking about it from the Columbia to the California boundary, Farrar informed Lane. "I have no doubt that a *majority* of the people would vote for a 'free state' Constitution, *if* there could be no agitation, no public discussion, of the merits of the slavery question. But, General, I verily believe that the agitation of the subject *cannot* be prevented, or silenced, or winked out of sight; and the discussion of the question will end in the introduction of slavery into Oregon." The *Times,* however, blamed

52. Lane to Bush, July 18, 1856, Bush Papers; Bush to Lane, Oct. 11, 1856, Lane Papers, InU; Bush to Lane, Oct. 31, 1856, Lane Papers, InU; Bush to Deady, Nov. 2, 1856, MS OrHi; *Oregon Statesman,* Nov. 4, 18, 1856.

"Abolition agitators" for the new activity and cited Webster's dictum that God and nature had already determined the limits of slavery so further discussion would be fruitless. The *Statesman* also attributed this increased agitation to the workings of abolitionism and estimated that proslavery sentiment had increased by as much as three hundred per cent in the past year and a half. Ridiculing the "negro-monomaniacs of the north, who would feign treat slavery as a *moral* question alone," Bush declared that the only issue was whether slavery was practical in Oregon and whether it would pay. Like Waterman, he rested his opposition with an appeal to Webster.[53]

Not all or even most Democrats favored slavery, but all proslavery men were Democrats, and the party's leadership found it difficult to refute charges that the Democracy was the party of slavery without appearing to sanction abolitionism. The *Statesman* invited signed communications, pro and con, from its readers, and both sides responded with arguments running the spectrum of opinion, although most free-state supporters seemed somewhat hesitant to jeopardize their chances of preferment with the national administration. The most cogent treatise came from the pen of Chief Justice George H. Williams, who disclaimed any objection to slavery in the abstract but opposed it for Oregon because of strong utilitarian and social reasons. This "Free State Letter" became the rallying point for antislavery sentiment within the Democratic party. The most effective champion of the proslavery forces on the other hand was the associate justice from the southern district, Matthew P. Deady.

The controversy over slavery held important consequences for political life in Oregon. Not only was it an issue in itself in the next territorial election, but it stimulated both sides to greater activity. Those determined to block the further extension of the slave power renewed their efforts and succeeded in organizing a territorial Republican party in the spring of 1857. The controversy

53. Farrar to Lane, Dec. 22, 1856, Lane Papers, InU; *Oregon Weekly Times,* Jan. 10, 1857; *Oregon Statesman,* March 31, 1857.

spawned a new proslavery press, realigning existing journals and creating new ones, the most important of which was Avery's *Occidental Messenger* at Corvallis. Eventually slavery significantly affected the realignment of factions within the Democratic party. It was by no means the only factor to determine political allegiance, but it turned out to be one of the most potent.

"I am sorry that you cannot read for I wish very much to talk to you, for at last there is no one that we can talk with, or write to, like a companion," Lane wrote to his wife in November 1856 in a rare communication that laid bare his most intimate thoughts. His "old complaint"—apparently his old shoulder injury, perhaps aggravated by arthritis—had plagued him sorely during the recent long and arduous presidential campaign. "For a month I spoke daily, some times twice, and some days three times a day, and often I left the stand so feeble that I could hardly stand, and upon one occasion had to quit in the middle of a speech, and tho I suffered much. . . . I can assure you that nothing but love of country would have induced me to work as I did. Money would have been no consideration, but the country was in danger, and I could not bear the idea of the election of Fremont to the Presidency so I went to work, and when I got at it, the people would not let me quit." Now he was rested and looking forward to seeing her in less than four months. "Home is at last the sweetest place of all."[54]

During the usual preconvention maneuvering, a number of promoters sought to bring Lane's name to the public eye, but there was no concerted attempt on his behalf at Cincinnati as there had been at Baltimore four years earlier. Lane was pleased with the convention's choice and after the election addressed congratulations to President-elect Buchanan together with a warning that "abolition, fanaticism, and sectionalism of the most dangerous character" had merely been rebuked and not buried and would require the utmost vigilance on the part of the new administration. He con-

54. Lane to wife (Polly), Nov. 17, 1856, typescript, Lane Papers, OrU.

cluded by asking Buchanan to make no changes in patronage for Oregon without consulting the wishes of Oregonians. A few weeks later, Lane and several other members of Congress from the west coast urged Buchanan to allow the Far West representation in the cabinet.[55] Speculation was rife in Oregon that Lane was in line for such an appointment, but nothing ever came of the idea.

The final, lame-duck session of the Thirty-fourth Congress, like its predecessor, was haunted by the specter of Kansas-Nebraska, the extension of slavery. "Nothing has been done but talk about niggers, niggers, and when this is to end no one can tell," Lane wrote to Bush after trying unsuccessfully to introduce several bills and a joint resolution to pay Bush's printing claim. "I will do the best I can for Oregon interests, and hope I may be successful, but if I fail it shall not be my fault." The next Congress, he went on, would be Democratic, and then justice would be done. "Now if these Black Republicans head me off in my efforts give me another show & my word for it I will succede."[56]

Lane was "in good working condition" when Congress turned to territorial business but was rather taken aback to hear the chairman of the Committee on Military Affairs asking to be released from considering the bill to pay the war expenses because neither Secretary of War Jefferson Davis nor the Board of Commissioners had yet reported on it. Lane objected that in past Indian wars Congress had always authorized the Secretary to pay all claims that were approved; he asked that the bill be referred to the Committee of the Whole for action. The commissioners, he continued, would recognize only claims that were "just, right, and proper," and if the Secretary had any doubt about a claim, he would not approve it. The chairman was unmoved. "The gentleman from Oregon assumes that the call for the volunteers was proper, & that the only inquiry now is as to the reasonableness of the pay to be allowed for their service," he replied. "He may be right, but I think, and the com-

55. Lane to Buchanan, Nov. 11, 1856, and Weller, Lane, et al. to Buchanan, Dec. 18, 1856, cited in Kelly, *Career of Joseph Lane,* p. 139.
56. Lane to Bush, Dec. 17, 1856, Bush Papers.

mittee think, that a wide scope of inquiry is left to the Secretary of War." The committee prevailed, and Lane's amendment went down to defeat.[57]

Bush's printing claim and the bill to authorize a state constitution met with better success in the House but were hopelessly delayed in the Senate. The House approved a joint resolution to pay Bush for the reprinted statutes, but the Senate was too pressed for time to consider it. Similarly, the House finally passed Oregon's enabling act, carried over from the first session, and referred it to the Senate for the second time in as many years. Lane expected opposition in the Senate but thought it would go through.[58] Douglas, chairman of the Committee on Territories, tried his best to oblige, making a last-minute attempt during the final session on the eve of the inauguration, but to no avail. Lane was clearly perturbed at the prospect of returning empty-handed to Oregon to face re-election and blamed Douglas for losing the bill by failing to press its consideration. "As I relied upon your aid & have been greatly disappointed & I fear wronged, I think it due to myself to ask some explanation of you of your seeming disregard of my wishes." Douglas replied at length to show that he had made every effort to secure passage of the bill. "You are at liberty to make such use of this communication as you may think proper to put you & myself right before the people of Oregon," he concluded. "I will add that no man could have done more than you did to ensure & deserve the success of your measure."[59]

Benjamin F. Dowell, an attorney from Oregon visiting the capital, wrote to Nesmith in a similar vein.

> Genl. Lane realy has great influence here. His recommendations go a long ways with the departments, and he is decidedly

57. Lane to Bush, Jan. 20, 1857, Bush Papers; *Congressional Globe,* 34 Cong., 3 Sess., pp. 386–90.

58. *Congressional Globe,* 34 Cong., 3 Sess., pp. 606–08, 455; Lane to Waterman, Feb. 4, 1857, *Oregon Weekly Times,* March 14, 1857.

59. Lane to Douglas, March 4, 1857, Lane Papers, InU; Douglas to Lane, March 4, 1857, Lane Papers, InU.

> the best man to send here to prosecute the Oregon War claims. ... No man from Oregon could have procured the appropriation from the last *Black-negro-worshiping* Congress. I attended the house several days. They were more like wild Geece than civilized enlightened Statesmen. Perfect confusion prevailed. Half the time, the only words I could hear was "Mr Speaker" from a dozen voices at the same time. Banks ought to be indicted for keeping a disorderly house.[60]

On the morning of the inauguration, as Lane prepared to leave for Oregon, a final reverse occurred. Superintendent of Indian Affairs Hedges had been forced to resign because of ill health, and Lane had submitted Nesmith's name for his replacement, but Senator Bright, with whom Lane had since broken, had blocked Nesmith's confirmation during the Senate's secret executive session in the early hours of the morning. Bright wanted the reappointment of Palmer. Although Lane would have to wait fifteen days for the next steamer to Oregon, he elected to remain in Washington to secure Nesmith's nomination. His influence with the new administration was at stake, but he attributed his action to loftier motives. "Nes. is in trouble," he explained to Bush, "and I have all my life made it a rule to never desert a friend."[61] When the *Columbia* docked at Portland, Lane was able to announce Nesmith's appointment.

60. Dowell to Nesmith, April 1, 1857, MS OrHi.

61. Lane to Bush, March 4, 1857, Bush Papers; *Oregon Weekly Times,* April 25, 1857.

Nesmith was not particularly grateful. Now that he had the job, he wrote to Deady (May 3, 1857, MS OrHi), he felt "very much like the lucky cuss who won the elephant at the raffle, and did not know what to do with him." And again (July 17, 1857, MS OrHi), "I dont believe a damned word of what the 'Senett' [Lane] Says about the charges aginst me in Washington. . . . I am inclined to think that he has manufactured the thing for the purpose of magnifying his efforts in my behalf."

# ILLUSTRATIONS

# PROCLAMATION.

***BY THE GOVERNOR OF THE TERRITORY OF OREGON.***

In pursuance of an Act of *Congress*, approved on the fourteenth day of August, in the year of our Lord one thousand eight hundred and forty-eight, establishing a Territorial Government in the Territory of Oregon :—

I, Joseph Lane, was on the eighteenth day of August, in the year eighteen hundred and forty-eight, commissioned Governor in and for the Territory of Oregon. I have therefore thought proper to issue this my Proclamation, making known that I have this day entered upon the discharge of the duties of my office, and by virtue thereof do declare that the Laws of the United *States* are extended over, and declared to be in force in said Territory, so far as the same, or any portion thereof may be applicable.

Given under my hand, at *Oregon City*, in the Territory of Oregon, this third day of March, Anno Domini 1849.

JOSEPH LANE.

1. PROCLAMATION ESTABLISHING TERRITORIAL GOVERNMENT IN OREGON, MARCH 3, 1849. *Oregon Historical Society.*

2. JOSEPH LANE IN THE 1850S. *Library of Congress.*

3. JOSEPH LANE IN OLD AGE. *Oregon Historical Society.*

4. MARY HART LANE. *Oregon Historical Society.*

5. ASAHEL BUSH. *Oregon Historical Society.*

6. JAMES W. NESMITH. *University of Oregon.*

7. MATTHEW P. DEADY. *Oregon Historical Society.*

8. DELAZON SMITH. *Oregon Historical Society.*

9. JOSEPH W. DREW. *University of Oregon.*

10. LAFAYETTE GROVER. *Oregon Historical Society.*

11. BENJAMIN F. HARDING. *Oregon Historical Society.*

*Chapter 5*

# THE STORM BREAKS

"It is pretty evident to my mind that the party is growing plethoric and costive, and needs a thorough course of Cathartics, and high toned tonic," Deady announced to Bush in the spring of 1856. The party had been well purged by the location controversy of 1851–52, he continued, but since then had been "accumulating inert and infected members" at a distressing pace. "You are somewhat celebrated for the heroic treatment, and political amputation is your forte. So cut and prune away until the encumbered hack of a party is again lanklean and hungry enough to be bridlewise and swift enough for anything under 2′ 40″."[1]

"You are getting to be more entertaining," Bush replied dryly, but he exhibited little inclination to borrow trouble at this time,

1. Deady to Bush, May 14, 1856, Bush Papers.

because opposition to the Clique was mounting rapidly. The Softs could pose a distinct threat in the off-year elections, in which case the next legislature would be anti-Bush; Waterman informed Lane that the only issue of the spiritless campaign was the attempt by Leland and other "sore heads K. N.s and *ismites*" to win control of the legislature and turn Bush out of the public printing. Democrats in Washington County openly protested against the "too dictatorial mandates of a self-constituted leadership," while their colleagues from Lane County publicly deplored the efforts of all who opposed the party merely because "they happen not to like Bush, Delazon Smith or other members thereof." Nesmith failed in an attempt to represent Polk County in the Legislative Assembly.[2] As the campaign progressed, James K. Kelly emerged as the leading contender for the Softs, while Delazon Smith appeared to be the Clique's choice for delegate should Lane choose not to run again. "Lane is in Washington," Drew complained to Deady, "and as usual is not identified with either faction, trying to get money for the pockets of all and in a better position for a compromise candidate than ever before."[3]

The election passed without excitement, and the Clique turned its attention to the next contest for delegate. Drew was willing to support "anybody to defeat Lane," but by the end of August, he reluctantly decided that Lane would regain the nomination. "But between us," he swore to Deady, "I will be damned if I ever vote for him again or for any other such a damned demagogue. My democracy shall never carry me that far again." If either Lane or Kelly were nominated, he concluded, he would stay at home on election day. Lafayette Mosher, who had just married Lane's youngest daughter Winnie, warned Lane that the *Statesman* had been all ready to attack him when Zieber's appointment was announced,

2. Bush to Deady, May 17, 1856, MS OrHi; Drew to Deady, May 18, 1856, MS OrHi; Waterman to Lane, May 27, 1856, Lane Papers, InU; *Oregon Statesman,* June 10, May 27, 1856.

3. Drew to Deady, May 24, 1856, MS OrHi.

and that the Clique was now planning to give Deady the nomination in the spring. Others predicted calm seas ahead. Smith, who had ambitions of his own, finally wrote to inquire of Lane's intentions, reminding him rather pointedly of the "doctrine of 'rotation in office,' " but promising to support him if he did run again. Lane replied that he would "leave it to the people"; he would be gratified to be returned but would support any good Democrat the party preferred.[4]

The fireworks began in December when the new state legislature convened. On the first evening the Democrats caucused to nominate the various legislative officers, and the following day two Softs who had not attended the caucus bolted the nominee for president of the Council and decided to support Kelly instead. Kelly won. By a similar procedure the Republican nominee for enrolling clerk of the Council defeated the Democratic nominee by a single vote. The *Standard* was jubilant at this repudiation of caucus rule. Leland argued that the Clique had no complaint, because "a Democrat of unimpeachable political integrity" was elected. "It is now generally conceded by all consistent Democrats," he continued, "that any man who does not go into a caucus of his party, may oppose the measures adopted by that caucus, and yet not jeopardize his political integrity by repudiating those measures."[5]

Bush opened with both barrels:

> Every man who claims to belong to the Democratic organization, is bound by the nominations of the Conventions and Caucuses of that party, whether he is present at them or not.

4. Drew to Deady, Aug. 3, 27, 1856, MS OrHi; Mosher to Lane, Sept. 25, 1856, Lane Papers, InU; Smith to Lane, Nov. 9, 1856, Lane Papers, InU; Lane to Smith, n.d., Lane Letterbook 8, OrHi.

5. *Democratic Standard,* Dec. 3, 18, 1856, cited in *Oregon Statesman,* Dec. 25, 1856, Jan. 6, 1857. Because few issues of the *Standard* are extant, one must frequently rely upon citations or comments from other newspapers.

> ... It is his right to attend the primary meetings, and his duty to do so if practicable; but it is his duty to support the nominations in either event, if fairly and regularly made, and if they consist of Democrats who do not set at nought the usages of the party. All Democrats cannot, and never do attend the primary meetings of their party, and under the interesting doctrine of the Standard, there would seldom, if ever, be a Democrat elected to office.

He concluded with a final finger-shaking warning: "We want Democrats to note these things."[6] Apparently Bush had decided it was time to make the party "lanklean and hungry" again.

Two days following this candid outburst, tried and true Democrats from all over the territory—three hundred were expected—attended a Jackson Jubilee dinner at Boon's Hall in Salem. Admission to the two tables that ran the length of the hall was three dollars, and the celebrants took their leave about midnight after drinking fourteen regular toasts—the fourteenth to Lane—and fifteen more that they volunteered spontaneously. They also passed four resolutions that effectually read the *Standard* out of the party, repudiating it "not only as *anti-Democratic,* but unworthy the confidence, respect or patronage of any portion of our fellow-citizens." A fifth resolution endorsed the *Statesman* as "the *old* and true standard of Democracy."[7] Two weeks later a Democratic legislative caucus confirmed the Jubilee's action by a close vote of fifteen to twelve, and the *Statesman* excoriated those Softs who opposed the measure for the sake of party harmony. Bush was satisfied, he editorialized, that the party could afford to slough off quite a number of tainted factions, and survive. "The sound corn will keep the longer by being separated from the rotten."[8]

6. *Oregon Statesman,* Jan. 6, 1857.
7. *Oregon Weekly Times,* Jan. 24, 1857. Cf. *Oregon Statesman,* Dec. 23, 1856, Jan. 13, 1857.
8. *Oregon Statesman,* Jan. 27, 1857.

Caucus rule and the "excommunication" of the *Standard* became the touchstones of preconvention maneuvering. Leland appealed to Lane privately while publicly predicting that the "oligarchists," notwithstanding their "noisy friendship" for Lane, would force him to endorse their "mad action of last winter" or deny him their support. Bush pooh-poohed the idea, stating that Lane would most certainly have sustained the resolutions had he attended the Jackson Jubilee and doubtlessly would do so as soon as he reached Oregon. Grover assured Lane that he would be renominated but that so much bad feeling had developed over the *Standard* that he ought to get home as soon as he could. On the other hand, Farrar advised Lane to lie low, claiming that there were fewer than fifty persons present at the Jubilee when the resolutions were introduced. "If this quarrel goes into our Territorial Convention *both sides* will attempt to make you commit yourself upon it. Would it not therefore be advisable for you *not* to be in attendance?" Most of the precinct and country conventions endorsed the proscription, but a few assumed a neutral stance. When the Multnomah County convention, chaired by Robert Thompson, passed resolutions commending Kelly and deploring "these local and personal controversies in which the Democratic press of this Territory have so wantonly indulged," Bush taunted Thompson for playing "Doctor of Democracy" and courting the Softs. "Speak out and let us know what you mean," he snapped imperiously. "If the *Statesman* is wrong, say so, and let us know of what you complain. If you mean any other paper, name it, so that you can be understood." It was high time, he declared, that the party "*spew out* the putrid matter which has collected on its stomach."[9]

Lane's replies to Leland were apparently too conciliatory for the Clique. "Bush is in good health, but not in any very amiable mood,"

9. Leland to Lane, Jan. 27, 1857, Lane Papers, InU; *Democratic Standard,* cited in *Oregon Statesman,* March 24, 1857; Grover to Lane, Jan. 22, 1857, Lane Papers, InU; Farrar to Lane, Jan. 26, 1857, Lane Papers, InU; *Oregon Statesman,* April 7, 1857.

Drew informed Deady. "My impression is that he does not enjoy the reading of Old Joseph's letters to Leland."

> It seems damned humiliating to be forced year after year to support a man, who affiliates and seeks support from those who not only abuse all other leading democrats in the Territory, but who only two years since called Lane himself a stupid Jackass.
>
> I believe the time is about coming when all the leading democrats here—the oligarchists—as Leland terms them, will exercise their rights, powers and duties and nominate one of their kind.

Smith also accepted the inevitable but with little relish; many persons, he told Bush, were repelled by the "idea of a *fourth* renomination."[10]

The territorial convention met at Salem on April 13. Three of the eleven resolutions adopted were directed squarely at Leland and the members opposing the previous caucus resolution; the fifth resolution repudiated "the doctrine that a representative or delegate can, in pursuance of the wishes or fancied interests of the district *he* represents, go into or remain out of a caucus or convention of his party and refuse to support the nomination thereof and still maintain his standing as a democrat"; the sixth proscribed as a "disorganizer and enemy" all who refused to support caucus nominations, even if re-elected by their constituents; the seventh officially discarded the *Standard* as a "hypocritical foe," and a special resolution recognized the *Times* as a "worthy" party journal. The final resolution concerned slavery:

> 11. *Resolved,* That each member of the Democratic party in Oregon may freely speak and act according to his individual convictions of right and policy upon the question of slavery

10. Drew to Deady, March 19, 1857, MS OrHi; Smith to Bush, March 15, 1857, Bush Papers.

> in Oregon, without in any manner impairing his standing in the Democratic party on that account, Provided, That nothing in these resolutions shall be construed in toleration of Black Republicanism, Abolitionism, or any other faction or organization arrayed in opposition to the Democratic party.

The convention nominated Lane unanimously, after Nesmith received two votes on the first ballot, but the candidate was requested to make public acceptance of the platform, "including the anti-Standard resolution."[11]

A newcomer to the convention was Ethelbert C. Hibben, Lane's former clerk, who had proceeded to Oregon alone when Lane was detained by the last-minute delay in Nesmith's appointment. "It was understood and so announced that he was to take charge of the 'Statesman,'" Nesmith chortled to Deady, "but the plan dont seem to meet with the views of the distinguished gentleman who at present 'drives that shit cart.'" Drew predicted Hibben might attach himself to the *Times* because Bush had no need of a "partner."

> He comes here for the openly avowed purpose of securing Lane's election to the U.S. Senate [Drew wrote Deady]. Nesmith and Bush have blackguarded him 'till he is homesick and I believe he will soon be ready to take the Steamer home. Hibben seems surprised to find that there are any other aspirants for the Senate except Lane. Indeed the fellow appears very much disappointed and is awaiting Lane's arrival with great anxiety.[12]

11. *Oregon Statesman,* April 21, 1857; *Oregon Weekly Times,* April 18, 1857.

12. Nesmith to Deady, May 3, 1857, MS OrHi; Drew to Deady, April 21, 1857, MS OrHi. Cf. Lane to Bush, March 4, 1857, Bush Papers.

Hibben (1824–76) was born in Ohio and at an early age moved to Indiana, where he studied law and was admitted to the bar. After working intermittently for Lane in Washington, he came to Oregon in 1857 solely to promote Lane's election to the Senate. He returned to Indiana late in 1859 and apparently resided there until his death, at which time he was employed as a deputy clerk in the circuit court of Marion County.

Bush hailed the convention as the best ever held in the territory and seemed especially pleased that no more than seven of the fifty-nine delegates had voted against the controversial resolutions. The convention was "decidedly *hard,*" Nesmith related to Deady; "a great amount of enthusiasm was exhausted upon the *platform* but not a damned bit upon the *candidate.*" "I think we got old Jo square on the platform this time, and got him where he can't play good Lord and devil in the same breath," Bush added. "He is helping the local organization some this time, a thing he has never done before."[13]

At two o'clock in the morning of Wednesday, April 22, 1857, the *Columbia* reached Portland, depositing Lane, healthy and relaxed, on Oregon soil. "We never saw him looking better," reported the *Times.* His reception proceeded as usual, according to the press, except for an accident during the firing of the salute. Somebody removed a finger from the vent while ramming the cartridge, and the cannon discharged prematurely, blowing the second mate overboard, injuring his face, shattering his arms, and mangling three fingers on each hand. An unfortunate incident.[14]

Unnoticed by reporters and less tragic in effect was an episode in the bar of the Metropolis Hotel, where another reception had been planned for the delegate. John McCracken described for Deady, whose residence in the Umpqua so often excluded him from the center of fun, how the Clique had arrived, "vi et *whiskey,*" and had taken the town in full force.

> I went to the wharf as usual when the "Express" arrived the other evening, and found myself suddenly surrounded by a

13. *Oregon Statesman,* April 21, 1857; Nesmith to Deady, May 3, 1857, MS OrHi; Bush to Deady, May 19, 1857, MS OrHi.
14. *Oregon Weekly Times,* April 25, 1857; *Oregon Statesman,* April 28, 1857.

> noisy, boisterous crowd and as soon as I recovered my usual self possession, and raised my hat from my eyes over which it had been summarily *"mashed"* I discovered Judge Bush, Genl Drew, Col. Nesmith, Gov. Curry, Lieut Grover, Maj [Victor] Trevitt and Mr. Hibben—a late arrival from *Indianny* a sort of "John the Baptist" to the *nominee* of the late Democratic Convention (Territorial). You may judge of the character of the greetings I received from the gentlemen above named, a portion of . . . whom . . . were sent here by the Convention to welcome Joseph, and lift him upon the platform. . . . about eleven oclock P. M. "old rye" beginning to effervesce, patriotism and devotion to "old Joe" rising accordingly, speeches were made in the bar room of the "Metropolis" and "Bank Exchange" and had the aforementioned individual arrived at that time he would have been duly recieved and honored. but alas! for the evanescence of human things nature demands repose and at two oclock AM all were *snugly stowed.* about three the Steamer's gun fired, but the drowsy god had both Committees fast. Joseph arrived and found none awake to do him reverence. some one that came up on the steamer tried to arouse a little inthusiasm, and knocked at the door of "a leading democrat" informing him that Genl Lane had arrived and was shivering on the wharf. the only response was, "let him shiver and be d - - - - d."

According to McCracken, Lane had then been on hand for about thirty-six hours and was still awaiting "speeches receptions or any thing of the kind."[15]

Lane's first act was to draft a public letter endorsing the Salem Platform and declaring it to be "both the right and duty of the people, through their delegates in Convention," to repudiate individuals or the press whenever they pursued a disorganizing

15. McCracken to Deady, April 23, 1857, MS OrHi. Cf. *Weekly Oregonian,* April 25, 1857.

course. To Leland's request for a specific endorsement or repudiation of the resolution against the *Standard,* he replied that he had too much confidence in the collective judgment of the party to question its decision, and he commended to the *Standard* a more harmonious course.[16] Lane probably was reluctant to have these letters pried out of him, because they brought a swift reaction. Dissenters in Yamhill County, calling themselves "National Democrats"—Bush preferred "bastard democracy"—bolted the regular county nominations and held their own convention to draw up a slate of candidates, refusing to support Lane unless he disavowed the Salem Platform. Softs in Multnomah, Clackamas, Clatsop, and Benton counties followed suit, and a first-class revolt was in the making.[17]

The fledgling Republican party having no contender to place in the field, Lane's only opponent was an independent Democrat from Yamhill, George W. Lawson, whom Lane had dismissed from the southern land office. The two men had quarreled shortly after Lawson's appointment as receiver, apparently because of Lawson's spiritualist activities, although his free-state proclivities or his intentions toward the fair fifteen-year-old Winnie may also have been involved.[18] Lawson was vigorous upon the stump, but no match for the more experienced Lane, and the campaign for the delegateship was the dullest yet. The *Argus* supported Lawson as a free-soil and temperance candidate, but the *Oregonian* showed

16. Lane to Drew, Bush, and James M. Pyle, April 24, 1857, reprinted in *Oregon Weekly Times,* May 2, 1857, and *Oregon Statesman,* May 5, 1857; Lane to Leland, April 24, 1857, *Oregon Weekly Times,* May 2, 1857, and *Oregon Statesman,* May 5, 1857.

17. *Oregon Statesman,* May 12, 1857; *Weekly Oregonian,* May 9, 1857; Woodward, *History of Political Parties in Oregon,* p. 106.

18. Bush to Nesmith, Sept. 7, 1855, MS OrHi. Lawson wrote to Lane (July 25, 1855, Lane Papers InU) asking to marry Winnie "if she approve me." Winnie, the "Belle of the Umpqua," had no shortage of suitors. Robert Metcalfe wrote to Lane (Feb. 28, 1856, Lane Papers, InU) that he and Winnie had decided to marry, but Winnie suddenly changed her mind and married Lafayette Mosher, July 1, 1856.

little interest in the contest.[19] Before the election, Bush left the *Statesman* in Drew's care and accompanied Nesmith (as a clerk) on a three-week inspection trip of the Puget Sound area; Lane was supposed to have gone along and was anxious to, but of course he could not then leave the campaign. The *Times* accorded Lane its usual attention and announced immediately after the election that Hibben was assuming the editorial chair.[20]

Since the referendum to hold a constitutional convention seemed certain to pass, the only issues in the campaign were caucus rule and slavery, now forcibly brought to the fore by the prospects of imminent statehood. Lane's proslavery sympathies were a matter of public knowledge, but he did not resort to incendiary speeches. He was not an agitator and did not consider slavery a moral issue. In Portland he took broad, conservative, constitutional grounds, declaring that the people of any state had the right to determine their domestic institutions, and that he would cheerfully acquiesce in the decisions of the people—although in the Umpqua, where proslavery sentiment was more pronounced, he did express doubts that a man could "be a good Democrat and vote against slavery in Oregon."[21]

19. *Oregon Argus,* May 23, 1857. *Weekly Oregonian,* May 2, 1857: "Let them run, it is an even fight—we shall vote for neither."

20. Nesmith to Stevens, May 9, 1857, Stevens Papers (University of Washington Library, Seattle); Bush to Deady, May 19, 1857, MS OrHi; *Oregon Weekly Times,* June 6, 1857. Drew told Deady (June 8, 1857, MS OrHi) that "Lane and Hibben did not understand why Bush & Nesmith went to Puget Sound on the very eve of election." After noticing their departure, the *Weekly Oregonian,* May 30, 1857, concluded: "*Won't be back till after the election, either.* Thereby hangs a tale."

21. *Oregon Weekly Times,* May 30, 1857; T. W. Davenport, "Slavery Question in Oregon," *Oregon Historical Quarterly,* 9 (1908), 218; Deady to Bush, July 14, 1857, Bush Papers. Davenport was a contemporary of Lane and held pronounced antislavery views. He thought many of the rank and file of the party were influenced by Lane's proslavery sympathies but had "no recollection or record of his writing a letter or making a speech *pro* or *con* during the pendency of the question."

Lane's majority, a healthy sixty-two per cent, would have been even larger had not the Softs registered so much strength in the northern counties, but Lawson's vote reflected rather accurately the extent of the opposition. Bush claimed a two-to-one majority for the regulars in the House and constitutional convention and a bare majority in the Council, whereas Leland claimed a plurality for the Nationals in all three bodies. The only certainty was that defecting Softs were substantially swelling the ranks of the opposition.[22]

The constitutional convention in August brought the agitation over slavery to its greatest frenzy as both sides redoubled their efforts. The controversy was intensified by news of the Dred Scott decision, which reached Oregon in April and by which the Supreme Court, backed by the Buchanan administration, denied to Congress any power to prohibit slavery in the territories. Proslavery Democrats were especially vocal, but free-state partisans—Williams was an exception—appeared reluctant to risk being identified with Black Republicanism. The *Argus* thought proslavery advocates so zealous that each would outshout ten free-soil men, who outnumbered them two to one.[23]

For four weeks the convention debated the constitution, sidestepping the slavery issue by referring it directly to the people, along with the question of admitting free Negroes and mulattoes. Lane favored the document but played no role in its drafting. Instead, he spent more than a month pursuing a small band of roving Indians who had been harassing settlers in the Umpqua Valley for more than a year. When the Indians killed a "gang" of horses belonging to an old and esteemed neighbor, who was unable to give chase, Lane and Bill Martin and a few others undertook to drive them back to the reservation. Consequently, he was unable to accept an invitation from Isaac Stevens to meet him in Salem in

22. *Oregon Statesman,* June 30, July 7, 1857. The vote for delegate (ibid., June 30) was 5,662–3,471.

23. *Oregon Argus,* Sept. 5, 1857.

late August. Stevens had just been elected delegate from Washington Territory and doubtless wanted to plot strategy for securing the war debt before leaving for Washington. And there may have been more to discuss. Lane declined with regret, saying he had "much to say" to his friend and advising him he would try to leave for the East on the steamer of October 5. "Keep an eye to windward while you are at Salem," he concluded enigmatically. Stevens had to leave on an earlier vessel but suggested that Lane consult with "our mutual friend Capt. [John] Cain, who will tell you my anxiety to have a long talk and a perfect concert of action with you in everything which relates to our business."[24]

When Stevens left Fort Vancouver, Lane was inspecting Indian reservations in the Willamette Valley with J. Ross Browne, a special agent of the Treasury Department. Browne was frankly fascinated by Lane's artless bonhomie, by his anecdotes of men and things, and by his reminiscences of Indian life, and looked back on the trip as one of those delightful episodes "to be treasured in the favorite nooks of memory."[25] His report was as favorable as his impressions of the Northwest. He found no evidence to sustain the "absurd and monstrous" charge that the war had been conducted for the purposes of speculation; the quarrel between Wool and the territorial administration was personal and should have no

24. *Oregon Weekly Times,* Aug. 8, Sept. 19, 1857; *Congressional Globe,* 35 Cong., 2 Sess., p. 254; Lane to Stevens, Aug. 16, 1858, Stevens Papers; Stevens to Lane, Sept. 19, 1857, Lane Papers, InU.

25. *Oregon Statesman,* Sept. 29, 1857; Browne to Lane, Nov. 4, 1857, Lane Papers, InU: "Can you not come back again soon, my dear General, and let us try it over? I want to hear once more those gallant speeches to the ladies who inhabit the log cabins by the roadside, those dexterous and insinuating compliments to the fond mothers and their beloved offspring, by the genial firesides, those inspiring aspirations, for all that is attractive to man! Consider yourself pledged for a grand deer hunt in the Rogue River mountains, during the coming spring, and then by the crackling camp-fire, with its ruddy glow, we shall conjure up the spirits of the past again!"

bearing in settling the war claims. Oregonians received his report with universal satisfaction.[26]

The *Commodore* was loading in Portland when Lane returned from his circuit with Browne, but he decided to lie over a few days for the *Columbia,* a much safer vessel. With him were his two youngest sons, John and Lafayette, who would continue their education in Washington; as usual, his wife remained at home. He also had a detailed statement from Bush regarding his claims on the national treasury and even a rough draft of a resolution for their payment by Congress. After a "hard & tedious" passage, they reached New York safely.[27]

Only after Christmas did Lane learn of the results of the referendum on Oregon's constitution, which the voters approved, 7,195 to 3,215. The margin against slavery was even larger, 7,727 to 2,645, and the vote against admitting free Negroes and mulattoes, an overwhelming 8,640 to 1,081. It was evident, as George Williams later recalled, that the proslavery advocates had "talked loud and made a good deal of noise"; and it was also evident that Oregonians wanted nothing to do with the Negro, bond or free. Lane's reaction to the vote was consistent with his stand in the campaign. To the *Statesman* he wrote:

> I am much pleased to learn that our Constitution has been ratified by the people, but am sorry to find that there are some still harping over the slavery question. It has been settled by a vote of the people, and with their decision all should be satisfied. Our motto was, in the late canvass, and in our platform, and it is the true principle of the Kansas Nebraska bill, "leave it to the people." They have decided against slavery,

26. Browne's report is cited in *Congressional Globe,* 35 Cong., 1 Sess., p. 2119; cf. *Oregon Statesman,* April 6, 1858; Hibben to Lane, Oct. 28, 1857, Lane Papers, InU.

27. Lane to wife (Polly), Oct. 4, 1857, Lane Papers, InU; Bush to Lane, Sept. 13, 1857, Lane Papers, InU; Lane to Bush, Nov. 16, 1857, Bush Papers.

> and certainly *no good democrat will now attempt to disturb the peace and success of the democratic party, on this question, settled, and for all time, so far as Oregon is concerned.*[28]

Hibben also accepted the verdict—as long as it was clearly understood that the Democratic party was not opposed to slavery. Arrogant and tactless, this brash young man had unfavorably impressed the Clique from the beginning but gradually won recognition by pursuing an editorial course befitting the "Oregon Style" of journalism. Like Bush he assailed the *Oregonian* and *Standard,* devoting his columns to elaborate editorializing and inelegant abuse. Dryer became "the dilerium-tremens-racked idiot of the *Oregonian,*" but it was the editor of the *Standard,* "this miserable carricature of humanity—this factious, trouble-brooding, and discord-creating Ishmaelite," who drew most of his fire. "If the doctrine of the transmigration of souls be true," he once quipped, "Leland's spirit, after death, will be found playing snapping turtle in a swill-tub." The Clique approved. The next issue of the *Statesman* cited part of a *Times* editorial arraigning a "manifesto" that Softs from Yamhill County had submitted to the *Standard* to justify their bolting the regular ticket.[29] Hibben's animosity to Leland culminated one day when the two met on the street. Hibben explained the episode to his readers:

> We observed . . . that we desired to cross over and spit in Leland's face, and at once passed over and carried out our purpose. Leland drew a revolver, which we grasped, and

28. *Oregon Statesman,* Dec. 22, 1857; Williams to George H. Himes, Aug. 26, 1907, cited in Charles H. Carey, "The Creation of Oregon As a State: II. The Convention and Statehood," *Oregon Historical Quarterly,* 27 (1926), 9; Lane to Bush, Jan. 3, 1858, Bush Papers, reprinted in *Oregon Statesman,* Feb. 16, 1858.

29. *Oregon Weekly Times,* March 20, 1858, Oct. 10, 17, 1857; *Oregon Statesman,* Oct. 20, 1857, citing *Times,* Oct. 10, 1857. Nesmith to Deady (Oct. 24, 1857, MS OrHi): "Hibben is puting in a little more powder"; Bush to Lane (Oct. 7, 1857, Lane Papers, InU): "Hibben is coming out all right. I knew he was *naturally* right—nature made him up that way."

> prevented him from his darling purpose of shooting us. In the scuffle, he succeeded in snapping his pistol, but a portion of his coat-skirt catching between the cap and the hammer, it failed to go off. We were soon separated, and thus ended the affair.

By the end of the year, the *Statesman* frequently found room for snippets from the *Times,* as Hibben continued to excoriate the Softs and advocate the blessings of party regularity. But winning favor with the Clique made him increasingly suspect to its opponents. "I am sorry to say that he is not popular, altho he [is] quite a clever gentleman," Thompson wrote to Lane. "I regret much to see so cold a feeling manifested towards him by a good many good Democrats."[30]

James O'Meara, a diminutive bachelor of thirty-two years, possessed literary talents of above-average merit and a fighting spirit worthy of his Irish name. He had launched a career in journalism at age eight when he delivered newspapers on the streets of New York City, and two years later he left a local parish school to apprentice himself in a newspaper office, serving as errand boy, typesetter, and finally reporter. Lured west with the Forty-Niners, he remained in California as a newspaperman and became interested in politics, particularly in the career of Senator William M. Gwin. In August 1857 he visited Bush in Salem—a short time before Stevens arrived—and announced that he was interested in purchasing the *Statesman.* What he neglected to say was that he was being financed to the amount of two thousand dollars by Lane.[31]

30. *Oregon Weekly Times,* Nov. 7, 1857; cf. Hibben to Lane, Oct. 28, 1857, Lane Papers, InU; Thompson to Lane, Feb. 7, 1858, Lane Papers, InU.

31. *Oregon Statesman,* Aug. 11, 1857.

O'Meara (1825–1903) had a varied career as a journalist and editor. Upon coming to Oregon in 1857, he edited papers in Portland, Jackson-

For several months Bush had wanted to dispose of the paper and take a rest, if he were sure it would go to some "*true*" man. He had tried to persuade Deady to take it over at the beginning of the new volume in March 1857, or even Grover or Drew, but nothing came of the proposals, although Nesmith was willing to supply Deady with the funds. Bush agreed to sell to O'Meara, but to his great annoyance, rumors of the transaction began flying before they could conclude the deal. "Nes . . . was asked at Portland if the Statesman had not been sold to O'Meara, and says some thought so," Bush wrote to Lane. "If anybody owns it but me, I don't know it, and I ought to know it as soon as anybody." The *Argus* and *Oregonian* both carried reports of the sale, prompting further denials, the *Argus* referring to the new owner as a "California pro-slaveryite."[32]

On October 25 Bush advised McCracken in Portland, O'Meara's agent, that he had decided to sell but preferred to retain editorial control until the end of the current volume unless O'Meara insisted on taking over immediately. Three days later in Portland, Nesmith met O'Meara, just returned from San Francisco, and inquired what paper he intended to buy. O'Meara gave him no answer, and Nesmith left for Salem that day at noon, despite heavy rain, and arrived the following day. That night Bush wrote to McCracken that he had changed his mind and the deal was off,

---

ville, Eugene, and Albany (all of them stridently pro-Southern in tone), before leaving for Idaho in 1863, where he edited the *Idaho World* and became active in politics. Returning to California, he interested Ben Holladay in establishing the Portland *Oregon Bulletin* in 1870, which he edited until 1875. The next year he returned to San Francisco, where he resided for the rest of his life (except for editing yet another daily in Portland, 1887–89), and devoted his time to historical writing.

32. Bush to Deady, Nov. 2, 1856, MS OrHi; Bush to McCracken, Aug. 30, 1857, cited in O'Meara to Lane, Nov. 18, 1857, Lane Papers, InU; Bush to Lane, Oct. 7, 1857, Lane Papers, InU; *Oregon Argus,* Oct. 3, 1857; *Weekly Oregonian,* Oct. 10, 17, 1857; *Oregon Statesman,* Oct. 20, 1857.

but before the letter reached its destination, O'Meara had already left for Salem. Saddened and angered by this unexpected reversal, O'Meara demanded that Bush reconsider his offer; O'Meara was prepared to close the deal that very day. Bush refused a final answer until he could consult Nesmith, who was out of town, explaining that several prominent Democrats had protested the sale until after the special election in June 1858 for the new state legislature, which in turn would elect the state's two senators. Nesmith was in his office the next day but slipped out a back way when O'Meara approached; Bush also avoided him later that afternoon, and the young Californian decided to return to Portland.[33]

At this point O'Meara appealed to Lane. If Bush would not sell, O'Meara would purchase a half interest in the *Times,* he said, confident that he could help Lane more than Hibben could.

> I desired Capt Cain to let me have a portion of the draft you were kind enough to give towards my purchase of the *Statesman,* and upon the same style of security, viz: the office and building, but he seems to think it not in accordance with your instructions. I shall therefore make the purchase without assistance, but I trust, General, that by return of mail, you will authorize me through Capt. Cain, or whomever else you care to appoint, to draw against you. . . . With this aid, I can get along handsomely, and I trust will be enabled to assist you proportionately. One thing you may rely upon. I shall never be caught up in any clique at whose hands you are likely to suffer, neither by accident nor design. I am satisfied that in your absence, a powerful organization is sought to be built up against you. Men who are really candidates for the highest

33. Bush to McCracken, Oct. 25, 28, 1857, cited in O'Meara to Lane, Nov. 18, 1857, Lane Papers, InU; O'Meara to Lane, Nov. 12, 1857, Lane Papers, InU. To McCracken (Dec. 21, 1857, Bush Papers), Bush complained that O'Meara could not "furnish any security except mortgage on the office, which is no security at all," and that he did not believe O'Meara "then had a dollar to pay."

> places, but who declared while you were here that they were not, are working strenuously to form such combinations as will defeat you. Williams, Deady, Nesmith, Smith and Kelly are positively in the field for the Senate, let them deny it now much as either of them may.[34]

Lane's connection with O'Meara was a closely kept secret, for throughout the transaction no member of the Clique suspected it. It seems evident that Lane was attempting surreptitiously to obtain control of the *Statesman,* but in this instance the initiative came from O'Meara, not Lane. O'Meara must have wanted to acquire a paper in Oregon but lacked the requisite funds, and Lane grasped this opportunity to ensure continued support by the *Statesman* in the forthcoming senatorial campaign. The arrangement was clearly a business transaction; O'Meara neither requested nor expected Lane's largess and offered full security for the loan. He was obviously acting independently in suggesting a half interest in the *Times.* And when O'Meara accused Nesmith and the Clique of further intrigues, Lane responded with cold disbelief. May not O'Meara's informer have "misjudged the conduct, misunderstood the words, [or] misinterpreted the actions of Mr. Nesmith?" Lane inquired, assuring him that if the charges proved true, he would certainly proceed to counteract them.

> But it cannot be possible that Nesmith Bush or Curry can feel unkind to me! You know that I love Curry, I have always been the friend of Bush, have stood by Nesmith. . . . I cannot even for one moment give room to suspicion, much less to act on such suspicion. I will however add that I accept your communication as a further proof of your kind feelings toward me. And allow me to assure you that I fully appreciate

34. O'Meara to Lane, Nov. 12, 1857, Lane Papers, InU. "To be sure you get this," O'Meara wrote substantially the same in a second letter of the same date, which he sent by a later steamer. The quote is from the first letter. Cf. Cain to Lane, Nov. 19, 1857, Lane Papers, InU, a confidential letter ending, "*burn this letter.*"

your friendship and hope that it will continue with increased vigor through out life.

Meanwhile, O'Meara filed suit against Bush for breach of contract, and instead of buying an interest in the *Times,* he suddenly selected a new course of action. On January 1 he announced to Lane that he had just purchased the *Standard;* several friends had assisted him, and Captain Cain had advanced $750 on Lane's behalf, which gave Lane a one-eighth interest in the proscribed journal. And O'Meara requested another $750 to help him meet notes that would fall due in ninety days.[35]

O'Meara was not long in entering the political fray. The defection of Softs sharply reduced the Clique's majority, and when the new legislature met in December 1857, the *Statesman* pointed to the "outrageously unequal" system by which delegates to the Democratic convention were apportioned according to population, the same as the legislature, rather than on Democratic strength in each county. Two weeks later the state central committee, chaired by Nesmith, voted to base representation to the next convention on the Democratic vote for delegate in 1857. A logical culmination to the expulsion of the *Standard,* this move would disfranchise the Softs from any voice in the party, as Bush freely admitted. "If men are anxious to be included in a democratic apportionment, they must learn to vote the democratic ticket," he editorialized on January 19. "We know of no other way. This view of the subject may not prove consoling to certain parties, but we cannot, and care not to, help it." O'Meara denounced the move in his first issue of the *Standard,* thereby tipping his hand and incurring the wrath of Hibben, who had resented him as an interloper from the beginning.[36]

35. Lane to O'Meara, Jan. 3, 1858, Lane Papers, InU; O'Meara to Lane, Jan. 1, 1858, Lane Papers, InU. Lane did not advance the additional $750. O'Meara to Lane, March 26, 1858, Lane Papers, InU.

36. *Oregon Statesman,* Dec. 8, 29, 1857, Jan. 19, 1858. Cf. *Oregon Weekly Times,* Jan. 9, 1858, ff.

The legislature of 1857–58 adjourned, reported one of Lane's correspondents, "having done but little except . . . to make a full disorganized mess of the political community." O'Meara visited Salem after Christmas as an observer and reporter. The Softs received him warmly and announced they would not support the nominees of the next convention, although they would support Lane—many of them eagerly—as long as he did not turn his influence against them. O'Meara then drafted an "Address to the National Democracy of Oregon," signed by nine of the most rabid anti-Clique members, which called for a boycott of the regular convention at Salem and the election of new delegates to a National Democratic convention in Eugene three weeks later. He told Lane he would circulate five thousand copies of the address throughout the territory, that the *Occidental* and *Sentinel* would follow his lead, that Cain was delighted with the movement, and that the men from Salem were "sorely alarmed." While at Salem he had talked to "sound Democrats" from every part of the territory and was convinced that "the feeling against Platform men [was] almost universal in a majority of counties."[37] Neither Bush nor Hibben knew who authored the appeal, and both completely befogged the issue by denouncing it as an antislavery, "Black Republican" move, which it certainly was not.[38] At this point the revolt was no more than a local struggle for power, and few, if any, could foresee what it might become.

The regular Democratic convention met in Salem on March 16. Besides endorsing the Cincinnati platform and the Buchanan administration, the delegates approved the principles of both popular sovereignty and the Dred Scott decision, refusing to acknowledge

37. Daniel H. Lownsdale to Lane, Feb. 6, 1858, Lane Papers, InU; O'Meara to Lane, Feb. 1, 1858, Lane Papers, InU.

38. The *Oregon Weekly Times* (Feb. 6, 1858) pronounced six of the nine bolters "arrant black republicans"; the *Oregon Statesman* (March 9, 1858) called the Nationals *"an abolition party,* and we will wager that *ninety-nine out of every hundred men in Oregon who next June vote the Eugene ticket, will in* 1860 *vote the regular black republican ticket for President!"*

any contradiction between the two. They also reaffirmed the caucus-sovereignty resolutions of the last convention and invited "those National men whose party associations have heretofore differed from ours" to support "our principles and nominations, and cordially aid us in contending with faction and fanaticism, and for the peace and stability of the Union."[39] The only discord occurred over the nomination for governor, in which Lane's closest friends defeated Drew by throwing their support to Curry, who for this very reason had consented to run only a few days before the election. But they could not elect Curry and so compromised on relatively unknown John Whiteaker, a proslavery delegate from Lane County, who was elected on the third ballot. The convention named Grover to run for Congress and Bush for state printer. A final resolution unanimously commended Lane's record as delegate. O'Meara was unimpressed. "At Eugene City," he promised Lane, "I am determined to have a resolution passed endorsing you as our . . . *first* senator to be elected, or I will break up the organization."[40]

The platform adopted by the bolting Nationals in Eugene, April 8, differed only in two major respects. While strongly endorsing the principle of popular sovereignty, it omitted any mention of the Dred Scott case, and repudiating caucus rule, it reaffirmed "the great principles of the right of the represented to instruct the representative, and proclaim it the bounden [duty] of the representative to obey the instructions of his constituents or resign whatever position he may at that time hold." The convention elected its own state central committee and unanimously nominated E. M. Barnum of Polk County for governor, Kelly for Congress, and O'Meara for state printer. The resolution endorsing

39. *Oregon Weekly Times,* March 20, 1858; *Oregon Statesman,* March 23, 1858.

40. *Oregon Weekly Times,* March 20, 1858; *Oregon Statesman,* March 23, 1858; cf. Curry to Lane, March 17, 1858, Lane Papers, InU, and Drew to Deady, March 23, 1858, MS OrHi; O'Meara to Lane, March 26, 1858, Lane Papers, InU.

Lane praised his record as delegate but made no reference to the coming senatorial contest.[41]

This naked quest for political power intensified as the elections for the new state legislature approached, and neither side dared to repudiate Lane. A year earlier, after Lane's renomination in 1857, the *Oregonian* had pointedly declared: "The plain and simple truth is that a half dozen party stock jobbers and political gamblers in and about Salem are engaged in a desperate game for OFFICE and SPOILS.... [They] have been *compelled* again to nominate Jo Lane, although there is not a man of them but would send him to Van Dieman's Land if they could, rather than to Washington. Lane is in their way." Dryer thought there were "at least ten aspirants" for each new state office and the two new senatorships, the greatest prizes of all. Nevertheless, he predicted:

> like the ghost of Banquo, Lane will rise at the official feast, and by his presence overawe those who have again attempted his political assassination. He has the party under his thumb, and uses them as any other selfish political aspirant or party demagogue would stepping stones, to enable him the more easily to vault into the saddle of power and ride over all opposition.

Hibben was also dismayed by the "political trappings" of politicians in Oregon and "finally concluded to suspect the whole camp." "I have never dreamed of such cold and unscrupulous selfishness as that I find here," he wrote to Lane. "There is more men here who are democrats *for office* than in all Indiana, Ohio & Illinois. I remember to have heard you allude to this peculiarity but then I had no idea of the extent to which the pestilence prevails here." After the convention in 1858, a long-time resident warned Lane that "each little band of aspirants" was seeking to place itself in

41. *Weekly Oregonian,* April 17, 1858; J. W. Mack to Lane, April 18, 1858, Lane Papers, InU.

the ascendancy, and that he had never before "seen any thing in Oregon equalling the present wire working and management."[42]

After Lane's re-election in 1857, Softs in Portland had promised to support him for the Senate if he would only repudiate the caucus-sovereignty resolutions. Before leaving for Washington, Lane agreed to favor Deady for the federal judgeship if Deady would not permit his name to be used for the Senate, but Lane had scarcely returned to the capital when he received reports that Deady's candidacy was being promoted along with others. This both Deady and Mosher denied.[43] The situation became even more confused after O'Meara espoused the National cause. Most of those jealous for Lane's success, including Nat and Mosher, remained in the regular organization and cautioned him not to be misled by rumors of National strength. Others like Cain and Bill Martin were absolutely convinced that Bush, Deady, and Nesmith were playing him false and plotting his overthrow.[44]

The final complication was the feud that developed between the *Times* and the *Standard,* in which both editors were equally sincere in their devotion to Lane but diametrically opposed over the most appropriate course of action. From the first, O'Meara thought that Hibben had "acted scurvily toward him, that he was too abusive to do Lane much good, and that he was "honey-fuggling" with Bush, who would surely outsmart him. Hibben had in

42. *Weekly Oregonian,* April 18, 1857; Hibben to Lane, Jan. 11, 1857 [i.e. 1858], Lane Papers, InU; Daniel H. Lownsdale to Lane, April 11, 1858, Lane Papers, InU.

43. [Signature missing] to Lane, July 2, 1857, Lane Papers, InU; Deady to Lane, Feb. 7, 1858, Lane Papers, InU; Lane to Deady, April 17, 1858, MS OrHi; Mosher to Lane, Dec. 31, 1857, April 18, 1858, Lane Papers, InU.

44. Nat to Lane, Feb. 28, 1858, Lane Papers, InU; Mosher to Lane, April 27, 1858, Lane Papers, InU; Cain to Lane, Feb. 5, 1858, Lane Papers, InU. Bill Martin, returning from the Salem convention, warned Lane (March 31, 1858, Lane Papers, InU): "thare is a deep laid plan to beate you for the Cinate, all thare loud professions to the contrare not with standing."

fact been increasingly supporting the Clique and had bitterly resented O'Meara's attempt to acquire the *Times.* After he bought the *Standard,* O'Meara arranged an interview with Hibben in which he produced Lane's letter to Cain as evidence of Lane's confidence; they were both working for the same end, he declared, although as a journalist he would pursue his own track. Hibben responded politely but coolly.

> I did not give him my confidence [he confided to Lane], for I thought that if you had desired me to cooperate with him for your election . . . it seems to me you should have said so. He even went so far as to tell me that you authorized him to confer with me in the premises. Your silence upon this point made me doubt him and so we stand.
>
> I shall go ahead in my present track until I hear from you so far then as the Standard is concerned.[45]

Relations between the two men improved slightly after the interview, but when O'Meara frontally assaulted the Clique-sponsored caucus-sovereignty resolutions, Hibben retaliated with a blistering rebuttal:

> The *Standard,* of the 28th inst., reveals the alarming fact that a change of grinder where the cylinder remains unchanged . . . produces no variation whatever in the music. . . . In one sentence, the issue of the *Standard* before us is a thorough and entire endorsement and advocacy of the disorganizing career of . . . Leland. . . . No one need now be mistaken about the *status* of that organ.[46]

Hibben was passionately and correctly—at least in the short run—convinced that O'Meara's strategy was sheer madness. To Lane he sent an elaborate statistical analysis of the vote by counties in

45. O'Meara to Lane, Jan. 1, 1858, Nov. 12, 1857, Lane Papers, InU; Hibben to Lane, Jan. 12, 1857 [i.e. 1858], Lane Papers, InU.
46. *Oregon Weekly Times,* Jan. 30, 1858.

the last election, showing that Lane was strong in the disaffected areas. "If regular democrats are elected," he argued, "they will go into democratic caucus for you, but if 'soft' candidates should be chosen they will be precluded from the caucus and the majority . . . in that event will be from counties in which you may not be the first choice. *Every success therefore of the 'softs' is an actual detraction from your strength.*" O'Meara was equally convinced that he was right and recoiled from Hibben's attack. To Lane he wrote:

> I take all back that I said about Hibben in my last, and go back to first impressions. Excuse me, General, but I honestly think him the damndest conceited fool I ever tried to work with. After Capt. Cain and myself privately talked with him, and told him what we deemed the best course for him to pursue towards me in the *Times* (no positive outbreak) in his last number he had two columns of the bitterest things he dare say against me. He must not attack me otherwise than editorially, for if he ever maligns me, I shall give him a happy time of it. He *shall* respect me.[47]

To this latest missive, Lane replied with a long, carefully worded letter that indicated his conclusions were essentially the same as Hibben's; it showed, too, how deeply his democracy ran.

> I am satisfied with your friendship [he wrote O'Meara], therefore may take the liberty of writing freely without any fear of offense; you are actuated by feelings of personal kindness as well as political considerations in the course you are taking in regard to the organization of the Democratic party, with an honest and earnest desire to secure the election of such democrats to the Legislature, as will support me for the Senate; you can hardly know how kindly, deeply, I appreciate your kind and generous feelings, wishes and efforts: but can

47. Hibben to Lane, April 5, 1858, Lane Papers, InU; O'Meara to Lane, Feb. 1, 1858, Lane Papers, InU.

any good come of a division of the party? With two tickets in the field for Governor, Member of Congress & c, put in nomination by [two] Democratic Conventions, the party would of course become divided . . . and place our new state in the hands of the opposition. Is this the view you take of the matter?

It strikes me that Union is indispensable to success and that everything ought to be done on all sides to conciliate, harmonise and strengthen the party, and if wrongs have been committed and injustice done to individuals of the party, there is the place to correct them. The honest Democratic masses will always correct errors of their own and of the party, while they will take good care to preserve the organization of the party, defend its principles and support the regular nominees. You are on the ground and ought to see and understand the true condition of things and I have no doubt, that you are pursuing such a course of policy as in your judgment is best. But I must be allowed to say, that I am most decidedly opposed to a division of the party. I would therefore advise that steps be taken at once to settle all differences and meet together in support of the same great principles; they are eternal and cannot be compromised; temporary dissensions and discord may beat us once, but our friends would soon rally and victory would again perch upon our banners. I look upon the organization and success of the Democratic party, as very essential to our state. We are about to organize a state government, and if we succeed in the election of reliable democrats to state offices, we will have success and prosperity, the party will become united and strong and all will be well. but on the contrary should the opposition succeed in getting power, who can judge better than yourself, of the consequences to the state and the Democratic party.[48]

48. Lane to O'Meara (copy), April 4, 1858, Lane Papers, InU.

Like a run-down boardinghouse in tourist season, Washington City opened its doors to the nation's solons returning in late autumn of 1857. Unlike European capitals, Washington offered neither cultural nor commercial advantages; it was simply the seat of the national government. Two great new wings of the Capitol, in the process of being remodeled since 1850, were now nearing completion, although still in the future were the steps to each wing, the huge vaulted dome, and the hundred Corinthian columns upholding the porticoes. The city was a show place of contrasts, with extravagance and display abounding next door to abject poverty and squalor. Even Pennsylvania Avenue was marred by unsightly "ornamentation," and the dust from its unpaved surface had become almost intolerable. Worse still was the menace to health presented by inadequate sanitary facilities and a climate that was regularly insufferable, except for a few sunny days in winter and a generally glorious spring. The Potomac seemed also to breed a peculiarly virulent strain of crime and vice from which even the people's representatives were not immune. As sectional tensions mounted, certain members of Congress, it was said, began to go armed to the Capitol each day; municipal authorities had recently prohibited the carrying of "deadly or dangerous weapons, such as a dagger, pistol, bowie knife . . . brass or other metal knuckles" within city limits.[49] The social climate, however, after the drab days of the Pierce administration, had brightened considerably with the inauguration of Buchanan, and the city's social elite planned an unusually brilliant "season" that would reach its zenith in Mrs. Gwin's grand ball, which was still recalled a half century later.

The eyes of the nation focused upon Kansas. An election for a constitutional convention, which met at the temporary capital of

49. *Oregon Weekly Times,* Jan. 23, 1858.

Lecompton, was boycotted by free-state settlers, so that the resulting constitution legalized slavery in Kansas, permitting a referendum only on the admission of future slaves. When Southerners demanded that this legal fiction be forced through Congress, the Administration quailed, and Douglas hurried to Washington to plead with Buchanan to resist this mockery of his cherished ideal. Four days before Congress convened, the Little Giant confronted the aging President, declaring he would denounce him publicly if he acquiesced on Lecompton. Buchanan, his mind already made up, was incensed at so blatant a challenge to executive leadership. "Mr. Douglas," he glowered, "I desire you to remember that no Democrat [since the time of Jackson] ever yet differed from an Administration of his own choice without being crushed." "Mr. President," rejoined Douglas, "I wish you to remember that General Jackson is dead."[50]

The President's message to Congress implicitly endorsed the Lecompton constitution, at the same time promising that all Kansans would have an opportunity to vote on the slavery clause. The next day Douglas rose to denounce the constitution for the fraud that it was and called, unsuccessfully, for a new constitutional convention in Kansas. Then while awaiting results of the Kansas elections, Congress turned to other affairs, especially the current Mormon "threat."[51] Lane used the opportunity to introduce a bill to pay Oregon's war debt, a joint resolution for Bush's printing claims, and some lesser bills.

There was little doubt that the heavy Democratic majority in the Senate would follow the Administration's lead, but no such certainty existed in the House, especially after the elections in Kansas (on slavery, December 21, and on the entire constitution,

50. Allan Nevins, *The Emergence of Lincoln, I* (New York, Charles Scribner's Sons, 1950), 253.

51. Lane was very intolerant of the Mormons. To Hibben (Nov. 27, 1857, Lane Papers, InU), Lane wrote: "I hate traitors & I want to see the mormon organization broken up and completely destroyed and the sooner it is done the better."

January 4) produced new evidence of irregularities and corruption. Nevertheless, Buchanan transmitted to Congress on February 2 an official copy of the Lecompton constitution along with a message urging its acceptance. Douglas made a herculean attempt to rally the opposition, bargaining, threatening, cajoling, pleading, and then voted with the Republicans on March 23 when the Senate passed the measure, thirty-three to twenty-five.

The House now became the scene of the most frantic activity since the hectic days of 1850, as anti-Lecompton Democrats attempted to join forces with Republicans and Know Nothings to force the constitution to be resubmitted to the residents of Kansas. Every indication promised a close vote. As the controversy raged, Lane found himself inexorably drawn into the debate, using some comments about the constitution of Oregon to launch a ringing defense of the Administration's policy.

Like most supporters of the Administration, Lane seemed totally blind to the gross inconsistency between the vaunted ideal of popular sovereignty and the grim reality behind the myth of Lecompton. He was sincerely convinced that party unity must be maintained at all costs, in Oregon and throughout the nation, for a breach in the ranks would be tantamount to handing victory to the Republicans. And a Republican victory, because of their unconstitutional doctrines of federal power, would just as surely mark the end of the Union—the Union, that is, as conceived by the Founding Fathers. He was not so concerned about slavery per se as he was about the threat to the inviolate rights of the states, which in his mind constituted the essence of popular sovereignty. It mattered not from which direction the threat might come. Should the South, for example, seek congressional action to extend the area of slavery, he would cry, "Hold, my friends, you have no right to extend slavery *by such means*."[52] But it was the North, not the South, that was making unconstitutional demands, and the

52. Italics mine.

North was responsible for this incessant agitation over the "perplexing" question of slavery, thereby menacing the existence of the "great sisterhood of States." Lane regretted that certain persons who "occupied high positions in the Democratic party" had elected to cooperate with the opposition in keeping the slavery question before the country for "political purposes." He particularly regretted the course of Douglas, whose candidacy for the presidency he had supported at Cincinnati; when the convention nominated Buchanan, he had loyally switched his support and campaigned actively for the party's nominee, and he was now glad that he had. He hoped Douglas would soon be working again for the good of the party; at least he had "not yet given him up."

> The question now to be decided for all time to come, is, whether another slave State shall be admitted? Everybody knows that Kansas will not be long a slave State. Her people have the right to change, alter, and amend their constitution as they please. Slavery will not long exist there; but . . . if that constitution says slavery shall exist, you are bound to admit the State with slavery, and leave the people free to change their constitution when the proper time arrives.
>
> I repeat, sir, that that constitution is before us. The people have had a chance to vote upon the question of slavery, and nine-tenths of those who have voted have voted in favor of slavery. I have no doubt that a majority of the whole people of the Territory, at the time the question was submitted, were not in favor of slavery. But their opposition to slavery did not go to the extent of recording their vote against it. What I mean to say is this, that in ascertaining the will of the people you are to look to the votes given for or against, not to the vote withheld, whether they be withheld on account of indifference to the result, or from factious motives. And when gentlemen say they are ready to vote for the admission of a slave State, if they are satisfied that the people of the

> State are in favor of slavery, and yet propose to vote against this constitution, I say . . . they are estopped in that argument. They cannot go behind that constitution. It is here legally; it is here legitimately; it is here properly. If there have been irregularities, bloodshed, and disorder in the Territory, you know . . . it has been caused by the instrumentality of men armed with Sharpe's rifles, sent out by the emigrant aid societies for the purpose of defeating the ends of justice, and thwarting the will of the people. The fault rests with them; and let the consequence rest upon the guilty. . . . Bring Kansas into the Union. Raise her to the dignity of a State. Place the sovereignty in the hands of her people, and they will regulate their own affairs as they please, and peace will be restored to the country. Let us not do injustice to our friends of the South, now, and for all time.[53]

In short, Lane was willing to overlook the wrongs committed at Lecompton for the larger stakes of party unity and states' rights. Lecompton might violate the rights of the majority of Kansans, but a Republican victory would jeopardize the very foundations of the Union. And he was so much the politician that he could close his eyes to Democratic iniquities and shift full responsibility for them to the Republicans and their anti-Lecompton allies. A fatal flaw, perhaps, but not uncommon.

In April the House defeated the Lecompton constitution, 120 to 112, but accepted by a vote of 112 to 103 a last-ditch compromise, the English bill, which referred the constitution back to the voters

53. *Congressional Globe,* 35 Cong., 1 Sess., pp. 1395–97, March 27, 1858. To Mosher, March 18, 1858, Lane wrote, "Is it not strange that our friend Douglas should take it in his head to give a Democratic Administration and the party so much trouble and inflict such terrible injury to the party. Who would again trust him?" Lafayette Mosher Family Papers (University of Washington Library, Seattle). Cf. Lane to Mosher, Feb. 4, 1858, Lane Papers, InU.

with the proviso that if they accepted Lecompton they would be admitted immediately, but if they rejected it they would have to wait until their population reached the average of all congressional districts, almost 93,000. That August, Kansans rejected Lecompton and the Administration by a decisive margin, 11,812 to 1,926.[54]

The controversy over Kansas adversely affected the prospects for prompt action on Oregon. The day before Buchanan forwarded the Lecompton constitution to Congress, Lane presented Oregon's constitution to the House for referral to the Committee on Territories. From time to time he checked with the committee's chairman, who, foreseeing no opposition to the bill, advised waiting until after the debate over Kansas was finished. When Douglas inquired about Oregon's constitution, Lane replied that he neither desired to "embarrass Kansas with Oregon, or to have Oregon mixed up with Kansas." As soon as the Senate voted to admit Kansas, Lane sent a copy of Oregon's constitution to Douglas, who apparently overlooked it because later in the Senate he complained that Lane had not yet made it available. After Lane demonstrated his innocence, Douglas apologized for doing him an injustice. When the Senate finally considered the constitution on May 5, opponents of admission questioned the size of the population and various constitutional provisions. Some objected to the clauses discriminating against Negroes and Chinese; others frowned at the ease with which other aliens were permitted the franchise. By and large, the objections were of a perfunctory nature, and when the vote came on May 18, the measure passed thirty-five to seventeen.[55] By this time, however, the damage had been done, for time was fast running out in the House. The House adjourned without acting, and Lane wrote defensively to the *States-*

54. For discussions of the Lecompton issue, see Nevins, *Emergence of Lincoln,* I, 250–304, and Roy Franklin Nichols, *The Disruption of American Democracy* (New York, Macmillan Company, 1948), pp. 150–76.

55. *Congressional Globe,* 35 Cong., 1 Sess., pp. 1395, 1415; cf. Douglas' earlier remarks, ibid., p. 1324; ibid., pp. 1474, 1963–70, 2203–09.

*man,* absolving himself and the House of any responsibility for the failure: the calendar was too crowded with business of higher priority. He had failed to get the bill reported but was sure the House would take it up "very early" next session. With this expectation, he advised Oregonians not to wait for congressional action but proceed immediately to organize as a state.[56]

Before the Thirty-fifth Congress convened, before Douglas crossed swords with Buchanan in the White House, Lane and Stevens had called at the War Department and had learned that Secretary John B. Floyd was prepared to recommend payment of the war claims as audited by the investigating commission, even though some of the prices seemed unusually high. Lane was delighted, because executive backing guaranteed eventual success. It was a source of some pride to Lane that when Congress convened, he was the first member of the House to introduce a bill. To Bush he professed that he "would rather be shot than defeated in the passage of my war bill." The Committee on Military Affairs agreed to report in favor of the bill except for the per diem allowance of four dollars, which they thought was too high, but Lane remained confident of success.[57] He attempted to amend a bill reimbursing Governor James Douglas of Vancouver Island seven thousand dollars for supplies advanced to the volunteers but was ruled out of order. Lane thought it "right and just" to compensate Douglas for his expenditures but demanded to know why Douglas should be given priority over "the people who so nobly turned out to save the settlements of Oregon and Washington from the tomahawk and scalping-knife of the savages." In the final week of the session, both the Senate and House committees agreed to recom-

56. Lane to Bush, June 18, 1858, Bush Papers.

57. Lane to Bush, Dec. 17, 18, 1857, Lane Papers, InU, reprinted in *Oregon Statesman,* Jan. 26, 1858; Lane to J. H. Reed, April 23, 1858, Lane Papers, InU; Lane to Mosher, April 18, 1858, Lane Papers, InU. To Hibben (Nov. 27, 1857, Lane Papers, InU), Lane declared: "The President is a just man. he is with us, and we will get the appropriation."

mend payment of the claims allowed by the commission,[58] but there was such a backlog of unfinished business that the war bill, like Oregon's constitution, was jettisoned for lack of time.

Lane's legislative accomplishments were minor: improved mail service, extension of the land laws to the area east of the Cascades, appropriations for completing military roads. The Committee on Territories was not disposed to report favorably on Bush's printing claim, so Lane asked that instead they make no report at all. "This request was granted and so the matter stands," he informed Bush, promising to "try it again" next fall. The House chopped nearly $100,000 from Nesmith's estimates for the Indian appropriation bill; Lane tried to amend the bill and restore the deficiency but was unsuccessful. Bush feared O'Meara might try to replace the *Statesman* or *Times* in publishing the acts of Congress and asked Lane to prevent this, which he did.[59] He also finally requested Postal Agent Thompson's resignation, appointing instead Shubrick Norris of Portland, who had been recommended by Bush and Hibben, although O'Meara supported Thompson.[60] Journals like the *Times* and *Oregonian* expressed the widespread dissatisfaction with the mails, but for some time the *Statesman* had been particularly withering in its criticisms. Bush finally appealed to Lane: "I have never written you one word, General, about Bob Thompson as postal agent. But, our mails are in a *hell of a condition.* You know he is not competent. . . . For Christ's sake, let us have *somebody,* and some man who can at least speak and write the English

58. *Congressional Globe,* 35 Cong., 1 Sess., pp. 2118–21; Lane to Bush, June 4, 1858, *Oregon Statesman,* July 20, 1858.

59. Lane to Bush, June 18, 1858, Lane Papers, InU; *Congressional Globe,* 35 Cong., 1 Sess., p. 2555; Bush to Lane, Feb. 23, 1858, Lane Papers, InU; Lane to Bush, April 2, 1858, Bush Papers.

60. Thompson to Lane, April 18, 1858, Lane Papers, InU; Norris to Lane, March 26, 1858, Lane Papers, InU; Bush to Lane, Jan. 2, 1858, Lane Papers, InU; Hibben to Lane, Jan. 10, 1857 [i.e. 1858], Lane Papers, InU. O'Meara to Lane, Feb. 7, 1858, Lane Papers, InU: "Like a damned fool as he is, Hibben has permitted himself to be used as a cat's paw in this measure."

language with ordinary correctness." Thompson, meanwhile, had independently offered his resignation; he was "willing to be a martyr" if it would assist Lane's cause.[61]

To Lane, as well as the nation, the first session of the Thirty-fifth Congress was a bitter disappointment. He had intended to summer in Oregon, presumably hoping to attend the state legislature, which would elect Oregon's first senators, and to study first-hand the changing complexion of political affairs. Payment of the war debt and statehood would have guaranteed a favorable reception, but their eleventh-hour postponements persuaded him to remain in Washington. "I shall remain and do all I can to aid the Hon. Charles I. Faulkner [chairman, House Committee on Military Affairs], in his examination of our war claims," he told Bush. "By placing facts and documents in his hands, I may be able to do something for the promotion of the just claims of our people, and besides this there are many things pending in the Departments that I will attend to, and [be in] perfect readiness for the next Session." Aside from a few weeks in Indiana, he passed the summer months in the capital, where his youngest son, Lafayette, had been enrolled for the past year at a Roman Catholic school. He had done even better for John, procuring for him an appointment to West Point. Besides his other duties, there was always the mail, which this year presented as many challenges as always. And as many requests. One correspondent had purchased eight thousand dollars worth of Kentucky thoroughbreds and requested his assis-

61. Bush to Lane, Jan. 2, 1858, Lane Papers, InU; Thompson to Lane, Feb. 11, April 18, 1858, Lane Papers, InU. Bush and Nesmith pulled another of their shady deals in which they signed a recommendation (Jan. 11, 1858, Lane Papers, InU) and then wrote to Lane (Jan. 15, 1858, Lane Papers, InU) asking him to ignore it. Curry, who favored the appointment, was outraged by this "damnable way of doing business" and protested to Lane (April 26, 1858, Lane Papers, InU): "It throws the whole burden of complaint against yourself. It ought not to be tolerated. And you would serve men right by holding them to their public acts and disregarding their private say so." As it turned out, the office in question was never created.

tance to transport them to Oregon; another wanted to send his children west with Lane. A friend of John's at West Point desired Lane to procure a sick leave for him from the Secretary of War. One poor old fellow was in particular distress—"as I am loosin all of my Hair and thaire is no possible way for me to get a Wig in this country."[62]

The open rupture of a major political party is an agonizing experience, and fortunate is he who needs not choose between principle and self-interest. In the breach between Douglas and Buchanan, Lane's convictions coincided with his instincts, rendering support of the Administration almost inevitable. These same instincts alerted him to the threat to his political future posed by the growing disruption of the party in Oregon. Throughout his career he had sought to minimize disaffection and dissension—to the annoyance of the Clique—and his response to this new challenge was completely in character.

Lane's consuming passion, which he concealed not at all, was to become Oregon's first United States senator. For that reason he sent out Hibben to edit the *Times,* and for that reason he agreed to support O'Meara. Although Lane did not approve O'Meara's independent course, the fact that he corresponded with him soon angered both Hibben and the Clique. In February, Bush issued a covert warning to Lane: "They claim you are *winking at* the 'new movement' (which is but the old movement) and O'Meara shows a letter from you with a significant air. Of course, I know how much importance to attach to a letter from you *a long time ago,* before he had declared for the opposition."[63] Here was the rub. The distance was so great that by the time Lane could reply to a letter—or newspaper—at least two months would elapse. Bad

62. Lane to Bush, June 18, 1858, Bush Papers; M. C. McLane to Lane, Dec. 25, 1857, Lane Papers, InU.

63. Bush to Lane, Feb. 23, 1858, Lane Papers, InU.

enough for ordinary communication, but intolerable in times of stress.

In a letter to Hibben, February 16, 1858, Lane attempted to nip in the bud the dispute between Hibben and O'Meara over the apportionment of delegates to the Democratic convention. At the time of writing, Lane had seen only a single issue of each paper. He was undoubtedly seeking to prevent an open rift between these two young lieutenants, but as innocuous as the letter seemed, it inspired such a reaction as to make it the most important yet of his political career.

> I have read in the *Times* and the *Standard* two articles on the apportionment . . . of the delegates to the State Convention. . . . I regret to observe . . . some diversity of sentiment at variance with what I conceive to be the harmony essential to the integrity and unity of the democratic party, and which, without a spirit of conciliation and a liberal toleration of each others views, *may* lead, as far as the influence of the above named able journals extend, to a fatal and irreparable breach in our ranks. It is well observed in a leading editorial in one of these papers [*Times,* January 9, 1858], that "there are periods in the history of individuals and communities where one erroneous action, a single false step, must inevitably be followed by years of suffering and misfortune; when the neglect or improper use of the right moment or right occasion infuses a poison into the entire circulation of after life, which no remedy may reach, no action purify and no atonement redeem."
>
> Unhappily for the peace and happiness of the country, there has grown up . . . an exuberant independence (if I may use the expression) of action and thought, as extravagant as intractable, and equally destructive of the efficiency of the press to do good, as of the efficiency of the political organization through which any good is to be accomplished. In all

countries where freedom of opinion is tolerated, there must necessarily be political organizations to give proper concentration and direction to the popular will for the attainment of any given end. Is it the true policy to give such direction to the instrumentalities by which such organizations are kept alive, as to impart to them greater energy and efficiency; or is it to magnify a difference on some minor issue into an irreparable breach, and thus insure a victory to the banner of the adversary? In union, we are told, there is strength. On the other hand, we have the highest authority for the assertion that "a house divided against itself must fall." Should the germs of discord now existing in the democratic party in Oregon be speedily eradicated or suppressed, all will be well—should they be fostered and cultivated, it is easy to foresee what bitter fruits they will bring forth.

The principal feature of our whole political system is its representative character. This is as essential to the action of parties as to the operation of governments and the enactment of laws. The general views of the *Standard* of the relation existing between the represented and the representative, all must assent to. There must be no usurpation on the part of the latter of powers not delegated by the former; the right of the people is paramount to all rights of those who are the creatures of the people. To redress grievances is an inherent right, an incident of the sovereign power which belongs to the people, and of which they cannot be lawfully deprived. None can question these fundamental truths—they are political axioms, enunciated at the dawn of civil liberty in the Old World, and successfully maintained and defended on the battlefields of the New.

There are, however, incident to popular rights, corresponding duties. And what duty is more imperative at the time of peril and difficulty than that of healing dissensions, harmonizing conflicting interests and passions, and working together

> for the common good and to secure a victory over a common enemy? We behold the Union at this moment surrounded with perils which never surrounded it before—the nation convulsed and shaken to its very centre upon a great and exciting question, on the decision of which, hangs our future destiny. At such a time, when such mighty interests are involved; when the support of the Union and Constitution is needed, who will stop to struggle over issues necessarily short-lived and ephemeral? Shall patriots hang back . . . where abolitionism unmasks its nefarious and traitorous designs. . . ? The issues now presented are of such a magnitude as should merge all minor differences in one common and patriotic effort, to bring the State of Oregon into the line of those old States . . . which stand by the Union and the Constitution. Let Oregon arise, a new star in the West to cheer the hearts of patriots; and may no cloud of black republican disunion obscure her brightness forever.[64]

When he composed this letter, Lane could not know that O'Meara had already rallied the Softs in the legislature with his "Address to the National Democracy"; when he learned of this, he dispatched a second and more vigorous appeal for harmony.

> I see, with much regret [he wrote to the *Statesman*], that division and discord exists in the ranks of the Democracy of Oregon, threatening in its character, and if persisted in, will result in defeat and overthrow. Fellow Democrats of Oregon, *division in the Democratic party will not do.* . . . If ever there was a time for *every Democrat to do his duty,* his *whole duty, it is now.* All Democrats should bear in mind that *the Democratic party* is the Union. I appeal to the Democracy to bury all private animosities . . . and unite as one man in support of the *regular nominees.*

64. Lane to Hibben, Feb. 16, 1858, *Oregon Weekly Times,* March 27, 1858.

> . . . I would be very glad to be chosen one of the first Senators from our new State, but I shall never desire it at a sacrafice of the harmony, honor and integrity of the party.[65]

From then on at two-week intervals, he wrote to Bush even more forthrightly, always professing his own regularity, deprecating division within the party, and advertising his availability for the Senate.[66]

65. Lane to ed., March 18, 1858, *Oregon Statesman,* April 27, 1858, reprinted in *Oregon Weekly Times,* May 1, 1858.

66. Lane to Bush, April 2, 1858, Bush Papers: "I shall never abandon the party or fail to give my most earnest support to the regular nominees of the party. . . . I could part with my wife and all my children as easy as I could do any thing to weaken the democratic party or disturb its organization. . . . I am anxious to be one of the first Senators, and . . . I have not a particle of doubt about the feeling of the Democrats of Oregon in regard to my self. nine out of ten of them would if the question was presented to them go for me for the Senate."

Lane to Bush, April 19, 1858, *Oregon Statesman,* June 1, 1858: *"I hope that by this time all efforts that are being made to divide the party have been so rebuked that no similar effort will be made in years to come.* You may bear in mind that I wish to be elected to the Senate . . . , but I don't want to go into the Senate at the expense of the peace, harmony, honor and integrity of the Democratic party. *I have not in a single instance in my life failed to support the nominees of the party.* . . . I am opposed to all efforts to divide the party."

Lane to Bush, May 3, 1858, *Oregon Statesman,* June 15, 1858: "The spirit of loyalty, harmony and good feeling which characterized in an eminent degree the Salem Convention, is most gratifying to me, as it must also be to the whole Democracy of our new State. The platform unanimously adopted will bear the most searching scrutiny, and even green-eyed jealousy cannot detect a flaw."

Lane to Bush, May 18, 1858, *Oregon Statesman,* June 22, 1858: "As it is not certain that a letter by the next mail would reach you before the Legislature of your new State will assemble for the purpose of electing 'United States Senators,' I have concluded to write you briefly in reference to the matter. I am, as is well understood by the whole people of Oregon, a candidate for the office of Senator. . . . I must, however, be allowed to say, that I do not wish a seat in the Senate at the expense of the peace and harmony of the Democratic party. I look upon the maintenance of the organization of the party as essential to success."

Hibben published Lane's letter in the *Times* the week following the convention at Salem. Coming as it did just after the Nationals' open challenge of the Clique, the letter created quite a stir. Nesmith read it to Delazon Smith, who was en route that morning to join Bush and Grover on an electioneering tour through southern Oregon; Smith wouldn't believe Lane had written it and upbraided Nesmith for trying to pass it off as Lane's. Smith was not the only doubter; even Nat and Mosher questioned its authenticity. It certainly was not in Lane's style.[67]

Three days before the Eugene convention, Nesmith replied to Lane, referring to the letter as "a senseless unmeaning mess of trash"—he was surprised Hibben would publish it—and professed that he would not believe it was Lane's "until I see it in *your hand writing.*" O'Meara was nothing but "an adventurer, with less character, principle, or ability than his predecessor. Notwithstanding you had seen fit to characterize his disorganizing sheet as an '*able Journal,*' while old Cain swears that you endorse him [O'Meara], and shows a letter wherein you offered to furnish him with two thousand dollars." Bush also rapped Lane's knuckles; he had not seen a "single democrat," he wrote, who had read the letter who was not "as mad as the devil" about it. *He* wouldn't have had it

67. Nesmith to Smith (copy), Jan. 9, 1859, MS OrHi. Mosher to Hibben, Salem, April 5, 1858, Lane Papers, InU: "I do not believe the General wrote it and if he did I think it was very bad policy to have published it. It is full of meaningless generalities and has been tortured into an approval of the Standard and is doing us much injury here. I regret that I did not know it while at Portland, but one thing is certain, the impression that the General has any sympathy with that party must be corrected *at once.* We shall of course receive such letters from him soon, but in the meantime we may lose much."

Lane replied to Mosher, June 2, 1858, Lane Papers, InU: "I must however be allowed to say that I thought you were too good a soldier to be frightened at trifles. The letter to the 'Times' is mine written with care and for a proper purpose and if it did not answer the purpose intended it was not my fault. I wish very much to be one of Oregons first Senators, but would not do one single dishonest, dishonorable, or improper thing for the sake of a seat in the Senate."

published at this time for one thousand dollars, and why Hibben should have published it was more than he knew because now, at the outset of the canvass, the Softs were using Lane's letter and other assorted bits of correspondence as proof that he was for them and against the regulars. Bush hoped Lane would not further embarrass the party by sending any more letters, unless they unequivocally favored the party and were absolutely incapable of being misconstrued. The *Standard* differed little from the *Oregonian* or *Argus,* and although Lane called it an "able paper," most Oregonians thought it "d - - - - d weak." Lane had obviously been taken in by O'Meara and Cain. "Don't be deceived, General, into the idea that these 'Nationals' would support you, if they had the Legislature," he warned. "They will not do it. You have not a friend among them. . . . They have no more chance of carrying the Legislature than I have of being translated to Heaven. They are contemptibly weak."[68]

There is no doubt that Lane had been vague and pontifical in wording his letter, that he had striven too hard for effect, and that he had deliberately tried to conciliate O'Meara without giving offense. Nevertheless, the Clique failed to appreciate that he was writing only about the earliest stage of the squabble over apportionment, and that he had no way of knowing what had transpired locally since writing the letter. Yet the Clique decided "there and then," Nesmith related later, that the "question as to which side Gen'l Lane was on" was more important than any part of their platform.[69]

The Clique may have made such a decision, but it certainly did not openly oppose Lane in the campaign. This campaign was the first in which the office of public printer was elective, and Bush was

68. Nesmith to Lane, April 6, 1858, Lane Papers, InU; Bush to Lane, April 4, 1858, Lane Papers, InU. Ironically, Hibben had warned Lane (Feb. 7, 1858, Lane Papers, InU) against writing further to O'Meara: "If you write him and he publishes your letter it will be an injury to you."

69. Nesmith to Smith (copy), Jan. 9, 1859, MS OrHi.

particularly anxious to win an endorsement from the electorate in order to silence criticisms of his dictatorial rule. When the leading Republican candidates withdrew three weeks before the election, the contest turned into a two-way battle between Hards and Softs. Bush published Lane's letters without comment and concentrated his attack upon the *Standard,* which had reprinted only a portion of Lane's letter to the *Times.*[70] Delazon Smith tried to explain away the letter by saying that since O'Meara had said he would make the *Standard* a Democratic paper, Lane had tried to encourage him in this course. On the election day, the regulars prevailed but by much reduced majorities: Whiteaker over Barnum, 5,545 to 4,407; Grover over Kelly, 5,859 to 4,190; Bush, running behind the ticket, over O'Meara, 4,958 to 4,557.[71]

As prescribed by the constitution, the first state legislature convened on Monday, July 5, but, uncertain whether its actions were legal, adjourned four days later, having done little but elect two U.S. senators. On July 1, Bush reported "considerable opposition" to Lane's election but thought the caucus would nominate him. On opening day Drew estimated Lane had thirty of the thirty-eight votes. That night in caucus Lane's supporters defeated Ben Harding, the Clique's candidate for speaker of the house, by a single vote, electing instead William G. T'Vault of Jacksonville. According to one participant, when they caucused the following evening to nominate candidates for the Senate, T'Vault led Lane's backers to announce they would bolt and join the Nationals if there were any attempt to defeat Lane.[72] Outmaneuvered and impotent to

70. Bush to Deady, Feb. 16, May 8, 1858, MS OrHi; withdrawal announcement, May 21, 1858, *Weekly Oregonian,* May 22, 1858. The *Oregon Statesman* (May 25, 1858) devoted almost the whole editorial page to O'Meara.

71. Lucien Heath to Lane, May 3, 1858, Lane Papers, InU; *Oregon Weekly Times,* July 24, 1858.

72. Bush to Deady, July 1, 1858, MS OrHi; Drew to Deady, July 5, 1858, MS OrHi; J. S. McIteeny to Lane, Dec. 20, 1858, Lane Papers, InU. Stephen F. Chadwick to Deady, Salem, July 10, 1858, MS OrHi: "T'Vault

alter the situation, the Clique capitulated, and one of its bitterest critics of Lane nominated Lane and Smith for the Senate. The vote was unanimous, and the next day in the legislature, Lane received an all-but-unanimous vote—Dryer dissenting—and Smith a slightly smaller majority. "The victory is won," exulted Mosher in a letter directed to intercept Lane at San Francisco. "There has been an *open* fight made against you. I cannot give you the particulars, but send you a list of your enemies to put you on your guard. . . . There will be a change in the rulers of the party hereafter or I am much mistaken." A few days later Drew reiterated similar sentiments to Deady: "The war has commenced, as you will see by the vote on T'Vault and Harding. As Bush says, it is impossible hereafter to seperate Lane & T'Vault."[73]

Shortly after the legislature adjourned, Nesmith and Bush received Lane's replies regarding his "much abused letter to the 'Times.'" He was "never more surprised" in his life, he wrote, than to see the style and manner of Nesmith's letter. It almost seemed that Nesmith had been "looking for an excuse to pitch into" him for some time, although Lane preferred to think that his friend had merely "gone off half-cocked," as was sometimes his habit. "I am, Sir, a Democrat, true as steel, from principle and conviction, and have therefore never flinched, and never shall, from the sup-

---

is chosen speaker of the House, over Ben Harding by one vote. How this happened I cannot state, but such is the fact. I am told that Gen Lane met with much opposition at first, and I am also informed that the friends of Lane considered this act as an endorsement of Lane before the Legislature. But as to the fact I cannot state. . . . I think Gen Lane will meet with much opposition hereafter."

73. *Weekly Oregonian,* July 10, 1858; Mosher to Lane, July 9, 1858, Lane Papers, InU; Drew to Deady, July 20, 1858, MS OrHi. Drew also stated that Mosher told Smith on the way to Salem that the Clique was determined to support Nesmith over Smith, and Deady over Lane, which may have been true—at least in Smith's case. The Clique certainly wanted Deady to run, but he was adamant; see Drew to Deady, Jan. 10, 1858, MS OrHi, and Bush to Deady, July 1, 1858, MS OrHi.

port of its principles." Certainly he had written the letter, but he categorically denied any attempt to sanction disunion, and "no honest sensible man" could find a single word that could be so construed. To Bush he also protested:

> no fair sensible man, honest disinterested man (not one), will say after carefully reading my letter to the Times that it endorses bolters, disorganizers, or disorganizing sheets.
>
> You know . . . I have never in a single instance failed to give my most cordial and earnest support to the nominees of the party, have never allowed myself to loose or mis an opportunity of voting for the nominees of the party.
>
> There is another thing I wish you most distincly to understand that is that I have never in my life encouraged dissension, discord, or trouble in the democratic ranks, nor have I ever given aid or comfort to any man who did.
>
> But enough of the much abused letter. I submit it and my interests to the hands of the people. I have been faithful in all things and they know it.[74]

The *Statesman* did not begin its attack upon Lane—and then only indirectly—until August 3, by which time Bush had received Lane's letter of June 18 explaining why admission and the war bill had miscarried. Not only did Bush fail to publish that letter as requested, except for one sentence urging the organization of a state government, which Bush opposed, but he published a report from "Metropolis," a Washington correspondent, criticizing Lane's efforts in the last session of Congress. The reporter professed not to understand why Oregon's constitution passed in the Senate, where the territory had no representative, but failed in the House, where there was no great opposition. But Oregonians might console themselves that this failure would benefit Lane, should Oregon be admitted at the next session.

74. Lane to Nesmith (copy), May 31, 1858, Lane Papers, InU; Lane to Bush, June 2, 1858, Bush Papers.

> It is presumed here that Gen. Lane will be one of the U.S. Senators, and in that case he will draw mileage and pay, amounting to over $8000 per session, both in the capacity of Delegate and Senator at the next session . . . making him the comfortable little sum of about seventeen thousand dollars, as his pay and mileage for the next three months session.

And even if Lane were not elected to the Senate, he would still draw his pay as delegate. Moreover, admission would be vastly more difficult the next year, because, as the debate over Kansas indicated, many representatives were prepared to insist that Oregon also wait until she had the population required by a congressional district, which after the census of 1860 might be from 130,000 to 150,000.[75]

Following the "Metropolis" letter, Bush replied to Lane with a lengthy private communication, a reply that marked the end of correspondence between the two men for nearly twenty years.

75. "Metropolis," June 17, 1858, *Oregon Statesman,* Aug. 3, 1858. The same day Nat, who had been on very good terms with Bush to this time, cautioned his father that Bush had recently suggested Lane had been unfair to him regarding his printing claim. Nat now warned Lane against the Clique: "*They intend to put you down.* . . . You gave them a good cudgel to use against you, by writing so positive about our admission. they are using that now, saying you didn't want Oregon admitted until you knew whether you was elected to the United States Senate or not. [They] say you wrote that and about our war debt for Buncomb. . . . I wish to let these *ungrateful dogs* know that there isn't a Lane of pure blood that will ever bow the knee to them. You must shape your course so as to sail clear, knowing you will have this Salem pack of hounds yelping at your heels. I hope to see them sink so d - - - - d low using D[elazon] S[mith's] language that it will require the arm of Omnipotence to elevate them sufficiently to challenge the contempt of a decent man." The next day Nat wrote again (Lane Papers, InU) that Grover had said Bush and Deady wrote the "Metropolis" letter. Grover wanted to heal the breach between Bush and Lane, but Nat was not at all sure it would pay to buy Bush's good will: "So far as I individually am concerned I wouldnt give a snap of my fingers for the good will of the whole possy of them. I would be afraid they would sell me out to some one who would bid higher for them."

Lane might question *Bush's* honesty or sense, he declared, but a good number of persons, including most of the bolters, believed Lane's letter expressly sanctioned the National party. O'Meara even claimed Hibben had submitted it to him for approval before publication, and rumors said that Lane had invested $700 in the *Standard.* The trouble with Lane's letter was that it never clearly endorsed the central committee's ruling on apportionment and consisted instead of "unmeaning generalities" that "meant nearly anything one would have it, or nothing, as one would have it." You say your subsequent letters set your position right, *if I published them,"* Bush continued, his temper rising. "I did publish every one of them, although you seem to imply doubt."

> You say "when you found that O'Meara had left the organization you dropped him, and had nothing more to do with him." Your "dropping" did not extend so far as to cut off political correspondence with him, for . . . I myself have seen in your handwriting a copy of a letter sent to O'Meara as late as April 4th, which was certainly a month after news reached you of his open connection with the opposition. In that letter you devote considerable space to thanking him for his friendship and devotion to you, though you close it by deprecating division and dissension. But you do not say *who* or *what* you refer to. . . . In none of your public letters, did you name the "National Party" and deprecate its organization.
>
> The letter of Ap'l 4th . . . would have enabled any one to read the *first half* of it, and convince an audience that you felt under obligations to him, and looked upon him as your devoted friend.
>
> You say you "attempted to heal dissension and prevent disruption in our party." With whom are you going to reconcile us? . . . . Men with whom we wanted no connection, and with whom we could have none, except at the peril of being corrupted and disorganized.

You say and repeat that you "have never in your life neglected an opportunity to vote the 'Democratic Ticket.'" I have not impugned your democracy, and it does not become me to do so. Your allusion doubtless is to my absence in Washington Territory at the Election of last year. Well, I was absent, and much has been said by your immediate friends . . . that I left you to avoid voting for you. I will not condescend to a denial of it. . . . If I had desired to vote against you I should have done it in the Nominating Convention where I voted for you.

But you say by way of Contrast with me that "you never neglected an opportunity to vote the Democratic Ticket." I'll tell you what I never did. I have not at every election failed to vote the Democratic ticket in Oregon. I was never claimed by the opposition, to belong to them, and my position towards parties was never so equivocal that the Democratic party was forced to declare that I was with it, while the Opposition party as stoutly affirmed that I was with *it.* The opposition never charged that I privately, to members of it denounced the democratic platform, or any portion of it. And my especial friends were never found running upon or voting the opposition Ticket, and averring that they did it *as* friends of mine and by my sanction.

I have written this letter in very much the spirit I conceive yours to be dictated in; I don't think my first letter called for the suspicions it evidently engendered in your mind. You had undoubtedly been constantly informed by "GO BETWEENS" —that this and that man was untrue to your personal fortunes, and I have come in with the rest.[76]

76. Bush to Lane, Aug. 16, 1858, Lane Papers, InU; cf. Nesmith to Lane, n. d. [ca. Aug. 1858], MS OrHi, for a draft of a letter expressing similar views. Bush predicted editorially (*Oregon Statesman,* Aug. 17, 1858) that Oregon's war debt would not be paid for another three years.

The failure of Congress to admit Oregon raised the question of whether the state legislature should convene in September as prescribed by her constitution and as Lane had urged. Bush opposed it, for valid reasons, and when Hibben followed Lane's lead, the *Statesman* slowly but firmly turned its guns on the *Times*. Eleven members only, mostly Lane's supporters, journeyed to Salem in September. T'Vault called the House to order and went through the motions of organizing but was forced to adjourn for want of a quorum, to the great delight of certain Hards who refused to participate and hurled raucous insults at the Softs from the lobby of the capitol.[77]

In December, Bush flung down the gauntlet in the *Statesman*. Without mentioning Lane by name, he lashed out editorially at delegates who conferred or withheld patronage appointments on the basis of personal fealty, "as is too often the case," instead of respecting the rights and wishes of their constituents. Thompson's appointment as postal agent was a case in point. "Public offices belong to no individual whose position may enable him to control them," Bush spat out. "They belong to *the Democratic party* and the people whom the officer serves." To whom were these remarks directed? To no one in particular; to any representative in Congress of any territory or state—"to whom it justly applies, *and to nobody else.*"[78]

The next week Bush featured a pointed front-page editorial, "Personal Parties—Man-Worship," reprinted from June 30, 1857, which condemned the "shameful endeavor on foot to build up a *mere personal organization* in the democratic party, and in the country." The following week Bush laid the axe to a lame suggestion Lane had made to the *Times* that the reason Oregon was not

77. *Oregon Statesman,* Sept. 7, 14, 1858; *Weekly Oregonian,* Sept. 18, 1858.

78. *Oregon Statesman,* Dec. 7, 1858. Dryer (*Weekly Oregonian,* Dec. 18, 1858) referred to Bush's editorial as "a sugar-coated pill with strychnine inside, for Gen. Lane."

admitted the previous winter was that Oregonians had not completed their state organization: how they could have organized when the constitution specified that the first election would not be until June was "not very clear." Moreover, why had Lane not championed organization before admission failed? According to reports from Washington, Bush continued, most persons there were surprised when the bill failed and thought Lane responsible; they thought he had not wanted the bill reported out of committee because he then might be defeated for the Senate; and Representative Samuel S. Cox of Ohio had stated he would have voted for admission had not Lane requested the vote be postponed. The conclusion was inescapable: "Lane . . . has proved unfaithful and false to his trust." At last the enemy was named. In succeeding issues of the *Statesman,* the dissatisfaction and frustration of past months—even years—spilled across the pages. The Marion of Mexico, the idol of the masses, the statesman so extravagantly puffed for the presidency was hereafter *persona non grata* to the Salem machine. Vehemence formerly reserved for Leland or Dryer was now heaped upon the delegate in Washington.[79]

Lane finally replied to "Metropolis" in January by circulating an open letter to the people of Oregon. He had never before found it necessary to vindicate his official conduct in this manner, he declared, and was sure that Oregonians now would be slow to convict him of any delinquency. He had never pretended to be infallible, nor did he imagine that all of his acts would be universally approved. Even now he was not prepared to reply to "every idle charge and false accusation," but after the "extraordinary produc-

79. *Oregon Statesman,* Dec. 14, 21, 1858; cf. Lane to ed., Nov. 1, 1858, *Oregon Weekly Times,* Dec. 11, 1858. Bush's strictures against Lane were largely contrived to veil the real quarrel between them. Earlier (*Oregon Statesman,* Dec. 1, 1857), he had declared, "We have no doubt of the admission of the State . . . during the next Congress, but we do not confidently expect admission before the last session thereof, which will not meet until a year from . . . December." For a catalog of Lane's "crimes," see *Oregon Statesman,* Feb. 1, 1859.

tion" in "one of the most prominent, influential, and orthodox" newspapers in the territory, he could keep silent no longer. He could make any sacrifice, submit to any wrong, but he would not have his honor impugned. After an elaborate defense of his efforts in Congress, he explained that the rules of the Senate were more flexible than those of the House, because the upper chamber could consider any bill at any time by a simple majority vote,[80] whereas the House required a *unanimous* vote except for one day a week when a two-thirds majority was required. Furthermore, once the House referred a measure to committee it no longer retained any control, and a single member's objection could prevent a committee from reporting any item until it appeared in the regular order of business. The charge that Lane would act from mercenary motives was doubly absurd; he already had refused any additional compensation. He thought it

> singular, indeed, that at this late day, after being often blamed by my friends for what they regarded as a culpable indifference to money, I should suddenly become such an ardent devotee of Mammon, as to betray a confiding constituency that I might put a few dollars in my pocket. . . . Betray my constituents for money! . . . None but the most sordid wretch could have brought such a charge against me.

Finally, he reviewed his many legislative achievements for the people of Oregon. And with them, "the highest tribunal on earth," he would rest his case. In the meantime, he would labor faithfully with Grover and Smith for the admission of Oregon, and they would "cooperate as one man" in all matters relating to the interest of the new state.[81]

80. The Senate required a two-thirds majority. Nichols, *Disruption of American Democracy*, pp. 222–23.

81. *Letter of Hon. Joseph Lane, to the People of Oregon* [Washington, 1859]. Lane was apparently scrupulously honest. Deady wrote Nesmith (March 20, 1859, MS OrHi): Lane "makes the most of that indiscreet

Delazon Smith, as Curry pointedly observed, had "a winning way to make men dislike him." His penchant for long and verbose sentences, filled with flowery metaphor and rhetorical allusion, had earned him the sobriquet, "The Lion of Linn County," but the more common denomination was simply "Delusion." Inordinately ambitious, he had early ingratiated himself into the good graces of the Clique, but his relations with Salem had suddenly cooled. Before leaving for Washington, he told Nat that he was *"down on the Salem movement"* and friendly to Lane. "I hope you and him and Grover will be able to get along well," Nat wrote his father. "If you do all the 'Salem Cliques' this side of Jordan cant prevent your reelection. . . . I dont think any of the Clique are to be relied upon, especially their good feeling towards you. But . . . I wouldn't let any of them poison me against Smith and Grover." Grover, on the other hand, enjoyed greater popularity among the electorate than any other prominent member of the Clique. He regretted the rapidly growing rift between Bush and Lane and was willing to do what he could to repair the breach.[82] In late September the two new representatives from Oregon departed for Washington.

Bush almost certainly expected his two colleagues to send back evidence to substantiate the *Statesman's* charges against Lane,[83]

---

insinuation about *money* in the Metropolis letter. I told Bush at the time that Ancient was not vulnerable on that point." Even Bush was circumspect; in the *Statesman* (Feb. 8, 1859) he declared, "We have not charged him with being influenced by motives of pecuniary gain, and do not believe he was." Nat once complained (Nat to Lane, Dec. 12, 1852, MS OrHi) that his father was "very much in the habit of paying debts [he] did not owe."

82. Curry to Lane, May 2, 1858, Lane Papers, InU; Nat to Lane, Sept. 10, Aug. 4, 1858, Lane Papers, InU.

83. The *Oregon Sentinel* ran a series of articles in 1859 charging that Bush had made an understanding with them to this effect. Carey, *Oregon Historical Quarterly*, 27, 29.

and Lane, for his part, was equally determined to afford them no basis for complaint. Oregon's delegation, he promised, would "act together, vote together, and stick together . . . for the common good of the common people." He had good reason to pursue such a course, for, as he told his son-in-law, Aaron D. Shelby of Portland, he might draw the short term in the Senate, which would expire early in March. "Now if you will stand by the friends of Smith, and his friends in that event will stand by me, all will be right . . . Bush to the contrary notwithstanding."[84]

From Washington, Smith immediately sent back predictions that Oregon would be admitted as soon as Congress assembled; all was in readiness, their desks and chairs already in place. But to Nesmith, who was worried that Lane might effect his removal, Smith protested that the press in Oregon, and the *Statesman* especially, was furnishing the opposition with all sorts of ammunition.

> *It requires more labor here in Washington to counteract the influence of the Oregon press, than it does to meet and vanquish all its* OTHER *enemies!* If we talk about the Admission of Oregon, the payment of our war debt, etc, etc, we are told to *look at the declarations contained in the Oregon Newspapers!*
>
> The position, tone and influence of even the *Statesman* is with Dryer & O'Meara *against the admission of Oregon!* What in God's name is meant by this?

Smith also declared that Lane had been much mortified by the blunt criticisms of his letter to the *Times,* that he had admitted it might have been unwise and impolitic to have it published when it was, and that he had desired only to unite the party but was misled and deceived by O'Meara's course. Lane had not sought to procure

84. Lane to Shelby, Dec. 1, 1858, Lane Papers, InU.

Nesmith's removal but, on the contrary, had spoken highly of him, both privately and in public.[85]

Early in December, Bush asked Grover about patronage, particularly whether Lane had promised any office to Hibben, who was then returning to Washington. After denouncing Lane for neglecting the admission bill, Bush requested Smith to get a copy of Cox's speech in Ohio before Lane got him "to plaster it up," and to furnish any other evidence that Lane had sought to prevent admission. "I have taken issue with him on that as you will see, and I should like all the proofs I can get. Since the break has been made you would be surprised at the number of men who have thought for several years that he was an old humbug."[86]

Grover replied rather guardedly that he did not think Lane had any intention, now or ever, of giving Hibben an appointment because he thought him not "steady enough." Moreover, Lane was disposed to give Grover and Smith an equal say in patronage once Oregon was admitted. "There is some Presidential talk here in view of '60," he added. "Lane has some strength that way—more than you would believe." Smith was less restrained, in part because he faced financial ruin if admission failed and he was unable to draw his salary and mileage. Some months earlier in the *Statesman* he had estimated Oregon's population in excess of 100,000, but Bush had since published certain "census returns" that listed the population at less than 43,000, which the opponents of admission were now citing with devastating effect. From what he had learned from leading members of Congress, Smith wrote Bush, he was convinced that Lane had been right and Bush wrong about proceeding

85. Smith to Bush, Nov. 18, 1858, *Oregon Statesman,* Dec. 28, 1858; Smith to Nesmith, Nov. 30, 1858, MS OrHi. Grover to Nesmith, Dec. 18, 1858, MS OrHi, further vindicated Lane's conduct toward Nesmith. See also *Congressional Globe,* 35 Cong., 2 Sess., p. 252, for Lane's defense of Nesmith.

86. Bush to Grover, Dec. 4, 1858, cited in Grover to Bush, Jan. 18, 1859, Bush Papers; *Oregon Weekly Times,* Dec. 4, 1858; Bush to Smith, Dec. 25, 1858, cited in Carey, *Oregon Historical Quarterly,* 27, 30.

to organize a state government.[87] He was willing to serve Bush, he said, but it would be folly to quarrel with Lane, even if he were so inclined, because Lane's influence with the Administration was enormous—"*no* man in Washington has more." Lane had not opposed the Clique in making appointments for the new federal offices to be created in Oregon; Bush had recommended the appointees for district attorney, marshal, and district judge, and he would not disapprove the replacements for the collector of customs at Port Orford and receiver of the land office at Oregon City. Smith had formed no "alliances" with Lane, he continued; he was merely doing the General simple justice against Bush's ill-timed and unjustified assaults.

> You speak of my "*excessive praise*" of Gen. Lane. . . . There is *not a man* in Washington who will not exonorate him from the charges against him. . . . *You* came to Washington a few years ago and returned home full of friendship and *admiration* for the General. . . . I came here [as] his colleague in the Senate. I was overwhelmed with the evidence of his innocence upon the matter charged against him, and I am bidden to keep silent. . . . If General Lane is *really* culpable—if he has been derelict in *fact,* then shew the facts, expose and denounce and I [will] have not one word to say.
>
> Of General Lane's prospects for the Presidency, you are also *very* skeptical. . . . I know that at this present writing his chances for the Charleston nomination are *better* than those of any other living man! . . . These suggestions may be "simply laughed at" in Oregon, but they are *not* laughed at in the Atlantic States.
>
> You say, "I firmly believe we did not go in at the last session because he did not know that he was Senator." I know that

87. Grover to Bush, Jan. 18, 1859, Bush Papers; Smith to Bush, Jan. 1, 1858, *Oregon Statesman,* Feb. 23, 1858; ibid., Nov. 16, 1858; Smith to Bush, Feb. 1, 1859, ibid., March 15, 1859. Bush's figures, whether "official" or not, were probably quite accurate. The population of Oregon in 1860 was 52,465.

> you are mistaken! And you must excuse me when I say that I *must* act upon my *knowledge* rather than your *belief!* And this, I take it, is the only point in which I have sinned.
>
> Of course, if what I have frankly written, and in the very best of temper and feeling, shall have the effect to alienate your friendship, I have only to say that whilst I shall regret it, I cannot help it.[88]

While these exchanges were transpiring, the second session of the Thirty-fifth Congress was well under way. Lane's first major setback came early in February when the chairman of the House Committee on Military Affairs reported Oregon's war bill, with the recommendation that the Treasury Department examine the vouchers, allow the same wages as for regular troops (eight to eleven dollars per month), and report back at the beginning of the next Congress. Lane was crestfallen. The report was "not what I expected when the chairman told me, at the last session, that he should report for action at the beginning of this present session. I supposed a bill would be reported to pay as allowed by the war commission, and as very properly recommended by the Secretary of War." He further objected that it was grossly unfair to expect volunteers to leave their homes at a moment's notice in return for compensation so obviously inferior to the level of wages in the territory. He suggested, to no avail, an amendment that would have provided each volunteer with a bonus equivalent to the cost of transporting a regular from the East. He declined an opportunity

88. Smith to Bush, Feb. 2, 1859, Bush Papers. Grover wrote to Bush "in strict confidence" (March 5, 1859, Bush Papers): "You ask about Genl Lane's course here. After a careful examination of his conduct here I cannot find but that he has done all he could to push forward our State Bill and war bill as fast as possible. . . . If I had any facts which would be of use to you in the line mentioned in your letter, at your request I should feel bound to communicate them. . . . My personal relations with Gen Lane are the same as they always have been. I am not his confident nor he mine." Smith also sent to the *Times* (March 12, 1859) a letter from Sam Cox (Jan. 29, 1859), denying he had said that Lane had requested postponing admission.

on the last day of the session to attach the war bill as an amendment to the civil appropriation bill in the Senate, because he was afraid of alienating members of the House who had requested more information.[89]

The bill for the admission of Oregon had been lying on the desk of Committee Chairman Alexander H. Stephens for some time, when on January 7 he announced that he desired to report it at the earliest opportunity. When a Republican member inquired if there would be an opportunity for debate, Stephens assured him of "as long a discussion upon it as it may require." That night the Republicans caucused and decided to oppose Oregon's admission as a means of forcing the Administration to reverse its policy toward Kansas.[90] Several days later the committee submitted for printing a minority report incorporating these demands, but only on February 10 was Stephens permitted to introduce the bill. The debate raged for three days, including one evening session.

In presenting the majority report, Stephens reminded his colleagues that two years earlier they had passed an enabling act for Oregon, that the Oregonians had drawn up a constitution and approved it by a sizable majority, and that the Senate accordingly had voted for admission. According to his calculations, the population of the territory approached 130,000, well above the ratio required for representation in the House. Opponents of admission countered with figures of their own—and those of the *Statesman*—to show that the population was actually less than half that number. Lane argued that there had been a very poor turnout in the last election, that the poll would have been doubled if the Oregonians participating in the Fraser River and Klamath Lake gold rushes had voted, and that the population was at least 93,000, exclusive of Chinese. He defended the constitutional provision excluding Negroes from Oregon and denying them access to the courts with the statement that Oregonians simply did not want Negroes around because they tended to ally with the Indians against the whites;

89. *Congressional Globe,* 35 Cong., 2 Sess., pp. 885–88, 1612.
90. Ibid., 266; Simms, *Mississippi Valley Historical Review, 32,* 364.

moreover, Negroes would need no protection from the law if they were not allowed in the state in the first place. In comparison with the generally high caliber of debate in which both sides offered some penetrating arguments, Lane's contributions were minor indeed. But the issue was not to be decided on the basis of eloquence or rhetoric. When the vote came, partisan advantage prevailed, for the most part, over principle or consistency, although fifteen Republicans abandoned their colleagues, thereby ensuring passage of the bill by a slender 114–103 majority.[91]

There was rejoicing that night in Washington as news of Oregon's admission spread. About half-past nine a large concourse of celebrants, led by the United States Marine Band, serenaded Lane at Brown's Hotel. From the balcony, Isaac Stevens introduced the new senator from Oregon, and Lane replied with a very brief speech, asking to be excused because "although a man of iron, I have been so constantly on duty, laboring day and night to bring about this glorious result, that I find myself worn out; and, for

91. For Lane's remarks, see *Congressional Globe,* 35 Cong., 2 Sess., pp. 943–46, 970–71, 1004–05, and *Appendix,* 108–10. For a summary of the arguments and an analysis of the vote, see Simms, *Mississippi Valley Historical Review, 32,* 365–74.

On May 28, 1859, both the *Argus* and *Oregonian* reprinted a letter (April 9, 1859) from Schuyler Colfax to a local resident, W. C. Johnson, suggesting that Lane's stand on Lecompton was responsible for alienating Republican votes. Lane, wrote Colfax, "was one of the men who had used all his personal influence in favor of that political iniquity, the Lecompton Constitution, and its equally worthy successor, the English bill. He, of course, refused now to say whether he would vote in the U.S. Senate, if admitted there, to repeal the English prohibition which he had so earnestly labored to impose on Kansas; and his political friends in the House refused also to assent to its repeal in any manner or form whatever. This, of course, impelled many Republicans to insist that Oregon, with her Lecompton delegation, should wait for admission till Kansas, with her Republican delegation was ready to come in with her. With a less obnoxious delegation from Oregon, the votes of many Republicans would have been different."

While Lane's vociferous support of Lecompton undoubtedly alienated Republicans, they would probably have opposed any Democratic delegation as Simms' analysis suggests.

once in my life, in need of repose." Hibben, who sent back a report to the *Oregon Weekly Times,* declared, "the very earth seemed to tremble beneath the shouts of applause with which he was greeted . . . at the termination of each sentence." Several other supporters of the bill responded with short congratulatory speeches, after which the procession marched on the White House. Buchanan appeared at a window, said he presumed from this demonstration that the Oregon bill had passed, congratulated Lane for the "honor that he had fairly deserved," and then called on the band for "Yankee Doodle." Continuing its rounds, the crowd paid their respects to other legislators who had supported the measure, including Republican Eli Thayer of Massachusetts, who had made a brilliant nonpartisan appeal in the House, Stephen A. Douglas and House Speaker James L. Orr, who had both retired, and Vice-President John C. Breckinridge, the presiding officer of the Senate, who admitted that "whenever he could, he gave the bill a push."[92]

On Monday, February 14, Lane and Smith took their seats in the Senate. George E. Pugh of Ohio presented Lane's credentials, and Gwin of California those of Delazon Smith. After they took their oaths, the secretary placed two numbered pieces of paper in the ballot box, number "one" for the term ending March 3, 1861, and number "two," the term ending March 3, 1859. Lane drew first and selected number "one," leaving Smith with a term of but eighteen days.[93]

92. *The Admission of Oregon. The Serenades—The Responses* (Washington, L. Towers, 1859?); Hibben to ed., Feb. 18, 1859, *Oregon Weekly Times,* April 2, 1859; *Washington Union,* cited ibid.

93. *Congressional Globe,* 35 Cong., 2 Sess., p. 1019.

In subsequent years, Lane must surely have pondered what the effect on his political career would have been had he drawn the short term. It appears almost certain that he would have campaigned for re-election, and if he had won, which at least seems possible, he then would have been entitled to a seat in the Senate until March 1865.

*Chapter 6*

# AFTERMATH AND FINALE

Compared to the big-tent performance by Buchanan and Douglas, the quarrel between Lane and Bush was merely a side show, although Oregonians regarded it as a feature attraction. Most of them closed their eyes to the larger contest, and even in late 1858 few discerned any relationship between the two struggles. Yet within a few months, the overpowering national issues supplanted all local differences and forced a complete realignment of factions in Oregon.

The Dred Scott decision, which denied the right of a territory to prohibit slavery, directly challenged Douglas' concept of popular sovereignty whereby a territory might decide for or against slavery at any time. After Oregon's referendum on slavery and the state constitution in November 1857, Bush attempted to reconcile this ominous contradiction by arguing that it was "the very gist of the Kansas-Nebraska principle that the *people* are called upon when they form a State government, to act upon the subject of slavery," which was the position taken by the Administration and Lane. Debates in the legislature that winter revealed that the Hards were divided about the status of slavery in the territories, an earnest of trouble, despite the efforts of the Clique to present a united front.[1]

Word of Douglas' break with Buchanan over Lecompton reached Oregon late in January 1858, causing, said the *Oregonian,* "a terrible fluttering in the democratic camp." The next week Dryer challenged Bush to "inform his numerous party and political *admirers* which side he is on; whether for Buchanan or Douglas." Despite his well-known admiration for Douglas, Bush hesitated to commit himself for fear of further dividing the party, already shaken by the Nationalist bolt, and of losing control of the public printing. "There is no difference between the President and Mr. Douglas in matter of any vital principle involved," he declared blandly, predicting that they would amicably resolve their quarrel before the end of the current session. "The Administration have taken a moderate, firm, and wise course, and will see to it, that justice be done to Kansas." He did, however, mention that Douglas denied the President's position and raised "issues of fact tending to vitiate [its] basis."[2] To Deady he wrote, "I think Douglas' position is undeniably correct in principle, and in strict conformity to *his* Nebraska bill. But the conduct of the free State men . . . leaves them without much right to complain, and I am not certain but

1. *Oregon Statesman,* Dec. 8, 1857. For the debates in the legislature, see *Weekly Oregonian,* Dec. 26, 1857, Jan. 30, 1858. There is no doubt that the Softs, led by William Allen of Yamhill County, were delighted to thus embarrass the Clique.

2. *Weekly Oregonian,* Jan. 30, Feb. 6, 1858; *Oregon Statesman,* March 2, 1858.

that I would vote for the Lecompton Constitution *if* I was in Congress." "For Gods sake dont say 'that Douglas is right in principle,'" Deady retorted. "He is neither right in 'principle' or 'policy.'" In like manner the judge urged Lane to stand by the Lecompton constitution, adding that Douglas' "political departure was only a question of time." From Astoria, John Adair prophetically warned that Bush's free-soil proclivities would soon spell trouble. "I have read his paper closely for the last four or five months, and every time he has made a foot-print upon the Slavery, or Kansas issue, it has been on the wrong side," he told Lane. "He has laboured hard to avoid exciting the jealousy or distrust of pro-slavery men, but it has been too clear that he is 'trimming his sails' to catch any but *landsmen*. He will not dare make a move before the election, but my word and judgement upon it, he will go for Douglass in 1860."[3]

Throughout the hectic campaign for the first state legislature, the subsequent election of United States senators, and the break with Lane that eventually became public, Bush continued to straddle the fence. Then in mid-December, news came of the elections in Illinois. Dryer reported that the announcement in the legislature of Douglas' victory over Lincoln produced among Democrats a "sudden conversion . . . almost equal to that of Pentecost." The first *Statesman* in January 1859 declared, "Heretofore, we Oregonians have taken little or no part in the discussion of the questions at issue between the great political parties which

3. Bush to Deady, Feb. 12, 1858, MS OrHi; Deady to Bush, March 7, 1858, Bush Papers; Deady to Lane, Feb. 7, 1858, MS OrHi; Adair to Lane, April 7, 1858, Lane Papers, InU. Bush to Deady (March 23, 1858, MS OrHi): "I didn't say that 'Douglas was right on principle.' I said he was right under the Nebraska law, or that, in substance. . . . If I was in Congress I think, under all the circumstances, I should vote for Lecompton. But if I had been a member of the Kansas convention I should have voted for submission, and had I been one of the 'sovereigns' there, I would have voted against it, for I think there are numerous objectionable clauses in it. Still, it is 'republican,' under the constitution."

are contending for the supremacy in our government."[4] Bush did not immediately break with the Administration, but in the next few months he came out strongly for Douglas.

The factional realignment crystallized further during the debates in the legislature that winter, but the head-on confrontation between the Bush and Lane forces occurred during the state Democratic convention in the spring. The struggle began in early January when the state central committee met to fix the date for the convention; the Clique wanted it as early as possible, but Lane's friends managed by a single vote to postpone it until April 20.[5] The Clique, however, succeeded in apportioning delegates upon Whiteaker's vote in the last election, which effectively excluded delegates from counties of greatest National strength and gave the six counties in which the Clique was strongest a clear majority in the convention. With both sides pursuing a collision course, each appealed to the power of patronage. For example, Nesmith, who controlled more patronage than any other officer in Oregon, allegedly sought to silence a critic of the Clique by offering him an Indian agency. But in this area Lane clearly held the upper hand. In response to repeated warnings, he chopped off the appointments of Nesmith and Zieber and replaced them with loyal partisans, Edward R. Geary and William W. Chapman of Lane County. About this time the Lane-Smith coalition began to jell. In February, Drew found Shelby busy at Albany in behalf of his "parent in law" and warned Bush that the voters there were greatly agitated lest the *Statesman* also attempt to "kill off" Smith. "*They* say Linn County will never consent to give up Delazon—that if Marion & Polk throw off on Delazon, Linn will throw off on Grover and

4. Deady to Nesmith, Nov. 11, 1858, MS OrHi: "Bush very adroitly dodges the attack upon his position or *want* of position on Lecompton." *Weekly Oregonian,* Dec. 18, 1858; *Oregon Statesman,* Jan. 4, 1859.

5. *Weekly Oregonian,* Jan. 15, 22, 1859; J. W. Mack to Lane, Jan. 10, 1859, Lane Papers, InU; *Oregon Weekly Times,* March 26, 1859.

*Bush! ! !* They threaten a great deal and use very unfair arguments and assume false positions and I fear Linn County is going to adhere to Delazon and support Lane with him."[6]

And so it was. When the convention met, prominent Lane men —Mosher, T'Vault, Shelby, Martin, and others—invited the ten delegates from Linn County to a secret caucus over the barroom of Burns' Saloon, where they drew up a slate of candidates calculated to unite all opposition to the Clique: Smith for the Senate, Lansing Stout (who had come to Oregon two years before as a partner in Farrar's law office in Portland) for Congress, Chapman for president of the convention, and W. Stewart Brock from Lane County for chairman of the state central committee. They also agreed to support Eugene City's aspirations to become the state capital. The next day the convention elected Chapman over Nesmith, forty-two to thirty, and Stout over Grover by an almost identical majority, forty to thirty-three. Four of the five members on the resolutions committee supported Lane; and their resolutions, apparently written by Mosher, endorsed the Cincinnati Platform, the Dred Scott decision, and the Buchanan administration, but said nothing about popular sovereignty. The fourth resolution, "that we approve of and rejoice over that thorough and harmonious union of the party, which has displaced past differences, and given assurances of future united action" was adopted, reported Bush, "amid much laughter"; a final resolution endorsing Oregon's delegation in Congress passed with thirty dissenting votes. Lane's supporters also gained control of the state central committee and elected Brock chairman.[7]

At last the tables were turned, and the Clique sang a new song. "You have doubtless heard of the Damnable outrage perpetrated by Lane & Smiths friends in our mis-called Democratic convention," Nesmith growled to Deady a few days later.

6. *Weekly Oregonian,* Feb. 19, 1859; Mosher to Lane, Jan. 6, 1858 [i.e. 1859], Lane Papers, InU; Drew to Bush, Feb. 15, 1859, Bush Papers.

7. Nesmith to Deady, April 25, 1859, MS OrHi; *Oregon Statesman,* April 26, 1859.

> I boldly denounced the *"dirty bargain"* in the convention, laid the thing open to public gaze—exposed Stouts know-nothingism in California. My friends say that I made two of the best speeches of my life, and I only wish that you could have heard them. We refused to ratify Stouts nomination by a unanimous vote, and denounced it openly before and after it was made. . . . So you may know Hell is broke loose.

Bush affected as calm a pose as possible in the next *Statesman,* but his editorial nonetheless bristled with venomous disdain at the "artful device, foul proscription, and unholy bargaining" by which Grover had been so ruthlessly sacrificed. "We candidly believe that Grover, in the next Congress, would be worth more to the interests of Oregon than all the service Gen. Lane could render there in a lifetime."[8]

Grover and Smith returned separately from Washington just as the campaign was getting under way; Lane followed later, debarking at the Umpqua rather than Portland, because he was suffering from a severe cold and wished to go directly home. After a few days indoors, he was sufficiently recovered to attend a debate in Roseburg between Stout and David Logan, a former Whig and an advocate of popular sovereignty whom the Republicans had nominated. "I was pleased with Stout," he wrote to Lafayette back in Washington; "he is a good democrat and will if elected make us a good member."[9] Shortly thereafter Lane left for Salem, where the state legislature was holding a special session to fill Smith's vacated seat in the Senate.

Lane arrived in Salem on a Wednesday afternoon and discovered that the party was hopelessly divided. A caucus on Monday had adjourned over the question of admitting former Nationals; they were admitted the next day, and the caucus yielded four identical

8. Nesmith to Deady, April 25, 1859, MS OrHi; *Oregon Statesman,* April 26, 1859.

9. Lane to Lafayette, May 18, 1859, Lane Papers, InU.

votes—Grover seventeen, Smith eleven, Curry seven, Williams four, and Chapman four. Caucuses on Wednesday and Thursday accomplished nothing, and on Friday seventeen ballots were cast in which Smith reached a maximum of sixteen votes. On Saturday night, so Bush charged, Lane threw a "liquor party," a "'sociable' at which the brandy and wine flowed freely," and on Monday, Smith was elected twenty-two to twenty-one. In the legislature, however, the Clique had the final word. After repeated wrangling in both houses, the Clique's adherents in the senate walked out on the next to last day of the session, leaving that body without a quorum and the state without a second senator for the next Congress. If a Democratic party still exists, moaned the *Statesman,* it is "an organized band of brainless personal adherents, freshly drawn from opposition ranks, and as vindictively determined as ever, to defeat and drive from public confidence every man whose record marks him as a faithful, consistent democrat."[10]

The campaign between Stout and Logan promised to be as heated as the senatorial contest. Bush gave halfhearted support to the Democratic nominee, although his sympathies were covertly with Logan. Lane plunged into the battle with desperate determination to "save the state from . . . the republicans," convinced that "Bush and his gang have prepared the way for going over to that party." Speaking once or twice a day and riding as much as fifty miles in twenty-four hours, he and Smith canvassed all of the counties in the Willamette Valley before proceeding to the southern portion of the state. The campaign was more bitter than any other in Oregon's history, and Lane encountered much abuse. Speeches formerly hailed by the *Statesman* as "sensible" or "sound" now became vehicles of "*coarse personal abuse,*" "disgusting egotism," "vulgar witticisms," and "shocking profanity." Bush declared that Lane's speech in Salem—"his old speech, a little more strongly interlarded with self laudation, than it used to be"—actually hurt

10. *Oregon Statesman,* May 31, June 7, 14, 1859. Cf. *Weekly Oregonian,* June 11, 1859.

Stout. In one other respect the campaign was unique: for the first time in Oregon an election was fought over principle, not merely personality. The *Statesman* and Logan championed Douglas' concept of popular sovereignty against the "*absurd* doctrine," represented by Lane, Smith, and Stout, that the people of a territory could exclude slavery only when forming a state constitution.[11]

Lane claimed he had never before "worked so hard and so anxiously, as in the late election," and he was much gratified by the returns. So close was the vote that it took some time to determine the winner, but the final tally gave Stout 5,646 votes to Logan's 5,630. Marion County, headquarters of the Clique, gave Logan a majority of 1,062 to 296.[12]

Lane returned to Washington before the final encounter between the Clique and the new masters of the party machinery. "What are you going to advise your friends to do," Drew asked Bush in August, "if the present central committee of the Lane 'Society' call a convention to assemble at Eugene this fall to elect delegates to the Charleston Convention—the representation being based on Stout's vote?" It was a pertinent question. Bush had already served notice that future apportionment must be based on the vote for Whiteaker, but Bush was no longer calling the tune. Drew thought that if Stout's vote were followed, the old central committee ought to call another convention based on Whiteaker's vote. "Would not the moral effect of a convention of democrats instructing against Lane have some influence abroad and at home also?" he queried. Another Hard from Lane County suggested instead that they revert to the old basis of apportionment by population, the basis used for the lower house of the legislature.[13]

11. Lane to Lafayette, July 2, 1859, Lane Papers, InU; *Oregon Statesman,* June 14, 21, May 21, 1859.

12. Lane to Lafayette, July 17, 1859, Lane Papers, InU; *Oregon Statesman,* July 26, 1859.

13. Drew to Bush, Aug. 15, 1859, Bush Papers. *Oregon Statesman,* July 19, 1859; W. W. Bristow to Bush, Aug. 18, 1859, Bush Papers.

When Brock called a meeting of the state central committee at Eugene in September, Bush replied with an editorial urging all members to attend, even though the committee had "no more authority to call a convention of the democratic party than have any other nineteen members," but to bolt if Whiteaker's vote were not accepted as the basis of representation. When the committee met—Nat served as secretary—it unanimously resolved to call a convention at Eugene, November 16, to elect delegates to the national convention in Charleston. Mosher then moved that representation be based on the returns of Stout's election, which Drew promptly amended to substitute the vote for Whiteaker. The amendment was defeated nine to six. Drew resolutely led the minority out of the meeting and proceeded to draft an "Address to the Democracy of Oregon," denouncing the committee as a "cabal intent on prostituting the democratic organization to a mere contemptible Lane Society," and recommending instead that each county send delegates to Eugene on the basis of Whiteaker's vote. "The result," said the *Statesman,* "is not different from what we had anticipated."[14]

Predicting an "exciting time" at Eugene, Dryer sent a correspondent to report the convention. He was not disappointed. Even before the convention was fully organized, a supporter of the Clique moved that the credentials committee accept members on the basis of Whiteaker's vote. Ignoring Grover's warning that adoption or rejection of this resolution would be regarded as a test case, Mosher moved to table the motion. When the credentials committee, overwhelmingly in favor of Lane, reported on the basis of Stout's vote, thus reducing the delegates from Marion by six and from Polk by four, Grover again rose to his feet.

> MR. GROVER—I wish to say that there is a portion of the delegation desirous at the present moment to withdraw. I am authorized by *eight counties* here, to say . . . that they

14. *Oregon Statesman,* Sept. 6, Oct. 4, 1859.

> retire from the Convention upon this decision. . . . They do not [do] so on any feeling. They are present here without authority to sit longer in the Convention.
>
> MR. MOSHER—I beg leave to call the gentleman (Mr. Grover) to order.
>
> MR. GROVER—(To Mosher) The gentleman is through. (Laughter.)
>
> A VOICE—You are [too] slow. (Laughter.)
>
> Here Mr. Grover withdrew amidst much laughter, followed by all the Salemites.

Thereafter, Smith was elected president of the convention, taking his seat "amidst cries and stamping of feet." That night the convention elected Lane, Stout, and Deady (who had left for Washington with Lane) as their delegates to Charleston, and Adair, John F. Miller, and John K. Lamerick as alternates—proslavery men all. The resolutions committee, of which Mosher was a member, reported shrewdly worded resolutions, recommending "our distinguished fellow citizen, Gen. Joseph Lane, as the first choice of the Democracy of Oregon for the Presidency, and our delegates are hereby instructed . . . to give a hearty and earnest support to the nominee of the Charleston Convention, whoever he may be." Mosher thus obtained a unanimous endorsement of Lane even though some delegates had come otherwise instructed. Even Bush grudgingly admired Mosher's skillful maneuver, a device "no less ingenious and successful than that with which he cheated the delegates and defeated the popular will at the State Convention last spring." "We think," continued Bush, "we never heard of a readier or more effective way of getting rid of express instructions."[15]

The past year had proved most eventful. What began as a private quarrel between Lane and Bush had blossomed into a full-fledged struggle for supremacy in the party along clear-cut ideological

15. *Weekly Oregonian,* Nov. 5, 26, 1859; *Oregon Statesman,* Nov. 22, 1859.

lines. Both sides had fought savagely with everything at their disposal. Lane wielded patronage with devastating effect, removing the Indian superintendent's office to Portland, the surveyor general's office to Eugene, and the land office in Winchester to Roseburg, whose residents had long coveted it. He may also have suggested a third land office for The Dalles. Drew complained that there were only two officeholders in Coos County that had not "sold out body & soul" to Lane, and one of them, his brother, expected to be dismissed at any time. "I think Lane would have the Light House removed if he could," he concluded petulantly.[16]

The factional realignment, which was exhibited so dramatically at the convention in Eugene, also affected the Democratic press. The *Statesman* became the leading spokesman for Douglas. In the *Standard,* until it suspended permanently in July, O'Meara's course was surprisingly equivocal and vacillating—Dryer protested that it was "difficult to tell which side O'Meara takes in the contest between Lane and Bush"—but he then went to the Jacksonville *Sentinel,* which became one of the most rabidly proslavery journals in the state. After Hibben's departure, the *Times* lost much of its political zeal and languished under a vague, noncommittal course. Delazon Smith, on the other hand, established a new paper at Albany, the *Oregon Democrat,* in a bold attempt to destroy the *Statesman* and promote the fortunes of Lane and himself. Several new papers were established following statehood, among which The Dalles *Journal,* the *Roseburg Express,* and the Corvallis *Oregon Weekly Union,* an indirect successor to Avery's *"Ox,"* all espoused the National cause. By November the *Oregonian* complained that every proslavery newspaper in the state had aligned behind Lane.[17]

Slavery also intruded upon personal relationships. After the

16. *Oregon Statesman,* July 26, 1859; Drew to Bush, Aug. 29, 1859, Bush Papers.

17. *Weekly Oregonian,* Feb. 5, Nov. 26, 1859.

"bust up" of the state central committee in September, Nesmith appeared almost to have lost his sense of humor.

> We have now a fair prospect of being represented at Charleston by a double set of delegates [he glumly wrote Deady]. The sentiment of oposition to Joseph is daily becoming stronger, and however much you may regrett it, I am satisfied that his career of humbugging, dishonesty, and deception, is rappidly drawing to a close. You inform me in your letter that "Genl Lane" is afflicted with a felon on his hand. I suppose that you refer to the individual who in our early correspondence used to be characterised as the "*Sen*ate," The "True principles [of the government]," "Old Humbug" etc, but as the poet says, "times arnt as they used to was." I have heard that his hand had become nearly as rotten as his heart. if it be true his situation is deploreable indeed.

No, times were no longer "as they used to was." The slavery issue, as Bush stated editorially in July 1859, had "overwhelmed and swallowed up all questions of minor magnitude and importance," even such matters as the tariff, internal improvements, and the Pacific Railroad. "As this question will be the principal, and perhaps the only issue in the Presidential campaign of 1860," he continued, "it will probably be determined definitely by the result of that campaign."[18]

"Speculations still continue as to who will be the next Candidate for the Presidency," wrote Buchanan in August 1859 to his Secretary of War. "I had not a very good opportunity of ascertaining the public sentiment of Penna. on this subject . . . nor has this been formed; but there is considerable talk both of Lane & Breckenridge." "Here as you found it in Pa.," replied John B. Floyd, con-

18. Nesmith to Deady, Oct. 7, 1859, MS OrHi; *Oregon Statesman,* July 5, 1859.

valescing at one of Virginia's famous spas, "the chief prominence is given to Breckinridge & Lane in the public conversation for the presidency. If Lane's friends make no mistake, his prospects will be better than those of any other man I know. There is a feeling of great kindness expressed for him by everyone, and those to whom the idea of his candidacy is new are strongly impressed with his availability." This preoccupation with kingmaking was not confined to the executive branch; the new Congress that assembled in December was just as much interested in electing the next president as it was in enacting legislation. For Democrats the first session of the Thirty-sixth Congress was merely a rehearsal for Charleston.[19]

Congress met in the shadow of John Brown's seizure of a federal arsenal at Harper's Ferry, Virginia, in an abortive attempt to incite a slave rebellion; the legislators answered the first roll call three days after Brown's limp body swung heavily from the scaffold. After the opening exercises in the Senate, the senior member from Virginia rose to demand a formal investigation of the late "invasion" of the Old Dominion, while members of the House plunged into a two-month contest for the speakership, re-enacting the sorry spectacle of 1855. The day after the House finally compromised on a speaker, Jefferson Davis of Mississippi assumed Calhoun's mantle as champion of Southern rights by introducing a series of resolutions in the Senate that directly opposed Douglas' doctrine of popular sovereignty. The resolutions denounced all Northern harassments and attacks of the South's institutions; declared that territories could exclude slavery only when ready for statehood; denied to Congress or a territory any right to legislate, either positively or negatively, against slavery in the territories; and, advancing even beyond Calhoun, asserted that Congress must provide all "needful protection" to slave property in the territories.

19. Buchanan to Floyd, Aug. 5, 1858, cited in Philip Gerald Auchampaugh, *James Buchanan and His Cabinet on the Eve of Secession* (Lancaster, privately printed, 1926), p. 57; Floyd to Buchanan, Aug. 8, 1859, ibid., p. 58; Nichols, *Disruption of American Democracy,* p. 270.

Modified slightly in a party caucus, the resolutions were then resubmitted for Senate approval, a Southern ultimatum just three weeks before the Charleston convention.

Although he made no major speeches, Lane took a more active role in debate than he had in the House, perhaps because his committee assignments involved him in more legislation, or perhaps simply because there were fewer members in the Senate. He introduced a bill to pay Oregon's war debt on the basis of the claims accepted by the commission; his membership on the strategic Committee on Military Affairs enabled him to get it reported favorably, but it failed in the House. He repeatedly foiled Republican attempts to increase retroactively the pay of Anson G. Dart, a former Indian superintendent in Oregon, but the Republicans eventually had their way. As a member of the Committee on Public Lands, he supported its homestead bill and showed unusual independence in voting for it, even after Buchanan's veto. He also favored such diverse measures as a military road between Fort Benton, Montana, and Walla Walla, Washington Territory; an arms depot for the Puget Sound area; a four-year term (instead of five) at West Point; an army signal corps, in which he took a particular interest; and two additional Indian superintendencies for Oregon and Washington Territory.[20]

On the great question of the day, he placed himself squarely in the Calhoun tradition. Even before Davis introduced his controversial resolutions, Lane had enunciated a similar devotion to the rights of the states. He realized that Douglas and "many good Democrats in the northern States" did not agree with him, but he would not rule them out of the party "when the salvation of our country depends upon the success of the Democratic party."

20. *Congressional Globe,* 36 Cong., 1 Sess., pp. 214, 522, 658, 1145–46, 1217, 1989–90, 2098–3000, 2467–68, 2558–61. The vote on the homestead bill, which failed by three votes to override Buchanan's veto, is ibid., p. 3272. Lane had opposed a more liberal bill in the previous session.

Nobody loved the Union more than he, and to preserve it he would willingly expend every drop of blood in his veins, "but to maintain that Union, the Constitution must be maintained in its spirit, in its letter, and in its meaning." And as much as he loved the Union, he would not have it "maintained by the violation of the Constitution itself." The only way to preserve it was to "deal fairly by every portion of the territory." "If the northern States of this Confederacy could not have equal rights with the southern States in the territories," he asked rhetorically, "would they remain in the Union?"

> I do not see how any man who loves the Union and the Constitution can discriminate between the sections of this country, and pretend to say that the common territory of all shall be given exclusively to free labor or to slave labor. The citizens of the States have equal rights in the Territory while it remains in the territorial condition; and when the people who inhabit it come to form a State constitution, then it is their right to prohibit slavery or to establish it as they see fit, and they have a right to be admitted into the Union as they shall decide.

He regretted that Douglas and his followers differed from him on this matter; he could agree with them "upon all essential questions, this only excepted." Yet he was confident that they would strive to prevent the election of a "sectional man" to the presidency and to "do all in their power to secure the election of the nominee of the Charleston convention."[21]

Like most Democrats, Lane regarded the coming contest at Charleston as crucial to the future of the Democratic party. It seems inconceivable that his own presidential ambitions had diminished, although his chances had been set back somewhat by the narrowness of Stout's victory over Logan. There is some indication that

21. *Congressional Globe,* 36 Cong., 1 Sess., pp. 184–85.

Lane was becoming increasingly apprehensive about his political future. As early as February 1859, after taking his seat in the Senate, he promised Lafayette but two more years to study in Washington. During the last campaign in Oregon, Lane reportedly stated he would not seek re-election to the Senate but would retire to his farm in 1861. ("Humbug," scoffed Bush, he will want to run "just *once* more.") Early in 1860 and frequently thereafter, he reiterated to Lafayette that he neither desired nor expected to return to the Senate.[22]

Whatever the strength of his own aspirations, Lane consistently refused to seek the nomination at Charleston, although the volume of correspondence from individual well-wishers suggests that he enjoyed greater support than in 1852. "Lane's room is full from morning till night with accomplished Knee-benders who look upon him as a sure card for the Presidency," Deady wrote to Nesmith from Washington. "He has a kind and acceptable word for them all and they go away thinking him the greatest man in the nation. I am not surprised from what I've seen that Bush lost his heart here in 54–55." The intriguing and socially prominent Rose Greenhow, an aunt of Mrs. Stephen A. Douglas, apparently "entertained" on his behalf, and Buchanan himself gave at least one caller reason to believe that Lane was his personal choice to succeed him.[23]

22. Lane to Lafayette, Feb. 17, 1859, Lane Papers, InU; *Oregon Statesman,* June 21, 1859; Lane to Lafayette, Jan. 6, 1860, Lane Papers, InU. First reports in the East gave Logan the victory. John B. Floyd to Buchanan, Aug. 14, 1859, Auchampaugh, *Buchanan and His Cabinet,* p. 59: "Your military candidate, General Lane, has sustained a sad blow in losing his State. I am sorry for it; but it may not prostrate him."

23. Deady to Nesmith, Jan. 4, 1860, MS OrHi; Nichols, *Disruption of American Democracy,* pp. 281, 314; entry for March 24, 1860, Edgar Eugene Robinson, ed., "The Day Journal of Milton S. Latham, Jan. 1 to May 6, 1860," *California Historical Society Quarterly,* 9 (1932), 13: "I thought I observed . . . that the President would favor 'Jo Lane'—or that if Mr [Robert M. T.] Hunter [of Virginia] was forced upon the Charleston Convention by the South—M Lane would get the nomination [for vice-president] with a view of carrying the Pacific Coast."

The *Statesman* might belittle his "insane chase after a Presidential nomination," but Lane nonetheless possessed qualities that made him a possible contender. Sheets like the New Orleans *Crescent* might puff him as "a very good rough fighter" with "excellent qualities of head and heart" and then decide that "he is no more fitted for the Presidency than a Commanche Indian. Destitute in administrative talent and education, uncouth as a bear and abrupt as a stump-tail bull in fly time, he would blunder his Administration into contempt and make us the laughing stock of the nations." But the American people, to say nothing of their representatives, have not usually selected their chief executives on the basis of administrative ability and education, and Lane could present the strong countervailing attributes of sheer availability and political appeal. Many observers who thought the time was ripe for a dark-horse candidate sent Lane encouraging letters from virtually every section of the country. He was one of the few Northerners who would be acceptable to the South and who could possibly retain just enough Northern strength to carry two or three of the critical states. He was also a Western man, which should ensure victory in California and Oregon. Moreover, except on the status of slavery in the territories, he had not committed himself on the pressing questions of the day. If he had few ideas, he had fewer enemies. More accurate than flattering was the correspondent who referred to his "superior availability over any other living man."[24]

A good measure of his appeal derived from his military record, which was distinguished enough to give ample opportunity to imaginative campaign orators. But even more powerful was the way in which his supporters identified him with Andrew Jackson, as he himself did. One booster who had traveled from Virginia to Georgia reported having heard "almost a hundred individual expressions of opinion that you would make 'a President like Gen Jackson' and that the south could rely on you as a Northern Man,

24. *Oregon Statesman,* Feb. 21, 1860; *Crescent,* cited ibid., May 17, 1859; F. Bigger to Lane, June 9, 1859, Lane Papers, InU.

and the only one they *could rely on.*" Numerous followers thought they saw in him those same qualities that had immortalized Jackson—that same iron will, unerring intuitive judgment, and devotion for the common man. Some even imagined he looked like Jackson. "General Lane is nearer what our imagination has ever conceived General Jackson to have been," reported the Raleigh (North Carolina) *Standard,* "than any man that we ever have or ever expect to see. He is a tall, muscular, bony man of sixty, possessed of all the vigor of thirty, with a high full forehead and well developed organization; very plain and very agreeable."[25] Like the illustrious Tennesseean, Lane was also a man of humble origins and simple ways, a man whose folksy mannerisms and bluff good cheer had made him popular in Congress and the departments. What stump speakers across the country could make of such materials was readily apparent.

The main obstacle—and it was a major one—to Lane's nomination was the want of a hard core of political managers as had acted in 1852, a group of men devoted to his interests and capable of consolidating and co-ordinating his strength in Oregon or Indiana, Texas or New York. As another correspondent complained, the leading politicians all admitted his popularity and availability but were committed to somebody else because they doubted he would get the nomination. For his part, Lane seemed content to bide his time and await developments. He consistently turned aside all who inquired of his intentions, yet carefully avoided giving offense. "How can I aspire to the high office of President when there are so many . . . who are better qualified to discharge its duties?" he replied to one inquiry. "I yield to no man in patriotism, or love of country, but to many, in point of qualification. . . . I cannot, there-

25. J. N. Goodall to Lane, Dec. 18, 1859, Lane Papers, InU; *Standard,* cited in Kelly, *Career of Joseph Lane,* p. 165. Bushrod W. Wilson to Joseph Wilson, Nov. 28, 1859, Wilson Papers: "When I say Old Jo is liked among the people I mean Among the real *Old rough and ready Oregonians,* who dont know anything politically but Dem, and think they are yet voting for *Old Hickory.*"

fore, seek a position that I should approach with great fear and doubt, of ability to discharge its high duties. The people, however, have a right to command and . . . while I shall not seek, I will not decline."[26]

Ironically, the committee that chose Charleston as the site of the next Democratic convention intended thereby to promote party harmony. Charleston, cultural metropolis of the slavocracy and quintessence of all things Southern, opened her doors to the nation's delegates but her heart to only a few. The Cincinnati reporter, Murat Halstead, thought that there were not enough Douglas men in the country to "prevent the Convention from 'wearing a southern aspect.'" Douglas' delegates, he reported, arrived from Washington "full of enthusiasm—rampant and riotous—'hot as monkeys'—and proclaim that the universal world is for the Little Giant. They have a desperate fight before them and are brim full of the sound and fury of boastfulness."[27]

Excitement in Washington, where Congress continued in session, ran almost as high as it did in Charleston. Many Northern delegations had trooped through the city on their way south, and members of Congress anxiously awaited each new report of the convention's activity. Lane remained in Washington, as did Douglas, assiduously tending his Senatorial duties. "I am the only person that I am acquainted with that remains cool and unconcerned," he professed to Mosher. "I cannot to save my life want or desire the nomination. the only wish that I have on the subject is that a good sound trustworthy man may be selected." Anyone but Douglas.

26. C. M. Bull to Lane, March 29, 1860, Lane Papers, InU; Lane to H. M. Phillips, July 20, 1859, cited in Kelly, *Career of Joseph Lane,* p. 157.

27. William B. Hesseltine, ed., *Three Against Lincoln: Murat Halstead Reports the Caucuses of 1860* (Baton Rouge, Louisiana State University Press, 1960), pp. 8–9. Halstead's account of the convention is indispensable.

"Certainly the Convention will not make a man the Standard bearer of the party that he so lately betrayed."[28]

When the convention assembled on Monday, April 23, the question uppermost in everyone's mind was whether Douglas could be checked. Every delegate, every motion, every maneuver was designed to promote or to resist him. Douglas' delegation was pledged not to accept a platform with a slave code; some Southern states were instructed to insist upon one. The North had sixteen delegations and the South fifteen; in a test of strength by states, California and Oregon could prove the difference. In voting for the permanent chairman, the two Western states combined with the South to seat a well-known opponent of Douglas, Caleb Cushing of Massachusetts. On Tuesday night the convention decided to adopt the platform before selecting a nominee, thereby placing the issue in the lap of the platform committee. While the convention marked time, the committee wrangled for two days and most of two nights, unable to effect a workable compromise. On Friday morning the committee wearily submitted conflicting reports, the majority from the West and South urging the substance of the Davis Resolutions, and the minority from the North advocating compliance with the Supreme Court decisions respecting slavery in the territories. By some minor miracle, the crisis was postponed over the weekend; on Monday, the seventh day, the convention accepted the Douglas minority platform, and the delegations from the lower South, led by Alabama, walked out of the hall.

Oregon's delegation was in a quandary. "We have stood by the South in defending their rights but were overpowered," Stout telegraphed Lane. "It is my judgment that Oregon should now withdraw and refuse to participate with Either wing of the party. What say you? . . . I say the South is right. . . . We must not pander in any manner to black republicanism as the northern states now propose to do." "Stand by the equality of States," Lane wired back,

28. Lane to Mosher, April 26, 1860, Lane Papers, InU.

"and stand by those States that stand by the constitutional rights of all. By all means go with them, go out and stand by them." Stout consulted with the delegations from Virginia, Kentucky, and Tennessee and offered to withdraw with them, but instead they all decided to remain and present the names of their favorite sons.

> Douglas cannot be nominated if we all remain [Stout again wired Lane]. you would have a fair chance of a nomination. Those who withdraw have . . . asked if you will accept a position on the Ticket to be nominated by those who withdraw. please answer immediately as they meet again this evening to nominate. I will do as you request. I hardly know what to advise. I am trying to do my duty to the country first & to you next.

Lane's reply gave Stout much leeway:

> My strongest desire is for the peace harmony & success of the democratic party if it can be had without a sacrifise of the principles of the equality & the constitutional rights of the States. You know the condition of things better than I do. act in the premise as in your judgment may seem best for the Country. Every thing for the country & nothing for self is my motto.[29]

As it turned out, the bolting delegates decided not to make any nominations, awaiting instead the outcome of the regular deliberations.

Early in the convention the *New York Times* reported a rumor that Buchanan had instructed his managers to make an effort for Lane, and throughout the week Lane's friends had been working

29. Stout to Lane, April 30, 1860, Lane Papers, InU; Lane to Stout, n.d., Washington *Evening Star,* cited in *Oregon Statesman,* July 3, 1850; Stout to Lane, May 2, 1860, Lane Papers, InU; Lane to Stout, May 2, 1860, Lane Papers, InU.

quietly and discreetly behind the scenes.[30] The day following the Southern "secession," the regular convention began balloting for a presidential nominee. Isaac Stevens, who headed Oregon's delegation by proxy,[31] nominated Lane, but in the twelve ballots cast that evening, Lane received no more than six votes, three from Oregon and three from Pennsylvania. Douglas could not muster more than a bare majority. That night the wire-pullers were busy. According to a story Stout related to O'Meara years later, both sides were ready to accept Lane as a compromise candidate when his telegram endorsing the seceders arrived; Douglas' friends got wind of it through a "leak" in the telegraph office, and the deal was off.[32]

30. *New York Times,* April 25, 1860, p. 1. Cf. W. B. Phillips to Lane, Charleston, April 23, 24, 25, 28, May 2, 1860, Lane Papers, InU.

31. Of the delegates elected by the state convention in Oregon, only Stout and Lamerick were able to attend. Besides Stevens, Justus Steinberger, Bob Metcalfe, and A. P. Dennison represented Oregon by proxy.

32. O'Meara, "The Pioneer Days," *Sunday Oregonian,* Nov. 30, 1890, p. 16. The story is garbled at least in detail. After calling Stout a "bedrock democrat" and Logan a former Know Nothing, O'Meara says in part: "On the grave trouble, just before the final disastrous division and adjournment, when it became apparent that neither Breckinridge nor Douglas would be nominated, a movement was broached to harmonize the two factions by nominating General Lane. It appeared to meet favor on both sides. The nomination was likely to be made the following day. That evening Stout received the memorable telegram from General Lane at Washington: 'Go out, and stand!' Stout did not reveal the dispatch to anyone. But a leak in the telegraph office had made it known to some of the friends of Douglas. Stout was interrogated. He could no longer conceal the fact. That settled the matter. General Lane had prevented his own nomination for president by the indiscretion of that dispatch. His nomination at Charleston at the time would have prevented the fatal split in the democratic party. Lane would have undoubtedly have been elected. The fortune of the whole country would have been changed. There would have been no secession of States; no colossal internecine civil war. The destiny of the Union was involved in that brief dispatch. It is a momentous matter to contemplate; a tremendous theme to dwell upon."

O'Meara implies that the wire came before the South had walked out rather than after the fact. Breckinridge did not permit his name to be used in the balloting at Charleston, and Stout obviously showed Lane's wire to the delegations from Va., Ky., and Tenn.

When the balloting resumed next morning, Lane's vote jumped to twenty, and on the fourteenth ballot, twenty and one-half, but it went no higher. For fifty-seven ballots the Little Giant's managers sought to win the prize for their candidate. Then in an unprecedented move, they recessed the convention for six weeks to reconvene at Baltimore, June 18. The seceders were wholly unprepared for this unexpected maneuver; they could do little but recess themselves, agreeing to meet again at Richmond on June 11 to plot further strategy.

The rancors of Charleston transformed Congress into a seething caldron of political turmoil, as both sides attempted to reform their ranks before reassembling at Baltimore. Southern moderates who had opposed the walkout in Charleston realized that two things must be done to reunify the party: they must stop Douglas and insist that the Davis Resolutions be the basis of the platform. "Douglas cannot nor will not be nominated," Lane declared to Deady, "or if he should be the south will bring out a candidate and run him with the certainty of giving him the entire south. We are in a muss," he added gloomily, "and I can hardly see how we can get out with whole bones, but we will see." During the long and acrimonious debate that followed in the Senate, Lane emphatically sided with his Southern colleagues. Davis' resolutions, he said,

> ought to have been asserted by the Democratic party in plain English ten years ago. If they had been, you would have had no trouble in this country to-day; the Democratic party would have been united and strong, and the equality and constitutional rights of the States would have been maintained. . . . It is the fault of the Democratic party in dodging truth, in dodging principle, in dodging the Constitution itself, that has brought the trouble upon the country and the party that is experienced to-day.
>
> Sir, it appears to me to be very singular indeed, that any man can hold that the territory of this country belongs to a portion

> of the people . . . and to say that all shall not have an equal right there, is to deny a fact so plain, a principle so just, a right so manifest, that I can hardly see how any man who professes to be a Democrat can deny it.[33]

While the Senate debated the merits of intervention or nonintervention, Lane's stock began to rise. In a post-mortem of the Charleston debacle, James Gordon Bennett's *New York Herald* thought Lane would have been nominated had the party "held together." "Stout kept back Lane's friends, some think, too long," reported the *Herald.* "No organized band of politicians worked for him, but he provoked, on that account, the less hostility. He stands a good chance at the Richmond convention. His name, and that of Jefferson Davis, are now most prominent among Southern men. It is a question with them which should head the ticket." Southern extremists were also prepared to accept Davis and Lane or men of their stripe. Secretary of the Treasury Howell Cobb, a moderate from Georgia, confessed to his brother-in-law that although he personally preferred another, he thought "old Joe Lane . . . the best man to make the fight on, both in the convention and before the people. He is as true as steel and then he has 'fought, bled and died for his country.' I believe that the best chance now is to take a northern man—any of them will be acceptable after we get clear of Douglas."[34]

By the time the seceders reassembled in Richmond, former Whigs and Know Nothings had met in Baltimore and nominated John Bell of Tennessee to a middle-of-the-road "Constitutional

33. Lane to Deady, May 13, 1860, MS OrHi; *Congressional Globe,* 36 Cong., 1 Sess., pp. 2323–24.

34. *Herald,* cited in *Oregon Statesman,* June 12, 1860; R. Barnwell Rhett to Porcher Miles, May 10, 1860, cited in Nevins, *Emergence of Lincoln, 1,* 263; Cobb to John B. Lamar, May 22, 1860, Ulrich B. Phillips, ed., *The Correspondence of Howell Cobb, Alexander H. Stephens, and Robert Toombs,* American Historical Association, Annual Report, 1911, 2 (Washington, Government Printing Office, 1913), 480.

Union" ticket, and the Republicans, the scent of victory strong in their nostrils, had met in Chicago and selected for their candidate a relatively unknown lawyer and rail splitter from Illinois. Lane appeared nervous and uneasy about the fate of the Democracy. His desire for the nomination may have been tempered by the troubles at Charleston, and he asked the delegates thronging through Washington on their way to Richmond not to use his name. He reminded Lafayette they would be leaving for Oregon in the spring; he would try to bring back enough law books for him to continue his studies there; and he even suggested that John might resign and come home with them too. "I dont wish to be nominated," he declared, "and would be very reluctant to accept if nominated, and I will say to you in all candor that I am very tired of public life. I want to retire and spend the remainder of my days in quiet, surrounded as I would be with my children and grand children. I think I could be happy."[35]

Most delegates to Richmond were determined to regain their seats at Baltimore, so they promptly adjourned to that city. Lane's friends made their headquarters at Eutaw House, confident that the party would soon be reunited. Stevens wrote Lane after the first day's sessions, predicting that the bolting delegations would be quickly readmitted and that "in no possible event" could Douglas be nominated. Lane was less sanguine and would not "even undertake to guess" what might transpire, although he thought it possible that the party could yet unite around some conservative candidate and win in November. But he told Lafayette he would "rather be right, than to be President by yielding to any wrong." Stevens soon repented his optimism when the credentials committee, of which he was a member, voted to exclude some of the bolters and to seat instead the Douglas delegations that had been newly elected from the seceders' states. Stevens replied with a minority report insisting upon the readmission of all original dele-

35. Lane to Lafayette, June 10, 1860, Lane Papers, InU.

gates, but the convention rejected it.[36] When the voting began, the anti-Douglas forces, now including Oregon and California, again walked off the floor; and the disruption of the party was complete. After the second ballot, the convention unanimously declared Douglas the regular nominee of the Democratic party.

The seceding delegates, new and old, withdrew to a nearby hall and organized themselves as the National Democratic Convention. With great harmony and dispatch, they adopted the platform they had striven for so tenaciously at Charleston and then proceeded to nominate their candidates: for president, by unanimous consent after the first ballot, John C. Breckinridge of Kentucky, for vice-president, by acclamation, Joseph Lane.[37] Stevens became chairman of the National Democratic Executive Committee.

Lane probably accepted the nomination with reluctance, as did Breckinridge, and both men gave positive assurances to the campaign managers that they would do everything in their power to prevent a secession movement should Lincoln be elected. In his formal letter of acceptance, Lane again subordinated the question of slavery to the great constitutional issue at stake.

> The platform adopted . . . embodies what I have been contending for as the only means of stopping the sectional agitation, by securing to all equality and constitutional rights.
>
> The Democratic party . . . does not propose to litigate for the extension of slavery, nor for its restriction, but to give

36. Stevens to Lane, June 19, 1860, Lane Papers, InU; Lane to Lafayette, June 19, 1860, Lane Papers, InU; *Minority Report of Mr. Stevens, Delegate from Oregon, Showing the Grounds upon Which the Regular Southern Delegation Were Entitled to Seats in the Convention at the Front Street Theatre,* Baltimore, Breckinridge and Lane Campaign Documents, No. 2 (Washington, National Democratic Executive Committee, 1860).

37. Stevens did Lane the honor of nominating him for president, but the sentiment of the convention was clearly for Breckinridge, and Oregon cast her three votes for the Kentuckian. Thomas S. Green of N.C. nominated Lane for the vice-presidency, which was unanimously agreed to by roll call. Hesseltine, *Three Against Lincoln,* pp. 274–75.

> to each State and to every citizen, all that our forefathers proposed to give, namely, perfect equality of rights, and then to commit to the people, to climate, and to soil, the determination as to the kind of institutions best fitted to their constitutional limits.

Above all, he declared, the Union must be preserved, the Constitution sustained.[38]

For all the drama associated with the conventions, the campaign of 1860 was surprisingly drab and spiritless. With the Democracy hopelessly divided, there was little doubt that the Republicans would win. Observers at Charleston had so predicted, and even Lincoln was supremely confident. "I hesitate to say it," he wrote to an Oregonian early in August, "but it really appears now, as if the success of the Republican ticket is inevitable. We have no reason to doubt any of the states which voted for Fremont. Add to these, Minnesota, Pennsylvania, and New Jersey, and the thing is done." He also expected that the division between Douglas and Breckinridge Democrats would give the Republicans "a fair chance" in Oregon.[39] As the campaign progressed, more and more National Democrats began to pin their hopes on an anomaly in the electoral procedure whereby the election might be transferred to Congress if the electoral college failed to give any candidate a clear majority.

Lane got off to a bad start in the campaign at a ratification rally on July 2 in Philadelphia, where a large number of Douglas' adherents attempted to break up the meeting with shouts and

38. Frank H. Heck, "John C. Breckinridge in the Crisis of 1860–1861," *Journal of Southern History, 21* (1955), 323–24; Stevens to Nesmith, April 23, 1862, MS OrHi; Lane's letter of acceptance is in *Minority Report of Stevens,* Breckinridge and Lane Campaign Documents, No. 2, and *New York Times,* July 11, 1860.

39. Lincoln to Simeon Francis, Aug. 4, 1860, MS OrHi.

jeers. When those in charge presented resolutions endorsing the National platform and nominees, the "Nays" were as loud as the "Yeas." Lane made a brief speech extolling Breckinridge's qualifications for president, attacking Lincoln's voting record during the Mexican War, and denouncing popular sovereignty "as taught by some" as a "heresy" that "never ought to have been introduced." Hisses and boos frequently interrupted the speaker, and at one point some Nationals tried to throw the Douglas men out, but Lane asked them to forbear. Eventually the police intervened and made more than a score of arrests.[40]

No incidents marred the rally in Washington City a week later when ten thousand persons reportedly demonstrated before the city hall. There were bands, fireworks, and numerous banners expressing the sentiments of the occasion: "Non-intervention by Congress or Territorial Legislatures"; "Democracy is good for all, And 'Old Abe' must have a dose next Fall"; "Let millions join the loud refrain—Hurrah for Breckinridge and Lane." As a climax to the evening's celebration, the crowd heard Buchanan declare that since neither Douglas nor Breckinridge had been regularly nominated by a two-thirds majority, he thought everyone "at perfect liberty to vote as he thinks proper." He then went on to explain his reasons for supporting Breckinridge and Lane.[41]

Custom decreed against a candidate campaigning actively, and none did in 1860, save Douglas, whose extensive itinerary became the sensation of the day. Lane made few speeches, preferring to let supporters at the state and local level speak for the ticket. He spent two leisurely weeks with friends and relatives around Raleigh, North Carolina, and took the opportunity to visit the birthplace of his father. At a gathering of the clan before he left, he

40. *New York Times,* July 3, 1860, p. 1.

41. *Speech of President Buchanan, on the Evening of Monday, July 9, 1860,* Breckinridge and Lane Campaign Documents, No. 4 (Washington, National Democratic Executive Committee, 1860). Former President Pierce also supported Breckinridge and Lane. Pierce to B. F. Hallet, June 29, 1860, *New York Times,* July 18, 1860, p. 3.

assured them of his support for the Union—the Constitutional Union, that is, for "a Union that did not protect the rights and privileges of all was not worth preserving." He parted with a promise:

> Should your rights ever be invaded, should your property ever be endangered, should your lives ever be jeopardized, I would fly to your relief from my far-off Pacific home and give all the powers of my arm and my head in your defence, in defence of the rights of the South. But I would come to fight your battles no sooner than I would go to Maine to fight her battles, if her citizens . . . were in jeopardy. I would maintain the Constitution as it is, and the rights of all sections as they are.[42]

Wherever he did speak, the message was the same, although as the campaign progressed, his appeal became more urgent. At Covington, Kentucky, in front of a local inn, he declared *the* issue in the election to be "whether or not all the people should have equal rights in the common Territories." He thought popular sovereignty "the sheerest nonsense ever uttered by mortal man . . . a heresy—a fundamental error."

> If the Government attempted to force an indignity upon Ohio, would not the Kentuckians rush to maintain her constitutional right? And should they not do the same for South Carolina? Even if any State or people should be willing to submit to an insult, or to surrender a right, he would stand alone if necessary, to protest against it. [Applause.] The blood of his ancestors shed in many a battle to defend constitutional rights ought to haunt the man who would relinquish one of them, and the bones rising from the battle-field ought to shake in his face and call him a coward.
>
> It should be remembered that the Breckinridge ticket was the only Union ticket in the field, for it stood by the equality

42. *New York Times,* Aug. 1, 1860, p. 3.

> of the States. . . . Whether that ticket were elected or not, the party must never abandon their right doctrine. Then, if defeated once, they could rise and fight for their principles. [Cheers.][43]

And so it was throughout Indiana, where he campaigned most extensively. Railroads, tariffs, homesteads, foreign affairs—all were forgotten. The all-encompassing question was the equality of the states. But the Hoosier Democracy had already cast its lot with Douglas, having sent a delegation to Charleston fully instructed for popular sovereignty. Each faction was prepared to go down with the ship before it would yield a single point to the other.

Nowhere was Lane more concerned about political developments than in Oregon, where continuing internecine strife threatened to play into the hands of the Republicans. Aside from the electoral votes involved, Oregon was particularly important because the new state legislature would elect two United States senators. "For God's sake let us have success . . . in the Election of democratic senators, and at the November Election," he implored Deady. As the election drew near and the National tide began running stronger, Stevens thought "the whole question whether Breckinridge and Lane are elected" might turn on the outcome in Oregon.[44]

Shortly after the election of delegates to Charleston, the Clique decided to concentrate its efforts behind Nesmith for the Senate. About the same time Colonel Edward D. Baker, a most distinguished orator from California and a close friend of Lincoln, arrived in Oregon at the invitation of local Republicans. After looking over the country and conferring with Bush, he decided to return for his family and settle in Salem. "His object is to go to the Senate," one of his supporters wrote to Lincoln. "The prospects now are that he will get one third or more of the Representatives and

43. *Cincinnati Gazette,* cited ibid., Sept. 14, 1860, p. 8.

44. Lane to Deady, July 15, 1860, MS OrHi; Stevens to Deady, Sept. 18, 1860, MS OrHi.

Senators at the election in June—and the Anti-Lecompton democrats will get about the same number, and that together they will elect the two Senators." A correspondent warned Lane that some persons were already offering bets that Oregon's next senators would be Nesmith and Baker.[45]

Oregonians had also to choose a new congressional representative, but the Bush and Lane factions disagreed over when the election should be. Lane's followers wished it as early as possible, at the time of the general election in June, which might assist them in retaining control of the legislature; the Clique sought to defer it until after the election of senators or even until the national election in November. The Democratic state convention in April nominated a strong proslavery man, George K. Sheil of Salem, to run for Congress, but most of the Clique or Douglas Democrats boycotted the convention, and Bush denounced it as illegal. When the Republicans in convention the next day responded to the Democratic challenge and also nominated a candidate, David Logan, the Clique was enraged. "I hoped they would keep still and, if they saw fit in June to vote for a Congressman, they would vote at least for some independent candidate—possibly a Douglas democrat," Drew complained to Bush. "They are a damned impracticable, brainless set of asses to attempt to push out a man on a republican platform just at this time."[46] In the ensuing campaign, the Republicans and Bushites—Lane men called them mulattoes—agreed not to run candidates against each other in certain counties, notably Marion and Linn. The vote between Sheil and Logan was so close that Eastern papers first announced that Logan had won, whereas Sheil was the victor by 103 votes. Lane Democrats elected nine-

45. Drew to Deady, Dec. 19, 1859, MS OrHi; *Weekly Oregonian,* Dec. 17, 24, 1859; *Oregon Argus,* Oct. 27, 1860; Simeon Francis to Lincoln, Dec. 26, 1859, cited in Johannsen, *Frontier Politics and the Sectional Conflict,* p. 117; Joseph T. Wagnon to Lane, Jan. 8, 1860, Lane Papers, InU. Cf. Edward R. Geary to Lane, Dec. 24, 1859.

46. *Oregon Statesman,* April 24, 1860; Drew to Bush, March 11, 1860, Bush Papers.

teen members to the new legislature, Douglas Democrats eighteen, and Republicans thirteen. On nearly every ticket, supporters of the Clique voted with the Republicans against the supporters of Lane. Illiterate old Bill Martin spoke for all Lane's sympathizers: "Douglas . . . has plaid hell with us heare."[47]

The final split in the Oregon Democracy occurred when the Douglas Democrats in the state central committee walked out of a meeting and called their own convention to name presidential electors. When the legislature met to elect the senators, the clash was acrimonious and stormy. The Clique would not under any conditions accept Smith, and the Lane men refused to support Nesmith unless Smith were elected. After a lengthy struggle, the bargain was made: fifteen Douglas Democrats threw their support to Republican Baker, and the Republicans voted for Nesmith.[48]

Lane's setback in his home state attracted national attention and further demoralized the Breckinridge movement. Even before the drama in Oregon concluded, Lane had not been at all optimistic of success. "Things are looking very bad just now," he bluntly informed Lafayette after returning from Indiana. To Mosher he predicted, "The entire South in my judgment will go for Breckinridge, and the entire North with the exception of the Pacific States and New York and they are doubtful will go for Lincoln. Douglas will not carry a single state. I have not yet dispaired of success, but cannot say that it will . . . follow." "I shall remain at my post until the close of the congress," he concluded, "and then I will go to my farm and go to work like a man." From New York, where Stevens was trying to effect a fusion with the Douglas and Bell forces, Lane wrote to his son Simon the week before the election that he was "not without hope but it is only *a hope.*" "Some days I *think* that Lincoln will be defeated and then again I feel dis-

47. *Oregon Statesman,* July 17, 1860; *New York Times,* July 10, 1860, p. 1; Woodward, *History of Political Parties in Oregon,* p. 173; Martin to Lane, June 13, 1860, Lane Papers, InU.

48. *Oregon Statesman,* Aug. 21, 28, Oct. 8, 1860.

couraged," he continued, adding that if Lincoln should be elected, "the Union will be broken up."[49]

The only hope for a Democratic victory was for the opponents of Lincoln to win enough electoral votes in the North (thirty-five) to prevent a majority in the electoral college and throw the election into the House, where each state would cast a single vote. Should the House deadlock, as the last House had over the speakership, the Senate would then elect a vice-president—almost certainly Lane, in view of the Administration majority—who would assume the office of President on March 4. A long shot, perhaps, but not an impossibility, as even certain Republicans recognized when they raised the cry, "Lincoln or Lane."

The results of the election were depressing for all but Republicans. Lincoln swept all the free states except New Jersey, which he split with Douglas, for a total electoral vote of 180; Breckinridge won 11 states, all in the lower South except Maryland and Delaware for 72; Bell won Virginia, Kentucky, and Tennessee for 39; and Douglas carried only Missouri and part of New Jersey for 12. In the popular vote, Lincoln won 39.9 per cent, Douglas 29.4, Breckinridge 18, and Bell 12.6. Even if Breckinridge had received all Douglas' and Bell's votes, Lincoln would have prevailed. Douglas and Bell got more votes in the South than Breckinridge, although Breckinridge got more votes in New England than Lincoln did in the South. Neither Breckinridge nor Lane carried his own

49. Lane to Lafayette, Oct. 18, 1860, Lane Papers, InU; Lane to Mosher, Oct. 19, 1860, Mosher Family Papers; Lane to Simon R. Lane, Oct. 30, 1860. Lane also told Simon, "The coalition between the Douglas members of our Legislature, by which Nes. and Baker were elected is most dishonorable and will consign those concerned to infamy. No honorable man would take a seat in the Senate upon the terms that Nes. has got his." Cf. Stevens to John A. Green, Jr., Sept. 29, 1860, Lane Papers, InU; Stevens to Lane, Sept. 29, 1860, Lane Papers, InU; and J. F. Hammond to James H. Hammond, Oct. 29, 1860, cited in Ollinger Crenshaw, *The Slave States in the Presidential Election of 1860,* Johns Hopkins University Studies in Historical and Political Science, Series 63, No. 3 (Baltimore, Johns Hopkins Press, 1945), 28.

state. For Lane the crowning blow must have been the 270 votes by which the Republicans carried Oregon for the first time in her history. Lincoln himself admitted he carried the state "by the closest political bookkeeping that I know of."[50]

Breckinridge and Lane failed in large measure because most moderates regarded the demand for congressional protection of slavery as an impractical abstraction and refused to make it the hallmark of party regularity. As Senator Robert Toombs of Georgia protested, the question of whether a territorial legislature could prohibit slavery had not been raised before the Supreme Court in seventy years and might well not be raised for another seventy, so why create a straw man? What great emergency demanded intervention by Congress? What territory in particular did the South have in mind? To all intents and purposes the status of slavery was settled. Few doubted that Kansas would be anything but free, and there was little other territory suited to the Southern institution. But intervention became the rallying cry of the champions of Southernness, and thus unwittingly did the campaign's leaders encourage the forces of disunion.[51]

Two days following the election, Secretary of War Floyd saw Lane and talked with him at length. "He was grave and extremely earnest," the Secretary noted in his diary; "said that resistance to the antislavery feeling of the North was hopeless, and that nothing was left to the South but 'resistance or dishonor.' . . . He thought disunion inevitable, and said when the hour came that if his services could be useful, he would offer them unhesitatingly to the South."[52]

50. Milton H. Shutes, "Colonel E. D. Baker," *California Historical Society Quarterly*, 17 (1938), 318.

51. Toombs to Alexander H. Stephens, Feb. 10, 1860, Phillips, ed., *Correspondence of Cobb, Stephens, and Toombs*, p. 461. See also Crenshaw, *Slave States in the Presidential Election of 1860*, pp. 44–58; James G. Randall, "The Blundering Generation," *Mississippi Valley Historical Review*, 27 (1940), 14; Charles W. Ramsdell, "The Natural Limits of Slavery Expansion," ibid., 16 (1929), 151–71.

52. Diary entry for Nov. 8, 1860, cited in John G. Nicolay and John Hay, *Abraham Lincoln, a History*, 2 (New York, Century Co., 1914), 316.

As the Thirty-sixth Congress assembled for its brief final session, Lane was virtually obsessed about the fate of the Union. To Deady he wrote late in the evening of December 2:

> Tomorrow Congress will assemble for the last time that a national Congress will ever assemble under the constitution as it now is, and it is by no means certain that such amendments can be made as will justify the south in remaining in the Union. I dont believe there is any chance for a satisfactory settlement of the trouble or difficulty, consequently, look upon the Union as broken up. It is virtually broken up now. You will not regard me as an alarmist, or sensationalist, for you will find that all I say will be verified.

He had earlier expressed his opinion to Simon that Lincoln would not be "President of the United States as they were before his election," and that he was "inclined to think that a fair division of the Republic would be the best for both sections." He was particularly concerned about the attitude of Buchanan. "It is said by some that he will take ground against secession, and ask Congress to afford him the means that will enable him to coerce any and all states that shall undertake to go out," he told Lafayette, but he doubted the President would pursue such a course. "If he does, then we part company, for I never will, by my vote give one cent to be used against a people who are contending for their rights."[53]

Like many Southerners, Lane regarded the disruption of the Union a national tragedy. The election of the Republicans ended the Union; secession was "the national result of the success of Black Republican principles." Unless they would repudiate their

53. Lane to Deady, Dec. 2, 1860, MS OrHi; Lane wrote substantially the same thing to Lafayette, Dec. 2, 1860, Lane Papers InU; Lane to Simon R. Lane, Nov. 11, 1860, Lane Papers, InU; Lane to Lafayette, Nov. 19, 1860, Lane Papers, InU.

platform, their *raison d'être,* and guarantee the states their constitutional rights, there was no honorable alternative but to let the Southern states go in peace. "I would do anything, sir, to save this Union," he announced in the Senate, "but it must be saved . . . upon the principles of the Constitution." The right of peaceable secession he thought irrefutable. The suggestion that the Administration should act promptly and decisively against seceding states filled him with horror. It would mean civil war, he protested, and "the man who shall inaugurate such a war . . . will be the foulest murderer that ever disgraced the form of man; and will go down to his grave covered all over with the curses of heaven to say nothing of the curses of widows and orphans that would follow him to his death. Our Union was not formed by force nor can it be maintained by force."[54] Lane was a secessionist in that he firmly believed the South could and, under the circumstances, should leave the Union, but he did not regard secession as desirable and worked very hard to accommodate the South and prevent her withdrawal.

In his annual message to Congress, Buchanan denied both the right of secession and the power of the federal government to coerce a seceding state. His only positive proposal was a constitutional amendment to conciliate the South. Lane approved "a very considerable portion" of Buchanan's views but warned that the Union would dissolve "unless something can be done very speedily." "To say that the people of fifteen States of this Union . . . shall not have rights equal with the other portion of the country, is a degradation that a proud, honorable, and just people cannot submit to; and if they should, I would not entertain for them that respect that I do to-day." Two weeks later he added his own remedy to the numerous peace proposals suggested in Congress. He introduced a set of resolutions calling for a new constitutional convention to

54. Lane to Simon R. Lane, Nov. 17, 1860, Lane Papers, InU; *Congressional Globe,* 36 Cong., 2 Sess., p. 8; Lane to Pliny Thayer, Nov. 30, 1860, Lane Papers, InU. Cf. Thayer to Lane (copy), Nov. 21, 1860, Lane Papers, InU.

revise the Constitution as their forefathers "in a similar difficulty" had rewritten the Articles of Confederation. Since the South was the aggrieved party, he suggested the Southern states first meet to agree on the "conditions necessary for their security and peace" and submit them to the states of the North. The final resolution stipulated:

> That the Federal Government will abstain from the employment of all or any force to prevent or interfere with any State or States which shall determine by itself or themselves on any course for their own prosperity and safety, which shall not be aggressive towards the other States; and in any case where there may be danger of collision between any State and the Federal forces stationed there, the forces be promptly withdrawn.[55]

His plea fell on deaf ears.

Senator Andrew Johnson of Tennessee had rendered yeoman service for the Breckinridge ticket, but he was not about to see the Union dissolved because of "the absurdity of the pretension that there is a right to secede." Ridiculing the idea that the federal government did not have the constitutional power to execute its own laws, he rebelled at the revolutionary suggestion that the states could simply scrap the Constitution and draw up a new form of government. How could the South demand "of the North a compliance with the Constitution . . . if we violate the Constitution by going out ourselves?" The South's only salvation lay in obtaining additional securities "in the manner and mode pointed out by the instrument itself." If South Carolina went out of the Union, she would go out in violation of the Constitution, and Congress would have the undisputed right to "pass her under the jurisdiction of the United States, and hold her as a province."[56]

55. *Congressional Globe,* 36 Cong., 2 Sess., pp. 8–9, 112.
56. Ibid., pp. 117–20, 134–43.

Lane was on his feet in an instant. He was sure that the Democracy of the North would continue to defend the constitutional rights of other states, he said, but he was also sure of one thing they would not do:

> they will not march under his [Johnson's] banner to strike down a gallant, chivalrous, and generous people contending for rights that have been refused them by the other States of this Union. They will not march with him under his bloody banner, or Mr. Lincoln's, to invade the soil of the gallant State of South Carolina when she may withdraw from a Confederacy that has refused her that equality to which she is entitled, as a member of the Union, under the Constitution. On the contrary, when he or any other gentleman raises that banner and attempts to subjugate that gallant people, instead of marching with him, we will meet him there, ready to repel him and his forces.
>
> I now serve notice that, when war is made upon that gallant South for withdrawing from a Union which refuses them their rights, the northern Democracy will not join in the crusade. The Republican party will have war enough at home.
>
> I understand this [Union] to be a voluntary association of States. I understand that our fathers met together at a proper time in the history of our country, and established a Government, a Confederation. . . . They lived under it a short time, and they found it would not answer the purpose. A few States . . . said that though it had been provided by the Confederation that the Government should be perpetual, they would break it up. . . . They were seceders then. George Washington headed the band.
>
> But, sir, understand me; I am not a disunionist. I am for the right, and I would have it in the Union; and if it cannot be obtained there, I would go out of the Union, and have that out of the Union that I could not obtain in it.
>
> I look upon a dissolution now as a fixed fact; I look upon

> it as inevitable; but shall we not all look forward with hope, with anxious and patriotic hope, to the day when a reorganization shall take place . . . ? If we would bring about that reorganization, if we would rebuild the fabric that has been stricken down, we must maintain peace. Inaugurate force, sir, inaugurate war in this country, and all hope of reconstruction has vanished forever.
>
> Why, sir, to break up such a fabric, to break up such a Union . . . is a matter of the deepest regret to every good man North and South. There is not one State in the South that would do it without cause. There is no State North, but for the influence of the Republican party, that would do it. . . . They have destroyed the Union; not the South. They have forced the South into dissolution.[57]

The day following this speech, one of the most important Lane ever made, South Carolina passed an ordinance of secession and proclaimed herself an independent commonwealth, initiating a movement that saw six other states follow suit by the first of February. Although he was convinced that the Union was irrevocably dissolved, Lane continued to hope for a peaceful accommodation. He was not sorry his term would soon be over, he told Simon, but while he remained he would work for peace. "I desire it understood by all parties . . . that dissolution, if it takes place, ought to be a peaceful one," he announced in the Senate in early January.

> If we will not deal fairly by our southern friends . . . for God's sake let them, if they must go, depart in peace. Let us have no war. No man ought to propose the use of force or bring about collision in this country.
>
> Mr. President, I am for peace. I want it understood that I would be very slow to draw a saber or a sword against an American citizen. If he lives in Maine, he is my brother; if he

57. Ibid., pp. 143–45.

> lives in New Hampshire, he is my fellow-citizen; and the same in every other State, he is my countryman. He has the rights that I have; and . . . I would not refuse the southern States their rights. . . . Upon these principles I intend to stand; and if they fall, I intend to go down with them.[58]

Lane's preoccupation with the impending dismemberment of the Union also affected his attitude toward certain measures of legislation. While he remained silent and refrained from voting on the admission of Kansas, he strenuously objected to the Pacific railroad bill passed by the House, which called for the construction of a central route by means of a large subsidy of land and money. "Violate the rights of the States; refuse them equality; trample upon the Constitution; disregard the decision of the Supreme Court, and do every other thing to the injury of nearly half the States of this Union," he lectured the sponsors of the bill, "and then come foreward and say [to the South]: 'We will buy you off; your principles are not worth much.' Is that the way to talk to a people who believe they have been injured?" He had favored a Pacific railroad for ten years, he said, and would gladly vote for one now if the Union were secure, if it would benefit Oregon, and if it would not promise fortunes to the incorporators, as this bill would surely do. When the bill again came up for debate, he protested against considering it "when every gentleman knows that the country cannot be held together unless something shall be done promptly." "Would the Senator have a railroad at the expense of the Union?" he asked Gwin of California, one of the principal backers of the scheme. When he found he could not postpone consideration of the measure, he amended it to extend a branch from Sacramento to Portland. Assuaging his own fears about the constitutionality of invading states' rights by federal appropriations, he rationalized that if it were "necessary for the defense of the country, to make the road to

58. Lane to Simon R. Lane, Jan. 8, 1861, Lane Papers, InU; *Congressional Globe,* 36 Cong., 2 Sess., p. 293.

the Sacramento," then it was also "necessary to make it into Oregon." His amendment passed, but the bill eventually failed, to be resurrected by the next Congress.[59]

Lane similarly objected that a protective tariff was sectional and unconstitutional and would heap coals of fire upon the South. It was all a part of a general plan: "They mean coercion; they mean to enforce the Federal laws; they mean to collect the revenue; they intend to carry on a policy that will inaugurate in this country a civil war." He suggested they re-enact the tariff of 1846 with certain modifications, but his amendment was rejected and protection sustained.[60]

The only ray of sunlight for Lane during the entire session was payment of Oregon's much-abused war debt. The House voted to reduce sharply the wage allowances of the Senate bill from the last session, returning it to the Senate the final week of the session. On Lane's motion, the Senate rejected the new amendments and called for a conference with a committee from the House. In conference, Lane agreed to accept the essential features of the House's proposal with the proviso that more time be granted claimants to furnish evidence of their claims. Half a loaf was obviously better than none.[61]

As a "doughface" in Washington, a Northerner with Southern principles, Lane became increasingly unhappy during that final, fatal session of Congress. Residence in the capital was no longer "as pleasant as in former days," he complained early in January. He was anxious to get home. The Union was fast "tumbling to pieces" because of "that infernal Black republican sectional hypo-

59. *Congressional Globe,* 36 Cong., 2 Sess., pp. 293–94, 382–83, 427–28, 433.

60. Ibid., pp. 1060–61.

61. Ibid., pp. 1157, 1205, 1266. Lane was prepared to accept a half loaf in the previous session. Ibid., 36 Cong., 1 Sess., pp. 2467–68. The final bill reduced by about half the recommendations of the war commission.

critical fanatical negro loving party." Lafayette suspected the authorities were beginning to censor his father's mail.[62] The departure of Southern senators further aggravated his minority position and forced him to abandon hope of an eventual reconciliation. "I am of [the] opinion that a reconstruction will never take place," he wrote to Deady. "If I am right in this there will be a Southern confederacy composed of fifteen States, one that will command the respect and confidence of all the nations of Europe. But what will be the fate of the Northern States, I will not undertake to predict." The burdens of the day also exacted a physical toll. To Lafayette he declared late in January, "I am nearly worne out, constantly on duty, sleep but little and eat but little. This morning I am so feeble that I can hardly walk."[63]

Throughout the session, friends of compromise had been working tirelessly but to little avail. Senator John J. Crittenden of Kentucky headed a movement to give the South certain assurances and prohibit slavery only in the territory north of latitude 36° 31′. Lane and some Southern senators supported the plan, but the Republicans rejected it, aided by Douglas, Gwin, and six Southern Democrats, who withheld their votes. A hastily summoned Peace Conference, February 4, tried to give new life to Crittenden's resolutions, modifying them in such a way as to discourage all hope of extending slavery to any new territory that might be added to the Union. These new proposals reached Congress four days before the end of the session, and Lane decided to draw the line. The Crittenden Resolutions, he stated, were "as low down as I could go. They did not secure to every State that right they have under the Constitution . . . but the resolution now before the Senate . . . is a cheat, a deception, a humbug—nothing that any State can take as a final settlement of the questions that are now

62. Lane to Simon R. Lane, Jan. 8, 1861, Lane Papers, InU; Lane to Mosher, Jan. 8, 1861, Lane Papers, InU; Lafayette to Lane, Jan. 10, 1861, Lane Papers, InU.

63. Lane to Deady, Jan. 27, 1861, MS OrHi; Lane to Lafayette, Jan. 31, 1861, Lane Papers, InU.

giving trouble in this country, nothing that can permanently settle these difficulties."[64] The Senate decisively rejected the plan, and in a major speech the final day, Lane expansively defended his position and replied again to Johnson of Tennessee.

Lane had been itching for an opportunity to reply to Johnson ever since the Tennesseean's speech of December 19; Lane's rebuttal then had been only the preliminary bout. Early in February, Johnson flayed Lane for exaggerating and misquoting his earlier speech. Peevish and irritable—he also clashed repeatedly during the session with his new colleague Baker—Lane bided his time. "I will not spare him," he promised Lafayette. "He is not a gentleman, and shall not be treated as a gentleman, but as a low contemptible wretch that deserves the scorn and contempt of all good men." Nesmith, waiting to take Lane's seat in the Senate, wrote back to Oregon that "Old Jo" was regarded with universal contempt.[65]

The frequently delayed encounter occurred during the closing hours of the session, as friends of compromise worked feverishly to perform a last-minute miracle. Never before had Lane prepared so elaborate a defense; never before had he delivered so protracted an oration. This was his swan song, and he determined to make the most of it. Rejecting the "ambiguous" and "deceptive" compromise proposals, he went on to argue that he had consistently acted for the rights of the states; that secession was constitutional, because the North had broken the solemn compact between the sections by enacting legislation against slavery; that coercion would eventually bring ruin to all parts of the country; and that Johnson's speech in December had contributed immeasurably to Republican aspirations. There were few ideas that Lane had not expressed previously, and except for occasional flashes of insight and anger, the speech was undistinguished.[66]

64. *Congressional Globe*, 36 Cong., 2 Sess., pp. 1254–55, 1318.

65. Ibid., pp. 748–50; Lane to Lafayette, Feb. 7, 1861, Lane Papers, InU; Nesmith to Harvey Gordon, Feb. 16, 1861, MS OrHi.

66. *Congressional Globe*, 36 Cong., 2 Sess., pp. 1342–49.

Johnson's reply was both brilliant and devastating. Protesting "the Senator from Oregon is more Southern than the South itself," he brought the galleries to their feet when he denounced secession as treason. "If individuals were pointed out to me," he said, after it was finally decided the galleries need not be cleared, "who were engaged in nightly conspiracies, in secret conclaves, and issuing orders directing the capture of our forts and the taking of our custom-houses, I would show who were the traitors . . . and that being done . . . were I President of the United States . . . I would have them arrested; and, if convicted, within the meaning and scope of the Constitution, by the Eternal God I would execute them." His concluding peroration to the Union brought great applause and shouts of "three cheers more for Johnson." Lane made no effort to respond, confident, as he wrote Lafayette, that he had done his duty.[67]

Two days later, the Sabbath intervening, the nation inaugurated its sixteenth president. General Scott had taken extraordinary precautions to ensure that no incident mar the occasion, stationing platoons of infantry along Pennsylvania Avenue, cavalry along the side streets, and concealed riflemen along the roof tops. Lane showed little interest in the solemn pageant, his heart heavy with grave forebodings.

> For the first time in the history of our country [he wrote] a President has been inaugurated under the cannons mouth. It augers no good for the future of our confederacy. The inaugural as I understand means war bloody terrible war and I would not be surprised if it commences befor June. Lincoln does not understand the principles or framework of our Government and the consequence will be war, fierce bloody & destructive. The fact is he is no account. he is a miserable

67. Ibid., pp. 1350–56; Lane to Lafayette, March 5, 1861, Lane Papers, InU.

> creature, and will be a mere tool in the hands of a miserable corrupt sectional party that will destroy and break the Country.[68]

So saying, he began packing his things to leave for home.

By some cruel irony of fate, the steamer bearing Lane back to Oregon also brought news of the firing on Fort Sumter and Lincoln's call for 75,000 volunteers to suppress rebellion. For past months the *Argus, Oregonian,* and *Statesman* had passionately represented Lane as a mere tool of Southern extremism. Bush had been particularly virulent. After featuring Lane's wire to the delegation at Charleston, he ran an editorial, "The Lane and Gwin Conspiracy," accusing the two "political gamesters" of conspiring with the South to take also the Far West out of the Union by forming a separate, independent republic. The idea of a Pacific republic was as old as Jefferson and had been recalled periodically whenever Westerners felt Washington's neglect too keenly. The sectional crisis gave new currency to the idea, especially among Californian politicians, who spoke of it openly in Sacramento and Washington. Although there appears to be no good evidence that Lane ever countenanced the scheme, it was natural for his political opponents to identify him with it. Peddling gossip from Washington to the *Statesman,* Nesmith wrote that Lane was returning to inaugurate a Pacific republic. And when the news of Fort Sumter jolted the nation to the reality of civil war, Oregonians were ill-prepared to tolerate a "live secessionist" in their midst.[69]

68. Lane to Lafayette, March 5, 1861, Lane Papers, InU.

69. *Oregon Argus,* May 4, 1861; *Oregon Statesman,* July 17, 1860; Nesmith to Harvey Gordon, Feb. 26, 1861, MS OrHi. See also Joseph Ellison, "Designs for a Pacific Republic, 1843–62," *Oregon Historical Quarterly, 31* (1930), 319–42, and Dorothy Hull, "The Movement in Oregon for the Establishment of a Pacific Coast Republic," ibid., *17* (1916), 177–200. Complaining that Congress seemed interested only in Kansans

There were no brass bands, no welcoming salutes, when the *Cortez* nosed to the wharf early in the morning of April 29. Shelby and some friends had reportedly planned to fire a cannon but were told that the cannon "at least" would be dumped into the river. According to a story circulated by the *Argus,* the drayman—the *Statesman* made him "an honest drayman"—refused to transport Lane's baggage to the hotel: he would not assist a traitor who had brought bloodshed upon the country. Pointing to two or three of Lane's stout boxes, a bystander with mock gravity pronounced them full of Sharpe's rifles to arm the Pacific Republic.[70] Some persons were concerned that Lane might try to deliver a speech. The *Oregonian* insisted he returned "with the avowed purpose of converting the people to the views of the negro-shriekers" but magnanimously declared that as long as he was "guilty of no overt act here in Oregon, let him speak." The *Argus* suggested a tableau instead:

> Enter, General, *solus,* in regimentals, and carrying two flags—the flag of our Union, and that other Palmetto affair. The glorious old Stars and Stripes held at arm's length with disgust and detestation, and the new Southern rag clasped fondly to his breast. Curtain to fall, leaving Joseph trampling the folds of our national banner under foot, and kissing the Palmetto rag.

---

and Mormons, J. H. Reed protested (Aug. 27, 1858, Lane Papers, InU), "we will be compelled either to hang some Federal officer in order to attract attention, or else we must establish a separate organization on the Pacific in order to enjoy the commonest conveniences of civilization."

70. "Nuevo" to ed., Portland, May 3, 1861, *Oregon Statesman,* May 6, 1861—probably a forgery; *Oregon Argus,* May 4, 1861. One of the boxes did contain rifles, at least one hunting rifle each for the personal use of Lane and Lafayette, but hardly the arsenal reported by the *Statesman* (Nov. 11, 1861) or Bancroft (*History of Oregon, 2,* 455–56). Cf. Lane to William S. Hawken, Dec. 24, 1860, Jan. 24, 1861, photostats, MS OrHi, and Lane to Lafayette, March 19, 1861, Lane Papers, InU.

Even former friends like Curry avoided him, but the ladies of Southern Methodist Church invited him to a May Day dinner, "strictly Southern" in character. "A few old women tried to get up a panic that he was going to *secesh* us," Deady informed Nesmith, "but it did not take. He walked about town very quietly. I had him . . . to dinner with us, and as nobody else did the like I took a particular pleasure in it."[71]

Procuring a wagon and team, Lane left Portland, May 2, with Lafayette and two nieces on the last two-hundred-mile leg of their journey. At Dallas, where they stopped the first night, they again carted their own luggage to the hotel. News of Lane's arrival flew through the hamlet, and a crowd hastily gathered, running up the Stars and Stripes and firing thirty-four salutes, one for each state in the Union. When Lane awoke the next morning, the first thing he saw was his effigy, wearing a hat with a black cockade, hanging from the tree in front of the hotel. It was boldly labeled, "Jo Lane, the Traitor."[72]

The reception at Corvallis, where they spent a few days with Nat, was quite different. The citizens there, whom the *Oregonian* chose to regard as "a little squad of cackling secessionists, and escaped negro-stealers," greeted his arrival with a salute and honored him with a public reception at the courthouse. In a brief speech, he reiterated his desire for peace, cautioned his listeners against undue excitement, and repudiated the idea of a Pacific republic.[73]

Four miles from Winchester, Lane suffered an unfortunate mishap. While climbing out of the wagon, he accidentally caught the hammer of his pistol, which discharged, sending the ball up through his chest and out the top of his right shoulder. Although

71. *Weekly Oregonian,* May 4, 1861; *Oregon Argus,* May 4, 1861; the Rev. J. L. Hopkins to Lane, April 30, 1861, Lane Papers, InU; Deady to Nesmith, May 16, 1861, MS OrHi.

72. "S.D.M." to ed., May 5, 1861, *Oregon Statesman,* May 6, 1861.

73. *Weekly Oregonian,* May 11, 1861; *Oregon Weekly Union,* May 11, 1861.

he was back on his feet in a few days, either the bone became infected or his shoulder was dislocated, for it still gave him severe pain three months later.[74]

Although Lane's return to Oregon was marked by bitter recriminations, and the calumnies were to continue for years, the initial storm was soon spent. Two weeks after Lane reached Winchester, Riley E. Stratton commented about the "astonishing change" that was taking place in the public sentiment, that Breckinridge Democrats were "getting as mild as New Milk." Lane himself was content to assume the life of a farmer, nursing his injured shoulder and taking a much-needed rest. He seemed a much older man than the senator who had left Oregon two years earlier; observers noted his hair had whitened considerably. He dropped from public notice in the press almost as rapidly as he had engaged it twelve years earlier. His career was now over, his repudiation complete. In July, Drew reported to Deady from Roseburg, "Ancient Joseph seldom goes from home."[75]

74. *Oregon Sentinel,* May 18, 25, 1861; Dr. A. M. Loryea to Lane, Aug. 17, 1861, Lane Papers, InU.

75. Stratton to Harvey Gordon, June 2, 1861, MS OrHi; Drew to Deady, July 11, 1861, MS OrHi.

## *Chapter 7*

# EPILOGUE

For ten years Joseph Lane spoke for Oregon in the nation's capital. Rarely absent from his seat during the entire decade, he was undoubtedly one of the most faithful and energetic members of Congress. Neither an orator nor parliamentarian, he was nonetheless an effective representative, especially among the departments and at the White House. Except for the issue of Southern rights, he conscientiously mirrored the wishes of his constituents. He was a colorful if not particularly attractive personality and a man of unquestioned personal integrity.

Egotistical, ambitious, demagogic, Lane was also a shrewd and able politician, who more than held his own in a very rough league. He was willing to subserve the interests of the Clique, but when they decided that he was expendable, he turned the tables on them and beat them at their own game. Lane won the critical struggle for supremacy in Oregon; the party was his, and, as George Williams declared, he might have "represented Oregon in the senate as long as he lived."[1] But in the larger, overpowering sectional controversy, he stood on the losing side.

As a man of principle, Lane was more consistent than any of his contemporaries and much more consistent than they would admit. "Sir, if I prize any thing highly and above price," he once replied to a charge that he was catering to the Softs, "it is the *jewel of consistency* as a Democrat."[2] When the Union began coming apart at the seams and the nation stood on the brink of civil war, he could truthfully say that the times, not he, had changed. That he would not surrender his principles was a virtue; that his principles were incompatible with the age was a tragedy. And like Jefferson Davis and others who began demanding that Congress actively protect slavery in the territories, he did not realize that he was shifting from nonintervention to intervention. Unlike Southern moderates who withheld their support from Breckinridge and Lane, he did not appreciate the constitutional implications of assigning to Congress the responsibility of protecting slavery. If the Constitution permitted Congress the decision to intervene in behalf of the South's "peculiar institution," it presumably also permitted the decision not to intervene.

In the final analysis, Lane was not even a full-blown Jacksonian. He had an abiding faith in the collective judgment of the masses, and he never questioned their ability to think and act intelligently. But Jackson, despite his deep respect for the rights of the states, was a nationalist, which Lane was not. Replying to Johnson that last day in the Senate, Lane made a strained attempt to deny that

1. George H. Williams, "Political History of Oregon from 1853–1865," *Oregon Historical Quarterly,* 2 (1901), 27.

2. Lane to Deady, April 18, 1858, Lane Papers, InU.

Jackson would have implemented the "Force Bill" against South Carolina during the Nullification Crisis of 1832–33. "Coercion may have been contemplated by General Jackson at first," he declared, "but his opinions afterward underwent a radical change. Every man who is well acquainted with the history of the country knows that he never would have struck a blow; he would never have fired a gun. His heart had relented after he had made his proclamation. He had approved the law, and then sent a commission, as we all know, to South Carolina, to use all possible means to avert bloodshed. If the question had to be decided by the bayonet, he never would have used it, in my judgment."[3] Fundamentally, Jackson was asserting a basic principle of democracy: that the majority have the right to rule the minority. Lane was asserting an important corollary: that the majority must not tyrannize over the minority.

When war came, Lane did not offer his services to the South, as during his more extravagant flights of oratory he had indicated he would. He probably could have obtained a commission in the Confederate army, despite his age, and several Southerners appealed to him to come to their aid. But although he gave his blessing to John, who left West Point to enlist in the ranks of the Confederacy, he remained aloof himself and took no part in the conflict. Like many of his generation, he did not anticipate that secession would lead inexorably to war; when hostilities commenced, he was probably realistic enough to sense the futility of bloodletting.

Lane spent most of his last twenty years in semiretirement on a farm near the mountains, seven miles east of Roseburg. In 1867 he was baptized and confirmed into the Roman Catholic faith, together with his wife Polly, Simon, Lafayette, and Winnifred Lane Mosher. He was at the side of his beloved Polly when in August 1870 she was seized with spasms and, after lingering a few days, sank into a

3. *Congressional Globe,* 36 Cong., 2 Sess., p. 1346.

deep sleep. "Mother was always a good pure person and died happy and confident in the Christian faith," Lafayette wrote to Nat, informing him of the event. "Poor Father, he loved her tenderly and deeply mourns her loss." He buried her on a grassy slope near the farmhouse and remained on the farm for another eight years, living as a hermit, his only companion a Negro lad, Peter Waldo, who had been committed to his care by the court of Josephine County in 1864. In 1878 his children persuaded him to build a little house in Roseburg, on the bank of the Umpqua, next door to his daughter, Emily Floed, where he spent his remaining days surrounded by books and reminiscing with old friends.[4]

Although his political career ended in March 1861, Lane's interest in politics never faltered. The Civil War years were unpleasant. The *Statesman* gave him an occasional "stir" for partisan reasons, and there were suggestions by the Clique that he be arrested for disloyalty.[5] He took an active part in the campaign of 1864, helping Lafayette win a seat in the state legislature, and taking a strong stand against the draft law. Two years later he again campaigned for the Democratic ticket and created a bit of a flurry by announcing that Congress would have to readmit leaders of the Confederacy if their constituents re-elected them. In 1875 he again mounted the stump for Lafayette, who won a seat in Congress, and the next year he supported the Democratic presidential nominee, Samuel J. Tilden. Some months later he urged the chairman of the committee investigating the fraudulent sale of state lands to conduct a vigorous prosecution. "Nothing but a complete expose of the whole affair will save us in '80, or even give us a reasonable hope of success," he declared. "Democrats must

4. Kelly, *Career of Joseph Lane,* p. 190; Lafayette to Nat, Aug. 21, 1870, Lane Papers, OrU; James A. Abbott to Lane, Aug. 25, 1864, Lane Papers, InU; "Autobiography," pp. 61–62.

5. Deady to Nesmith, Aug. 19, 1862, MS OrHi. Cf. Deady to Nesmith, Oct. 30, 1866, and telegram from Harding et al. to Nesmith, Feb. 22, 1862, MS OrHi.

be honest, and if not honest, they must be disgraced and punished."[6]

In the summer of 1878, Jesse Applegate spent the better part of two days with Lane, and the two men conversed freely about past struggles and the perils currently facing the Republic. "Tho he has been a Democrat of the State-rights school," wrote Applegate, "he accepts the results of the war as settling the questions embodied in the amendments of the Constitution finally and forever, and thinks the preservation of the Union the greatest good to all sections. In short he is a true patriot and always has been. . . . Has no future but God and his own fame to look to, and he earnestly wishes for peace and prosperity to all the world."[7]

So thoroughly had spirits mellowed and old animosities melted that in 1880 Lane's former associates persuaded him to run for the state senate. In his seventy-ninth year and without adequate funds for the canvass, the old warrior nevertheless made a valiant but vain effort. Among those who helped to finance his campaign were Nesmith and Bush. Lane and Bush sentimentally exchanged photographs, and Lane entertained Nesmith and his wife when Nesmith campaigned that fall in Roseburg.[8]

Death came gently to Joseph Lane at nine o'clock in the evening, April 19, 1881, after a brief illness. For weeks he had been satisfied that the sun was setting and had addressed short farewell notes to his former companions. Deady spent a few hours with him before he died. According to Lane's wishes, his body was buried without religious ceremony in the Masonic Cemetery in Roseburg; his wife's body was exhumed and placed in the same vault. The funeral cortege was the largest witnessed in Douglas County. Deady, Nesmith, and Bush attended; at Lane's request Nesmith delivered the eulogy, and Bush served as pallbearer. "When the

6. Lane to William Galloway, undated newspaper clipping, Lane Papers, OrU.

7. Applegate to Deady, June 7, 1878, MS OrHi.

8. Lane to Nesmith, April 26, 1880, Bush Papers; Nesmith to Bush, April 28, 1880, Bush Papers; Lane to Bush, Nov. 19, 1880, Bush Papers.

history of this country is written," wrote Deady at the conclusion of Lane's obituary, "Oregon's first senator must occupy a prominent place. . . . In his grave are buried the memories of the frailties incident to human nature and the asperities of life's hot conflicts; and the passage of time will brighten his name and enhance his renown."[9]

9. *Daily Oregonian,* April 21, p. 2, April 23, p. 1, 1881.

# NOTE ON SOURCES

There are two major collections of Lane materials, one at the Oregon Historical Society, Portland, and the other in the Lilly Library, Indiana University, Bloomington. Although the two collections are similar in nature, a large proportion of the papers in Oregon relate to the period prior to 1855, and of the papers in Indiana, to the period after 1855. The collection in Indiana is especially valuable for the light it sheds on the precise nature of the split between Lane and the Clique. The activities of the Clique are well documented in the rich collection of the Oregon Historical Society and in the Asahel Bush Papers at the Oregon State Library, Salem. The record of private correspondence during the period of this study is amazingly complete. The historian is doubly fortunate that Deady's remote location from Salem during most of the territorial period obliged him to rely heavily upon correspondence for news of the Clique's activity, and that he preserved this information in his personal "archives," from which he intended one day to write a history of the period.

After correspondence, the newspapers of the time furnish the most illuminating account of political life. Although the early press in Oregon achieved a national reputation for its forthright and uninhibited style, frontier journalism was frequently good journalism in many respects. By far the most important newspaper in Oregon was the *Oregon Statesman,* which was published at the seat of government, wherever that might happen to be. Historians have hitherto largely ignored the Portland *Oregon Weekly Times.* Although it was a relatively minor paper, it is valuable as an anti-Clique, Democratic journal, and later, when Hibben assumed control, as the organ most dedicated to Lane's advancement. It is unfortunate that more issues of the other anti-Clique paper, the Portland *Democratic Standard,* have not been preserved. The leading opposition paper of the time was the Whig Portland *Weekly Oregonian;* even more influential in the latter part of the decade was the Oregon City *Oregon Argus,* the first Republican paper, which supplanted the Oregon City *Oregon Spectator,* a much weaker paper. Of the several newspapers that began later in the decade, the Corvallis *Occidental Messenger,* the Corvallis *Oregon Weekly Union,* and the Albany *Oregon Democrat* reflected significant viewpoints on political issues.

Lane's "Autobiography," as related to Hubert Howe Bancroft in the Clarendon Hotel, Portland, June 21, 1878, and supplemented by later letters from Lane, is insignificant and disappointing. Most of his remarks relate to his role in the Mexican War and skirmishes with the Indians in southern Oregon and northern California. He remained silent about politics in Oregon and his activities in Congress.

Bancroft got a poor impression of Lane and had little sympathy for him. Perhaps the chronicler was too much a product of the generation of the "bloody-shirt" to be objective about Lane. Frances Fuller Victor, who prepared the draft of *History of Oregon* (2 vols., San Francisco, History Company, 1888), afterward complained to Deady that Bancroft had edited her text to the disparagement of Lane. "But Lane is dead," she concluded, "and will never buy a set of the histories." On the other hand, Sister M. Margaret Jean Kelly, in *The Career of Joseph Lane, Frontier Politician* (Washington, Catholic University of America Press, 1942), strove too hard to counteract Bancroft, glossing over human frailties.

Kelly did important spadework and deals most effectively with the early aspects of Lane's career, but she did not have access to the Lane materials in Indiana and is superficial and unsatisfactory in many ways.

The pioneer work on early political developments in Oregon is Walter Carleton Woodward, *The Rise and Early History of Political Parties in Oregon, 1843–1868* (Portland, J. K. Gill Company, 1913). Woodward is still valuable for his description of political maneuvering and his demonstration that the Democratic party split over local issues, which soon became subordinated to the larger issue of slavery. A more recent study, Robert W. Johannsen, *Frontier Politics and the Sectional Conflict: The Pacific Northwest on the Eve of the Civil War* (Seattle, University of Washington Press, 1955), takes a broader scope than Woodward while covering much the same ground and emphasizes the national context of local politics, showing how political organization and patronage integrated the frontier with national affairs. From the evidence available to him, Johannsen suspected that Lane deliberately began laying the groundwork as early as 1855 to challenge the Clique and obtain control of the party.

The national scene is admirably portrayed by Allan Nevins, *The Ordeal of the Union* (2 vols., New York, Charles Scribner's Sons, 1947) and *The Emergence of Lincoln* (2 vols., New York, Charles Scribner's Sons, 1950), the first four volumes of a projected ten-volume monumental work under the overall title, *The Ordeal of the Union.* Nevins is much more catholic in his approach to the period than is Roy Franklin Nichols in *The Disruption of American Democracy* (New York, Macmillan Company, 1948). Nichols focuses upon the rupture of the Democratic party during Buchanan's administration and is particularly helpful in his analysis of the maneuvering in Congress and in the various states.

Of the more specialized studies, Henry L. Simms, "The Controversy Over the Admission of the State of Oregon" (*Mississippi Valley Historical Review, 32* [1945], 255–74), analyzes the shifting opposition to statehood. Emerson David Fite, *The Presidential Campaign of 1860* (New York, Macmillan Company, 1911) is a standard, descriptive account; more provocative is Ollinger Crenshaw, *The Slave States in the Presidental Election of 1860* (Johns Hopkins University Studies in Historical and Political Science. Series 63, Number 3 [Baltimore, Johns Hopkins University Press, 1945]). Murat Halstead's report of the political conventions of 1860 is a classic and has been recently edited by William B. Hesseltine, *Three Against Lincoln: Murat Halstead Reports the Caucuses of 1860* (Baton Rouge, Louisiana State University Press, 1960). A thoughtful, revealing account is Frank H. Heck, "John C. Breckinridge in the Crisis of 1860–1861" (*Journal of Southern History, 21* [1955], 316–46).

# INDEX